CW01261693

A Text-book of General Bacteriology

A TEXT-BOOK

OF

GENERAL BACTERIOLOGY

BY

WILLIAM DODGE FROST

ASSOCIATE PROFESSOR OF BACTERIOLOGY IN THE UNIVERSITY
OF WISCONSIN

AND

EUGENE FRANKLIN McCAMPBELL

PROFESSOR OF BACTERIOLOGY IN THE OHIO
STATE UNIVERSITY

ILLUSTRATED

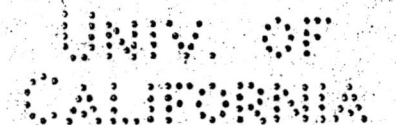

New York
THE MACMILLAN COMPANY
1911

All rights reserved

THIS BOOK

IS DEDICATED

IN GRATEFUL APPRECIATION

TO

BENJAMIN CUTLER FROST

AND

JAMES McCAMPBELL

PREFACE

BACTERIOLOGY, in the few years of its existence, has become one of the great subjects of the day. A knowledge of it is important to students of many different branches of science. At the present time it is usually taught, in English-speaking countries at least, with special reference to some particular application, such as medicine or agriculture. There is a growing demand for treatises on the subject of general bacteriology. The authors have attempted to meet this need in the present volume.

The material presented here has been used in college classes for a number of years with interest and profit.

The authors wish to express their sincere acknowledgment for the particular help received from the works of Fischer, Lafar, E. F. Smith, Wells, and others mentioned in the body of the text, and for the ideas and inspiration imparted by their former teacher, Dean H. L. Russell, of the University of Wisconsin. For suggestions and assistance in the revision of the manuscript, we are indebted to Professor M. P. Ravenel, of the University of Wisconsin.

W. D. F.
E. F. McC.

JULY, 1910.

TABLE OF CONTENTS

PART I. INTRODUCTION

CHAPTER I

THE HISTORY OF BACTERIOLOGY

	PAGE
Introduction	1
Historical	2

CHAPTER II

SPONTANEOUS GENERATION

Introduction	8
Early period	8
Second period	9
Third period	10
Modern period	12

PART II. THE MORPHOLOGY OF BACTERIA

CHAPTER III

THE FORM AND STRUCTURE OF BACTERIA

Introduction	14
Haplobacteria	15
Cocci	15
Bacilli	17
Spirilla	19
Trichobacteria	21
Involution forms and pleomorphism	24
The dimensions of bacterial cells	27
Locomotion of bacteria	29
Rapidity of motion	35

Brownian movement	35
Capsules	35
Sheaths	37
Mass grouping	37
Zoogloea and pseudozoogloea	37
Pellicle	37
Colony	37

CHAPTER IV

Reproduction of the Bacteria

Introduction	42
Haplobacteria	42
Fission	42
Rate of multiplication	43
Spore formation	46
Endospores	46
Arthrospores	50
Trichobacteria	50

CHAPTER V

The Minute Structure of Bacteria

Introduction	52
Histology	52
Cell wall	52
Protoplasm	53
Metachromatic and polar granules	57
Nucleus	59
Chemical structure	60

PART III. THE METHODS USED IN THE STUDY OF BACTERIA

CHAPTER VI

Culture Media

Introduction	66
The character of food required	67

TABLE OF CONTENTS xi

	PAGE
The composition and preparation of media	67
Liquid media	68
Solid media	71
Liquefiable solid media	73
Synthetic media	75

CHAPTER VII

Sterilization

Introduction	77
Sterilization by physical agents	78
Sunlight	78
Cold	78
Dry heat	79
Direct flame	79
High dry heat	79
Moist heat	80
Streaming steam	80
Steam under pressure	82
Disinfection	84

CHAPTER VIII

Culture Methods and Apparatus

Introduction	85
Methods of isolation	86
Fractional methods	86
Physiological methods	86
Dilution methods	87
The use of liquefiable solid media	88
Subcultures	91

CHAPTER IX

The Microscopical Examination of Bacteria

The history of the microscope	93
The bacteriological microscope	93
Oil immersion lens	93
Abbe condenser	93
The examination of living bacteria	94
The principles of staining	98

PART IV. TAXONOMY

CHAPTER X

THE CLASSIFICATION OF BACTERIA

	PAGE
Introduction	102
The classification of Migula	104

CHAPTER XI

THE RELATIONSHIPS OF THE BACTERIA

Introduction	115
Bacteria defined	116
The points of resemblance to other forms of life	117
The relationships to the plants	119
Classification of plants	119
Relationships to the Eumycetes	120
Relationships to the Cyanophyceæ	122
Relationships to the Euphyceæ	123
Relationships to the Myxomycetes	123
Relationships to the Myxobacteria	124
The relationships to animals	125
Protozoa	125

PART V. GENERAL PHYSIOLOGY

CHAPTER XII

THE RELATION OF BACTERIA TO ENVIRONMENT

Introduction	127
The functions of bacteria	127
External conditions	128
The food of bacteria	128
Chemical composition	129
Water	129
Oxygen	131
Anaërobic culture methods	132
Temperature	134
The thermal death point	138

TABLE OF CONTENTS xiii

	PAGE
The action of chemicals on bacteria	140
Formaldehyde, etc.	148

CHAPTER XIII

The Relation of Bacteria to Environment (*Continued*)

The Effect of External Conditions

Light	155
Electricity	159
Rontgen rays	162
Movement	163
Pressure	163
Association	164

CHAPTER XIV

The Metabolism of Bacteria

Introduction	165
The general character of life processes	165
Anabolism	166
Catabolism	167
Respiration	168

CHAPTER XV

The Products of the Metabolism of Bacteria

Introduction	171
Bacterial enzymes and their mechanism of action	176
Autolytic bacterial enzymes	181

PART VI. THE BIOLOGY OF SPECIALIZED GROUPS OF BACTERIA

CHAPTER XVI

The Prototrophic Bacteria

Introduction	183
Nitrifying bacteria	183
Nitrogen-fixing bacteria	185

	PAGE
Sulphur bacteria	186
Iron bacteria	188

CHAPTER XVII

THE CHROMOGENIC BACTERIA

Introduction	190
Range of color	190
Location of pigments	191
Solubility	194
Historical allusions	196

CHAPTER XVIII

THE PHOTOGENIC BACTERIA

Introduction	198
Distribution	198
Food requirements	199
Oxygen requirements	200
Temperature requirements	200
Methods of isolation	201
Pathogenesis	201

CHAPTER XIX

THE ZYMOGENIC BACTERIA

Introduction	202
Organized and unorganized ferments	204
Lactic acid fermentation	206
Acetic acid fermentation	208
Butyric acid fermentation	209
Methane fermentation	211
Higher alcohols, aromatics, and fatty acids	211
Bacterial fermentations in the arts	214

CHAPTER XX

THE SAPROGENIC AND SAPROPHILIC BACTERIA

Introduction	216
Proteolytic enzymes	217

TABLE OF CONTENTS

	PAGE
The mechanism of putrefaction	220
The products produced	221

CHAPTER XXI

THE PATHOGENIC BACTERIA

Introduction	228
Diseases, infectious and contagious	232
List of specific infectious diseases	232
List of nonspecific infectious diseases	235
List of diseases of unknown cause	238
The means by which bacteria are transmitted	239

CHAPTER XXII

THE PATHOGENIC BACTERIA (*Continued*)

The mode of action of pathogenic bacteria	243
Proof of the etiological relationship	245
The effects of the pathogenic bacteria on the body	246
The poisonous products of bacteria	248
Ptomains	249
Toxins	251
Endotoxins	254

CHAPTER XXIII

THE PATHOGENIC BACTERIA (*Continued*)

The toxic bacterial proteins	256
Anaphylaxis to bacterial proteins	257
Bacterial hemolysins	257
Antitoxins	258
Antibacterial substances	261
Agglutinins	262
Opsonins	263
Antienzymes	265
Table of antibodies	265
The factors which influence and modify infections	267
Virulence of bacteria	267
Number of bacteria	268
Avenue of infection	269

	PAGE
The subject infected	270
Immunity to pathogenic bacteria	271
The theories of immunity	272

CHAPTER XXIV

THE BACTERIAL DISEASES OF PLANTS

Introduction	274
Early conception	274
Present conception	276
The method of infection	278

PART VII. THE DISTRIBUTION OF BACTERIA

CHAPTER XXV

THE BACTERIA OF THE SOIL

Distribution according to habitat	281
Distribution in the soil	281
The species of bacteria	283
Bacteria in the surface layers	283
The legume or nitrogen-fixing bacteria	285
The nitrifying bacteria	288
The denitrifying bacteria	288

CHAPTER XXVI

THE BACTERIA OF THE AIR

Introduction	289
Condition in the air	289
The origin of the bacteria of the air	289
Quantitative distribution	291
Seasonal distribution	291
The species of bacteria in the air	291

CHAPTER XXVII

THE BACTERIA OF WATER AND SEWAGE

Introduction	293
The number of bacteria in water	293
The origin of the bacteria in water	294

	PAGE
Water analysis	299
The purification of water	301
Sewage	302
The purification of sewage	302

CHAPTER XXVIII

THE BACTERIA OF MILK AND ITS PRODUCTS

Introduction	305
The bacteria of the udder	305
The number of bacteria in market milk	305
The source of bacteria in milk	306
The contamination of the milk from the animal	307
The entrance of bacteria into the milk from the air	307
Cleanliness of milking utensils	308
The milker	308
The care of the milk	309

CHAPTER XXIX

THE BACTERIA OF MILK AND ITS PRODUCTS (*Continued*)

The species of bacteria in milk	311
Lactic acid bacteria	311
Slimy milk	312
Blue milk	313
Red milk	313
The disease-producing bacteria in milk	314
Pathogenic bacteria in milk after it is drawn	316
Typhoid	316
Asiatic cholera	317
Diphtheria	317
Scarlet fever	318

CHAPTER XXX

THE BACTERIA OF THE HUMAN BODY

Introduction	319
The bacteria of the skin and exposed mucous membranes	319
The bacteria of the mouth	322
Dental caries	326
The bacteria of the stomach and intestines	327

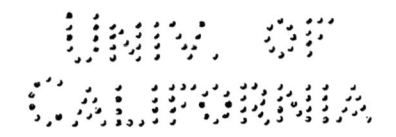

PART I. INTRODUCTION

CHAPTER I

HISTORY OF BACTERIOLOGY

Introduction. — Bacteriology is that branch of biological science which treats of bacteria. Bacteria are a definite and circumscribed group of microörganisms lying near the base of the ladder of life. They will be accurately described in the following chapters. It is frequently found desirable to discuss other microörganisms with the bacteria, both on account of the fact that they are closely related, and also because they produce similar changes, or are studied by similar methods. The more inclusive term "microbiology," which is used by the French, would be much better than the term "bacteriology" to describe the subject-matter discussed in this book. Custom, however, has fixed the word "bacteriology" in this country, and it will be used here, but not infrequently in the broader sense. While bacteria are associated with disease production, the majority of them are not disease-producing, and if there were no disease-producing bacteria in the world, bacteriology would still be a great science. In this book bacteria will be considered from a biological standpoint, and their structure and functions studied without any particular application in view. It is therefore a general bacteriology and paves the way for the applied phases of the subject. The applications of bacteriology are of particular service in medicine, agriculture, either in the departments of dairying, animal husbandry, horticulture, or soils, sanitation, engineering, home economics, and the commercial industries. Whatever the application, however, certain fundamental facts and methods must be considered, and an attempt is made to present these in this general work.

History. — The existence of bacteria on the globe antedates that of man, and yet their presence was not suspected until a few centuries ago and their actual existence was not demonstrated until much later. Probably the first authentic observation of microorganisms was made by Kircher in 1659, who demonstrated "minute living worms" in putrid meat, milk, vinegar, cheese, etc., but he did not describe their form or character. Anthony Van Leeuwenhoek, a Dutch naturalist who lived from 1632 to 1723, discovered bacteria about 1683. Leeuwenhoek was a linen weaver by trade, but as a man of some leisure he learned to grind lenses for a pastime, and made them so perfectly and used them with such keenness that he was able to see many microscopic objects for the first time, and among them the bacteria. Leeuwenhoek not only saw them, but he accurately described them and made drawings of them as well. In a letter to the Royal Society of London in 1683 he said: "I saw with wonder that my material contained many tiny animals which moved about in a most amusing fashion; the largest of these (*A*, Fig. 1) showed the liveliest and most active motion, moving through the water or saliva as a fish of prey darts through the sea; they were found everywhere, although not in large numbers. A second kind was similar to that marked B (Fig. 1). These sometimes spun around in a circle like a top, and sometimes described a path like that shown in C–D (Fig. 1); they were present in larger numbers. A third kind could not be distinguished so clearly — now they appeared oblong, now quite round. They were so very small that they did not seem larger than the bodies marked E, and, besides, they moved so rapidly that they were continually running into one another; they looked like a swarm of gnats or flies dancing about together. I had the impression that I was looking at several thousands in a given part of the water or saliva mixed with a particle of the material from the teeth no larger than a grain of sand, even when only one part of the material was added to nine parts of water or saliva. Further, the greater part of the material consisted of an extraordinary number of rods, of widely different lengths, but of the same diameter. Some

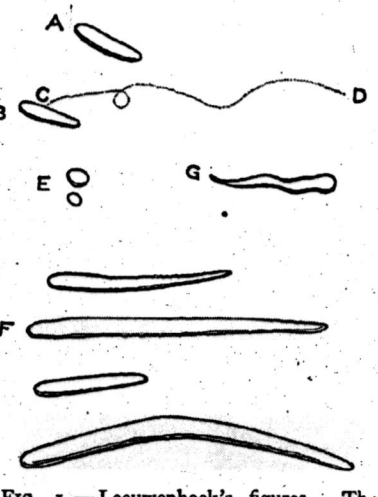

FIG. 1.—Leeuwenhoek's figures. The oldest known figures of bacteria. After Fischer.

were curved, some straight, as is shown in F; they lay irregularly and were interlaced. Since I had previously seen living animalculæ of this same kind in water, I endeavored to observe whether there was life in them, but in none did I see the smallest movement that might be taken as a sign of life." Leeuwenhoek's observations were purely objective, and lacked the speculative entirely. Other writers, however, within the next century theorized upon his discoveries and worthy of particular mention is Marcus Antonius Plenciz, a physician of Vienna. Plenciz proposed a germ theory of disease in 1762, and taught the etiological relationship of Leeuwenhoek's animalculæ to various diseases. He likewise insisted on a causal relationship of these minute and unnumbered forms of life to the processes of decomposition. Important discoveries regarding bacteria were made by O. F. Muller, a distinguished Danish zoologist. Müller made many important observations in regard to the form and structure of bacteria, and studied several types so closely that they can be placed in one or another of the present form types. He first used such terms as bacillus, spirillum, and vibrio, which are in common use now. He also made an attempt to work out (1786) a classification, and in so doing made an observation which has been appreciated by all later workers in this field; namely, " The difficulties that beset the investigation of these microscopic animals are complex; the sure and definite determination (of species) requires so much time, so much of acumen of eye and judgment, so much perseverance and practice, that there is hardly anything else so difficult." Another worker who deserves special mention is Ehrenberg (1795-1876). In 1836 he published his great work on Infusoria, and in this treated of the bacteria as no one had before him. He recognized quite accurately the limitations of this group and differentiated them from the true protozoa. He also recognized the principal form types in which the bacteria are usually divided. Another worker still should be mentioned, Ferdinand Cohn (1828-1898). He was Professor of Botany in the University of Breslau. His works contributed greatly to the advance of our knowledge of bacteria. A new era in the history of bacteriology began with the work of Louis Pasteur (1822-1895). Pasteur, although by inclination and training a chemist, was early led by his chemical researches to the study of the relation of microörganisms to various natural processes, such as fermentation, decay, and putrefaction, and later to the relation of these organisms to disease processes in man and animals. Later still he took up the study of the scientific methods of preventing and curing these diseases. Viewed from any stand-point, his researches are of the profoundest importance. He introduced the experimental method and used it with telling effect in the study of bacteria and allied microörganisms. From an obscure position, interesting only to the professional biologist, Pasteur raised these microörganisms to a place of greatest interest on account of their significance in the production of changes of greatest importance to man. Pasteur may well be considered the founder of bacteriology, but it remained for Robert Koch (1843–1910), by his epoch-making discoveries, to place bacteriology in the position of an independent science. In 1876, Koch, an obscure German physician, published his article on the relation of Bacterium anthracis to splenic fever in cattle. The relation was stated so clearly and the arguments were so convincing that the paper attracted wide attention and furnished a model for investigation of the relation of microorganisms to disease processes. Six years later he described a new method for isolating bacteria. This was by means of a cleverly devised liquefiable solid medium and is known as the gelatin plate culture method The importance of the discovery of this method to the development of bacteriology cannot be overestimated. About this time also Koch aided and encouraged the development of the bacteriological microscope provided with an oil immersion lens and an Abbe condenser. He also developed and applied the use of the anilin dyes, first introduced into microscopical technique by Weigert. Following this work, the discoveries in bacteriology have been rapid and almost continuous. In a general way, however, the important discoveries have been grouped about discoveries or modifications of technique. For example, following the use of the anilin dyes and the perfected microscope, the bacteria of a considerable number of the important diseases were discovered, as, for instance, those of relapsing fever, pneumonia, typhoid fever, and the protozoan of malaria. Following the introduction of the plate culture a considerable number of microörganisms, related to important diseases, were grown artificially, and their relation to the disease process definitely established, such as those of cholera, diphtheria, typhoid fever, and those associated with suppuration. More recently, with the discovery of Novy that certain protozoa could be grown artificially, there has been a great awakening along this line and important discoveries have been made. In 1880, Pasteur discovered that he could protect an animal from an attack of a disease by inoculating an attenuated culture. The work was first done with the germ of chicken cholera but later with Bacterium anthracis, and this was the beginning of the scientific development of protective inoculation, empirically discovered by Jenner, when he devised the smallpox vaccination. In 1895, Behring and Roux discovered the anti-toxin for diphtheria. This was the beginning of the important work on serum therapy which is being developed at the present time, and it was also the starting point for much of the important work which has been done on the theories of immunity.

CHAPTER II

Spontaneous Generation

Introduction. — In early times it was the general belief of most people who did not accept as literal the Biblical account of the creation of the world that many forms of life could arise *de novo*. This idea or theory is usually spoken of as the theory of spontaneous generation, or abiogenesis.

Early Period. — At first it was supposed that many higher forms of life, including some of the birds and mammals, could arise in this way. For example, among the early Greeks we find that Anaximander of Miletus held that animals were formed from moisture, and Empedocles of Agrigentum believed that all of the living beings on the earth arose through spontaneous generation. Aristotle, while not having such general belief in this theory, does assert that "sometimes animals are formed in putrefying soil, sometimes in plants, sometimes in the fluids of other animals." He also stated that "every dry substance which becomes moist, and every moist body which becomes dry, produces living creatures, provided it is fit to nourish them." Later we find Ovid defending this doctrine, and in the Middle Ages Von Helmont gives directions for the artificial production of mice which were something after this order: An old piece of cloth and some seed corn were to be placed in a jar, and after standing the proper length of time would surely produce mice. Kircher actually figures animals claimed to have been produced under his own eye.

During this period the theory of spontaneous generation was universally accepted. In the seventeenth century Alexander Ross, commenting on Sir Thomas Brown's doubt as to whether mice were bred by putrefaction, says: "To question this is to question reason, sense, and experience."

Second Period. — The first experiments which seriously questioned this theory were those devised by Francisco Redi, in 1668. Redi was a physician to the Grand Duke of Tuscany. In watching meat pass from the fresh to the putrid state he noticed that before the maggots appeared, which were commonly supposed to be the result of spontaneous generation, flies could invariably be seen buzzing about the meat. The idea occurred to him that these maggots might be the progeny of the flies, and he put some meat in a jar and covered the mouth of the jar with a piece of paper, and found that although the meat putrefied maggots did not appear. Later the paper was replaced by gauze. Meat protected in this way would putrefy, but would not develop maggots. The flies would deposit their eggs on the gauze, which would not allow them to reach the meat. This first serious blow to the theory of spontaneous generation was followed by other conclusive experiments by Swammerdam, Vallisnieri, and others, so that it was not long before the idea that the higher forms of life arose in this way was discarded.

Third Period. — When the scientists of the day began to study the microörganisms which Leeuwenhoek had discovered, the theory of spontaneous generation was revived, chiefly as the result of experiments by Needham (1713–1784), and one of the fiercest battles known to science was fought over this theory. It was very difficult to understand how it was that putrescible fluids would spoil after they had been heated if it were not true that the life which appeared in them was spontaneously generated. It was generally believed that the temperature of boiling water was sufficient to kill all forms of life, and the wide distribution of microorganisms or their spores in the air was not generally understood. One of the first of the crucial experiments which pointed out the error of Needham's experiments and led to the overthrow of the theory of spontaneous generation was made by Abbe Lazzaro Spallanzani (1729–1799), a fellow-countryman of Redi. In 1777, he filled flasks with organic solutions, boiled them for three quarters of an hour, and then sealed them and placed them under conditions favorable for the growth of microorganisms without, however, having them develop. Spallanzani's critics objected to his experiments on the ground that air had not been admitted, which they claimed was essential to the life of these microorganisms. Franz Schulze, in 1836, set aside the objections of these critics of Spallanzani by arranging a flask with two glass tubes bent at right angles so arranged that air could be drawn through the flask. The air, however, was first drawn through sulphuric acid, and it was found that when this was done spontaneous generation did not occur in previously boiled decoctions (Fig. 2). The critics,

FIG. 2. — Schulze's Experiment. Bulbs contain sulphuric acid through which air was drawn before it was allowed to enter the bottle. After Lafar.

however, said that the sulphuric acid in some way had changed the air. Theodore Schwann, the next year, performed experiments similar to those of Schulze, except that he substituted for the sulphuric acid, metal tubes, which were heated red hot when the air was drawn through (Fig. 3). Perhaps Schwann's most important observation was the fact that when certain chemical substances — potassium arseniate, etc. — were added to these solutions putrefaction did not take place. Schwann may therefore be regarded as the founder of the science of antiseptics. One of the most important experiments supporting the theory of biogenesis was performed by Schröder and Von Dusch in 1854. These workers substituted cotton for the sulphuric acid and heat which had formerly been used and showed that when air was drawn through cotton and allowed to come in contact with putres-

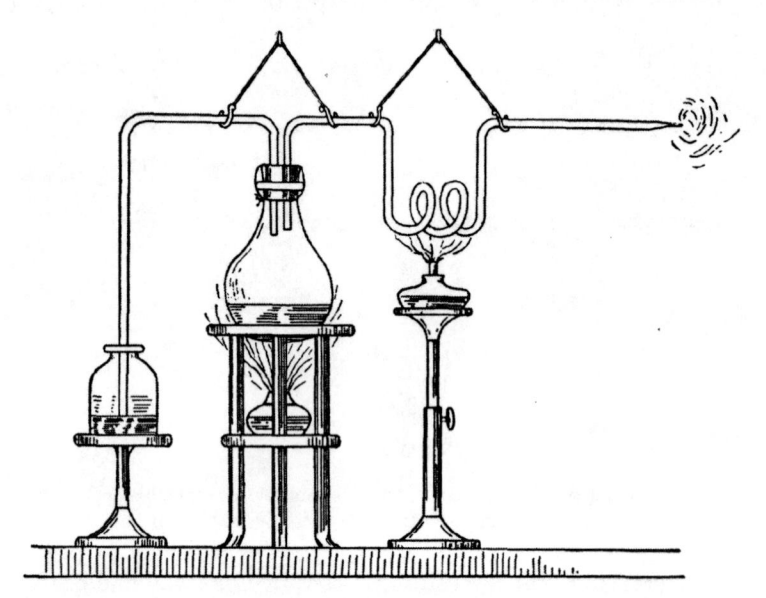

FIG. 3. — Schwann's Experiment. Air is allowed to enter the flask only after it was heated in the hot coiled tube. After Lafar.

cible material that had been sufficiently heated there was no putrefaction. These results were regarded by scientific men as definitely settling the question.

Modern Period. — A Frenchman, Pouchet, director of the Natural History Museum of Rouen, reopened the question in 1859 upon theoretical considerations. Pasteur, in 1860, entered this field, and with remarkable ingenuity and skill refuted the conclusions of Pouchet and his followers. While

Pasteur added little that was new, his experiments were of such a nature that they left little doubt in the minds of those who became acquainted with them that spontaneous generation had no foundation in fact, and, since his time, it has generally been believed that however life formerly originated it does not now originate spontaneously, and that the law of Harvey *omne vivum ex ovo,* or its modification *omne vivum ex vivo* applies to the lower as well as to the higher forms of life.

PART II. MORPHOLOGY

CHAPTER III

FORM AND STRUCTURE OF BACTERIA

Introduction. — The form, and to some extent the structure, of bacterial cells is subject so some variation depending upon the temperature at which cultivation takes place and

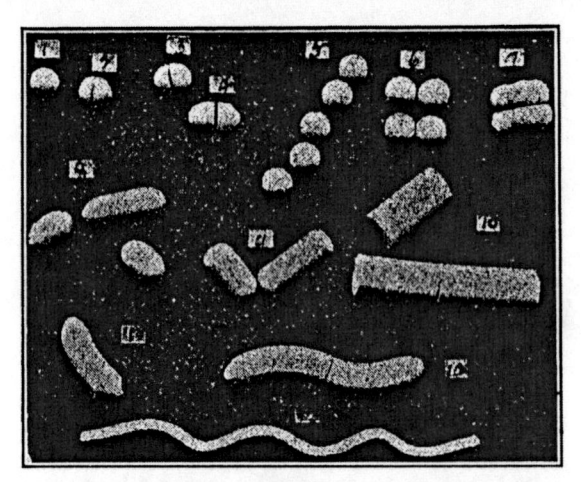

FIG. 4. — Form types of bacteria. Photograph of models, showing form and relative size. 1, M. pyogenes var. aureus; 2, 3, 4, micrococcus undergoing fission; 5, Str. pyogenes; 6, tetrads; 7, sarcina; 8, B. typhosus; 9, B. subtilis; 10, Bact. anthracis; 11, 12, Mps. comma; 13, Sp. obermeieri.

the chemical constitution of the media on which the bacteria are grown. In order that accurate information may be gained in regard to form and structure it is necessary that the various species of bacteria be grown on standard media. The variation in form and structure is often slight with some species and pronounced in others. Bacteria are conveniently divided into two orders, the Eubacteria (Migula), or true bacteria, and the Thiobacteria, or sulphur bacteria. The true bacteria, with which we are chiefly concerned, may be conveniently divided into two suborders, a lower and simpler form known as the Haplobacteria (Fischer), and a higher and more complex form called the Trichobacteria (Fischer). Bacteria vary greatly in shape according to the genera and species.

Haplobacteria or Lower Bacteria

The different form types of the haplobacteria are shown in Fig. 4.

Cocci. — In the active or vegetative stage all the lower bacteria are composed of single cells of minute size. The simplest of these is a round ball-like or globular form in which all the diameters are equal. To this form type the term "coccus" has been given. The group is subdivided according to the characteristic method in which the cocci reproduce in different planes (Chap. VI). If a coccus divides so that its successive division walls are parallel, the result is a chain of cocci. Cocci which reproduce in this manner are called *streptococci* (Ex. Strep. pyogenes) (Fig. 5). The individual cocci in the genus streptococcus remain connected or glued together in a chain by a gelatinous secretion. If a coccus divides in two directions at right angles in one plane, the resultant is a mass usually irregular because reproduction (fission) does not take place in every coccus at the same interval. Bacteria (cocci) which reproduce in this way are called *micrococci* (Ex. Micrococcus pyogenes var. aureus). If, by reason of the gelatinous envelope which often surrounds bacteria, the clump of cocci of a certain species are held together, they are called *staphylococci* (Fig. 6). The mass formed is not unlike a bunch of grapes. If a species exhibits a tendency for two cocci to stick together, the term *diploccoci* (Fig. 7) is applied; and if groups of four cocci or multiples of four occur together, the term *tetracocci* is used. This formation is also known as *merismopedia* (Fig. 8). The coccus may reproduce in three different diameters, all at right angles to each other and in two different planes, and as a result, providing division takes place at equal intervals, a cube will be formed. Bacteria (cocci) reproducing in this characteristic fashion are known as *sarcina* (Ex. Sar. aurantiaca) (Fig. 9). The size of the

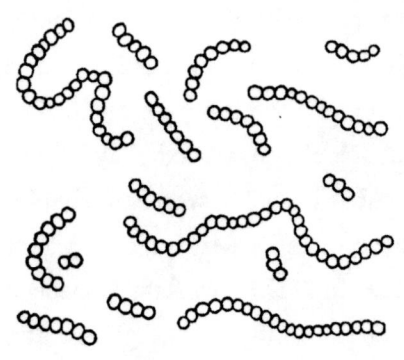

FIG. 5.—Streptococcus pyogenes. After Schmidt and Weis.

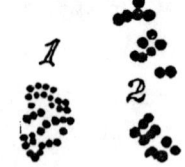

FIG. 6.—Staphylococci.

FIG. 7.—Diplococci (M. gonorrhœæ). After Schmidt and Weis.

FORM AND STRUCTURE OF BACTERIA

members of the genus known as the cocci varies from 0.15 micron to 2 microns in diameter. Micrococcus progrediens (Schröter) is said to be as small as 0.15 micron in diameter. Cocci do not produce spores. A few species of cocci are motile and possess flagella (Ex. Micrococcus agilis).

FIG. 8.—Merismopedia (Planococcus littoralis). After Schmidt and Weis.

Bacilli.—If we conceive of a coccus becoming elongated so that one axis is of greater length than the other, there results a cylindrical rod. To bacteria of this type the term *bacillus* is applied. According to Migula's classification, the term bacillus means a definite, motile, spore-producing, rod-shaped bacterium. We apply the term here, however, in its general sense to all rod-shaped bacteria. Bacilli may possess rounded ends (B. subtilis) (Fig. 10) or square ends (Bact. anthracis) (Fig. 11). The members of this form type vary greatly in length. The length varies from 1 to 80 microns, and the width from 0.1 to 6 microns (see *infra,* Size). Spores may

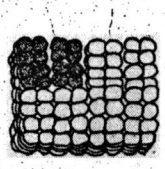

FIG. 9.—Sarcina ventricli. After Schmidt and Weis.

be found in certain species of bacilli at definite periods (see *infra*, Spores). These spores may occur in various positions in the rods, changing their contour somewhat. Some bacilli may also possess flagella, or whiplike processes, which serve as a means of locomotion (see *infra*, Flagella). To those rod-shaped bacteria which do not possess flagella Migula applies the term *bacterium*, *e.g.* Bact.

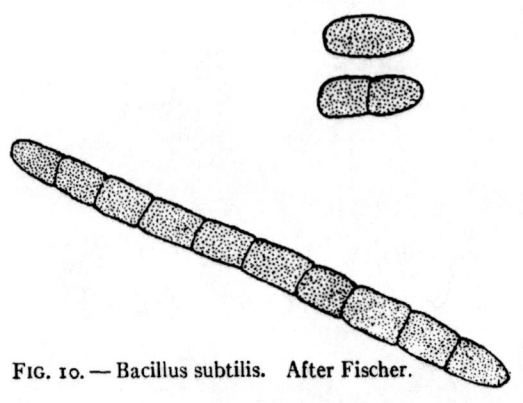

FIG. 10. — Bacillus subtilis. After Fischer.

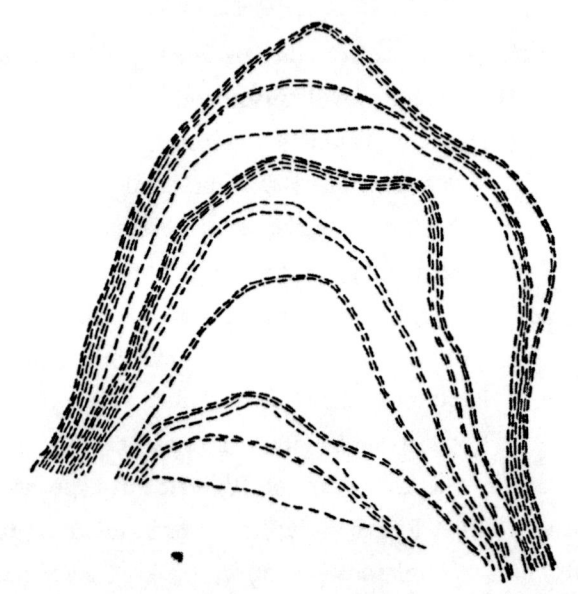

FIG. 11. — Bacterium anthracis. Chain formation. Note the square ends on the enlarged cells. After Schmidt and Weis.

anthracis. The motile spore-producing forms are called bacilli by Migula, as noted above. Not infrequently are bacilli surrounded by gelatinous capsules, *e.g.* B. capsulatus. It is quite common for some bacilli to grow in chains and form long threads under certain conditions, *e.g.* Bact. anthracis, or B. subtilus in beef broth (Figs. 10, 11). On careful examination it will be seen that the long threads or filaments are made up of individual bacteria, although at first sight the thread may appear to be homogeneous throughout.

Spirilla. — Besides the cocci and bacilli there is one other common group of lower bacteria known as the *spirilla*. These bacteria, as their name indicates, are spiral or corkscrew shaped. They are composed of rods, not unlike bacilli, but in addition they are twisted so as to make them appear as spirals. The spiral may be a short, one fourth turn or less (Microspira comma) (Fig. 12), or may be long and possess several turns (Spirillum rubrum). The name *microspira* or *vibrio* has been applied to those spirilla which are very short, and make but a fraction of a turn. The Microspira comma of Asiatic cholera is frequently called the Vibrio of Asiatic cholera. Koch called this last-mentioned organism the "Comma bacillus," on account of its resemblance to a print-

FIG. 12. — Microspira comma. After Schmidt and Weis.

20   MORPHOLOGY

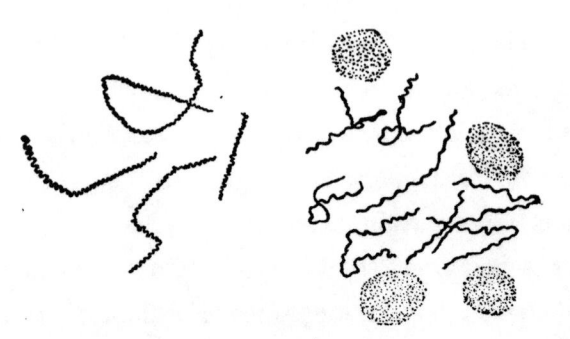

FIG. 13. — Spirochæte plicatilis. (*On left.*) Spirochæte obermeieri. After Schmidt and Weis.

er's comma when stained. Long, closely coiled spirals are called *spirochætes* by some writers (Fig. 13). A true *spirillum* is rigid and shows itself on a slide as a semicircle of spirals (Fig. 14); a *spirochæte* is a continuous line of spirals which often attain great length, and a *microspira* or *vibrio* is a short, curved rod similar to a comma. The spirillum and vibrio are rigid, and the spirochæte is usually a flexible spiral.

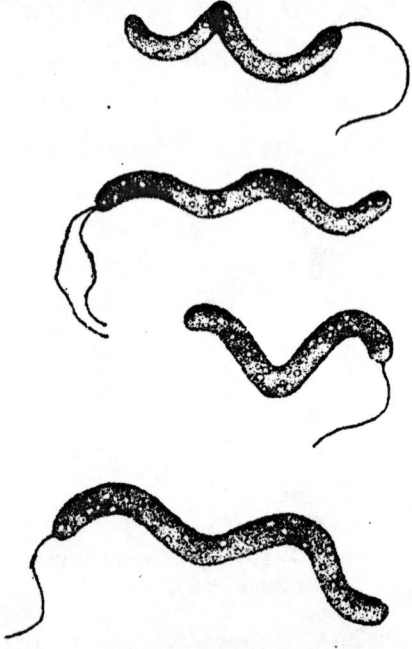

FIG. 14. — Spirillum . sanguineum. After Schmidt and Weis.

The size of a spirillum varies from 0.3 micron to 20 or 30 microns in length, and from 0.2 to 4 microns in width, according to the species.

The spirilla are motile, usually possessing flagella at one or both poles. The common method of locomotion through a medium is by rotation on the long axis, attended in the case of spirochætes by some lateral motion. The flagella or flagellum precedes the cell when in motion. A few motile spirilla do not possess any flagella.

Most spirilla do not produce spores. The method of reproduction among this group of bacteria is by fission, being similar in this respect to the cocci and the bacilli.

Trichobacteria or Higher Bacteria. — The trichobacteria or higher bacteria consist of filaments of varying length. The filaments show both true and false branching. The filament can by special stains be shown to be made up of individual cells separated from each other by definite septa. Frequently all the individual cells in the filament are surrounded by a common sheath or membrane (Fig. 15) (see *infra*, Sheaths). Certain cells at one end of the filament are used to attach the filament to other filaments and to various objects. At the free end of the filament

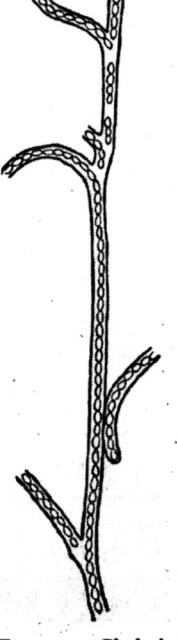

FIG. 15. — Cladothrix dichotoma. Showing "false" branching typical of trichobacteria. After Schmidt and Weis.

there are certain other cells which are set aside for the purpose of reproduction. These cells are called *gonidia* or conidia (Figs. 16 and 17). There is, therefore, a division of labor or a differentiation in function among the cells of a filament in this group.

The most highly organized group of the higher bacteria is represented in Streptothrix actinomyces, a form under the Chlamydobacteriaceæ (see Fig. 17, *A*). In the actinomyces the filaments do not appear ordinarily to be composed of separate individuals. Occasionally, however, the protoplasm breaks up into rods similar to bacilli. There is true branching similar to that in the mycelium of a fungus (Fig. 18). The filaments often produce small round bodies (gonidia), which in turn produce new individuals. There is often a club-shaped swelling on the end of a filament. In all probability this is a degeneration product and not an organ of reproduction, as was formerly thought by some writers. These round bodies are not similar to spores, as is shown by the staining reaction and power of resistance. It has been suggested that the members of the actinomyces group constitute a connecting link between the lower bacteria, on the one hand, since the filaments occasionally break up into bacilli-like rods, and the fungi on the other, since branching similar to that in the mycelium of a fungus occurs.

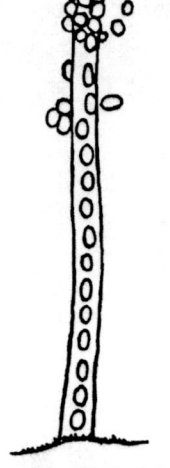

FIG. 16.— Cladothrix hyalina. Showing gonidia formation. After Schmidt and Weis.

There are several modifications in form and function among the higher bacteria. The members of one group (Beggiotoaceæ) are free from attachment and usually move by un-

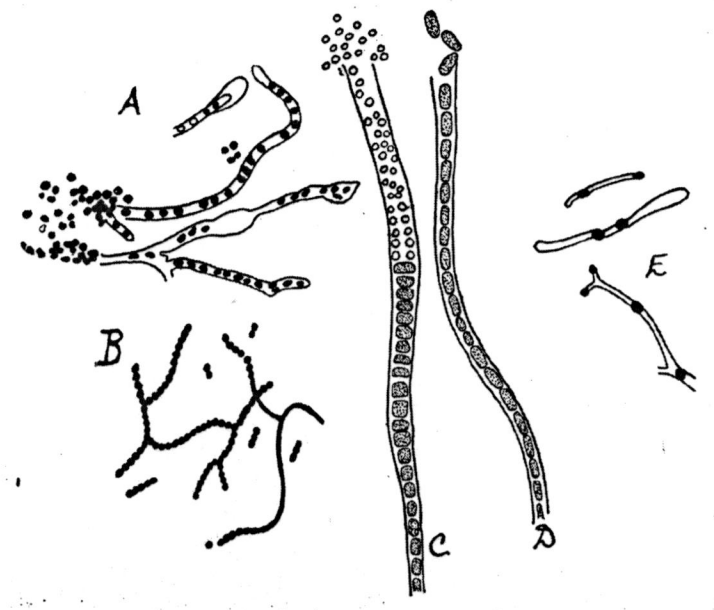

FIG. 17. — The formation of gonidia. (A) Streptothrix actinomyces, after Lehmann and Neumann. (B) Streptothrix chromogena, after Mace. (C), (D) Crenothrix Kuhniana, after Kopf: (C) microgonidia; (D) macrogonidia. (E) Gonidia-like bodies in Bact. tuberculosis.

dulative movements of their protoplasm. Some authors have ascribed to them an undulating membrane which during motility alternately contracts and relaxes. There is no common sheath around the cells. The cells contain granules of sulphur. Closely related to the above group is the group Thiothrix. This group is similar in structure to the Beggiatoaceæ, but one end of the filament is attached to some

24   MORPHOLOGY

substance and at the other gonidia are formed. When the reproductive cells (gonidia) burst out of the sheath and are thrown off, they usually are endowed with flagella temporarily and swim about freely. In still another group (Sphærotilus or Cladothrix) there is developed what is known as "false branching" as contrasted with the true branching of a fungus or weed. The appearance is due to the end cell of a filament dividing twice. The second division pushes to one side the product of the first division, and each cell goes on dividing separately, producing the so-called "branch" (Fig. 15).

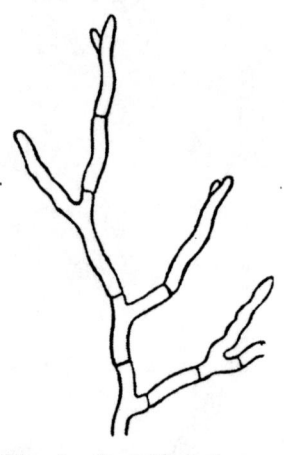

FIG. 18.—Penicillium glaucum. Showing the true branching of a fungus of higher order. After Fischer.

Further description of the Trichobacteria will be given in connection with the chapter on classification.

Involution Forms and Pleomorphism. — Among the bacilli, some spirilla, and certain trichobacteria, there frequently occurs protoplasmic degeneration and modification in form in some species. This degeneration of the protoplasm within the cell usually distorts the contour of the cell membrane, producing what are known as "involution forms." This degeneration occurs when the bacterial cell is not provided with suitable food, is being subjected to temperature changes, or to presence of a superabundance of excretory products.

The cocci do not seem to vary perceptibly under any conditions. It is possible to cause a regeneration of these "involution forms" in certain species when favorable conditions are provided. *It is not possible to cause any permanent change in the morphology of a bacterium and thus originate a new species of bacteria.* For example, it is not possible to cause a bacillus to change into a coccus and *vice versa*. This idea of *pleomorphism* was held for years by certain bacteriologists (Zopf. *et al.*). They explained the origin of new species by means of this phenomenon. Pleomorphism does not exist in its true sense; that is, there is no permanent change in form of a definite species of bacteria. The bacteria if modified from their normal shape will, when supplied with the requisite conditions of temperature, food, etc., as before stated, return to the normal. There may be a change in the characteristic form of growth of some bacteria under certain conditions. Bacterial cells may form themselves into pellicles, zoöglœa, chains, filaments, etc., but the type of cell remains the same. Chloride of lithium, and certain other chemicals, when placed in a medium containing bacteria, will cause a modification of their shape from the normal.

In certain species of bacteria the individual cells are more prone to change their shape under varying conditions than others, *e.g.* Bact. diphtheriæ, Bact. tuberculosis, bacteria in the root tubercles of clover, etc. (Figs. 19 and 20). Various species of bacteria produce "involution forms" under different conditions. For example, the acetic, lactic, butyric acid producing bacteria show great distortion in shape when the acids produced are increased above a certain percentage. Others show a change in shape when temperature is kept above

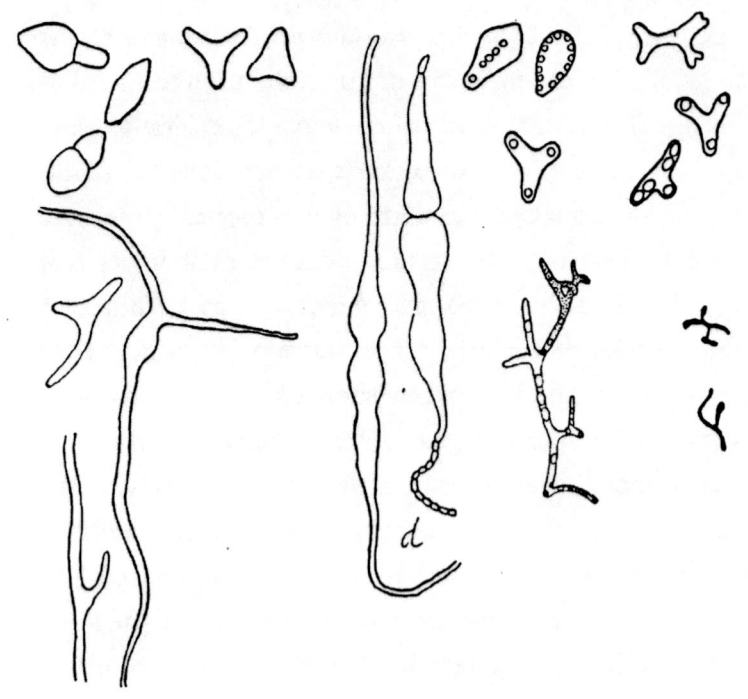

FIG. 19. — Involution forms. B. subtilis, water bacteria, Bact. aceti, Bact. pasteurianum, bacteroids from root nodules, Bact. tuberculosis, Bact. diphtheriæ. All forms shown are very different from the normal forms. After Fischer.

the normal for any period of time, and others show change in shape when food is lacking and excretory products have increased to a high percentage. Too rapid reproduction may cause aberrant shapes among some species. The conditions which produce " involution forms " among bacteria also

FORM AND STRUCTURE OF BACTERIA

attenuate the bacteria as far as their ability goes to produce fermentation, putrefaction, disease, etc.

Another theory — the theory of *pleogony* — was also formerly held by certain bacteriologists. This theory dealt with

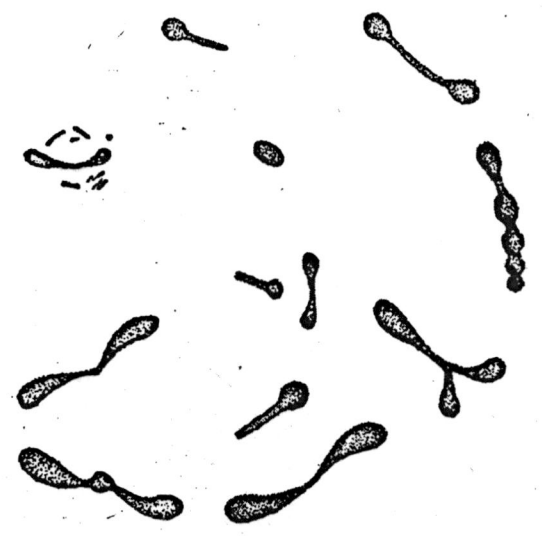

FIG. 20. — Involution forms. Bact. tuberculosis, two months' old culture. After Schmidt and Weis.

the development of new physiological characteristics among bacteria. The typical, normal, and physiologically active bacterial cell will, however, always return when the necessary conditions are provided. The passage of some bacteria through animals causes a return to the normal virulence and typical form of the bacterium.

Dimensions of Bacterial Cells. — The size varies with the species. In most instances it is fairly constant within the limit of the same species. In some species the size of the bacterial cells varies as greatly as does the shape. Within the same species a variation in certain cells of 0.1 and in others to 3 or 5 microns in length has been noted. Temperature, reaction, and composition of the media, and, in addition to these, the age of the cell are responsible for these variations.

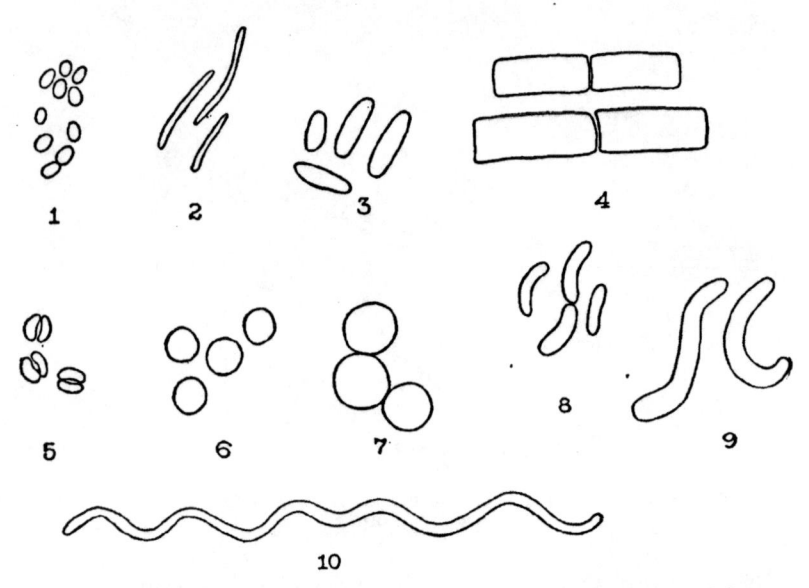

FIG. 21. — The comparative size of bacteria. (1) Bact. influenzæ. (2) Bact. tuberculosis. (3) B. typhosus. (4) Bact. anthracis. (5) M. gonorrhœæ. (6) M. pyogenes var. aureus. (7) M. freudemeichii. (8) Msp. comma. (9) Sp. undula. (10) Sp. obermeieri.

The size of the cells differs when introduced into animals and plants and on the various culture media used for the study of bacteria. It does not seem that breadth is any more constant than length among species of bacteria which vary in size.

It is interesting to note that one of the smallest observed bacteria, Pseudomonas indigofera (Voges) Mig., is only 0.18

micron in length and 0.06 micron in width. Bacillus dentrificans Mig. is a rod 1 to 1.5 microns in length by 0.1 to 0.3 micron in width. The Micrococcus progrediens (Schröter) is 0.15 micron in diameter. A bacterium described by Nocard and Rouxin pleuropneumonia is said to be still smaller. Without doubt there are still smaller organisms which are ultramicroscopic. Some of the largest bacteria have been reported by Errera and Schaudin. They describe a spirillum of the dimensions 23 to 28 microns in length by 3 to 3.4 microns in width, and also a bacillus 24 to 80 microns in length and 3 to 6 microns wide. Some very large cocci have been reported by various writers.

Fischer makes the estimate that it would take 30,000,000,000 pus cocci to weigh one gram. In a drop of water one cubic centimeter in size 1,700,000,000 pus cocci would have plenty of space. Bujwid counted the number of Micrococcus pyogenes var. aureus cells in a milligram of a pure culture and found that there were approximately 8,000,000,000. Fischer states that if an anthrax bacillus is 3 to 10 microns long and 1 to 1.2 microns broad, that 8,000,000, at least, would be required to equal a mass the size of an ordinary cigarette. Nägeli gives the weight of an average bacterium as a 10,000,000,000th part of a milligram.

Locomotion of Bacteria

Flagella. — Certain species of bacteria possess the power of locomotion. The degree of motion depends upon the age of the bacterium and the temperature of the surrounding medium. The faculty of moving about from place to place is possessed by only a few varieties of cocci, *e.g.* Micrococcus agilis, etc., but is quite common among the bacilli and spirilla. Motile bacteria progress by means of the vibration of long, whiplike appendages called flagella or cilia.

Ehrenberg was the first to describe flagella on bacterial cells. In 1838, he described appendages on B. triloculare. In 1870, Cohn described flagella on Spirillum volutans. In 1875, Warming described flagella on Spirillum undula, Spirillum rugula, etc. In 1877, various stains were used to demonstrate their presence. By means of stains it was found that a large number of bacteria possessed these organs of locomotion. By the year 1880, all bacteriologists had agreed that there were appendages of this character on certain bacterial cells. The method of locomotion by flagella is used by practically all motile lower bacteria. Among some of the higher bacteria the existence of an undulating membrane is claimed in certain species, *e.g.* Beggiaotoa. It is supposed that these species move by the alternate contraction and relaxation of their undulating membrane.

The flagella on a bacterium vary in number and arrangement according to the species. They are usually quite constant in number for the species. The flagella may vary in position on the different bacteria, and Messea, in 1890, proposed dividing the flagellate bacteria into the following classes: —

FORM AND STRUCTURE OF BACTERIA

(1) Monotrichous — one flagellum at one end (Ex. Pseudomonas pyocyanea) (Fig. 22).

(2) Lophotrichous — several flagella at one end in a bunch (Ex. Spirillus rugula) (Fig. 23).

(3) Amphitrichous — flagella at both ends, one at each (Ex. Bacillus butyricus) (Fig. 24).

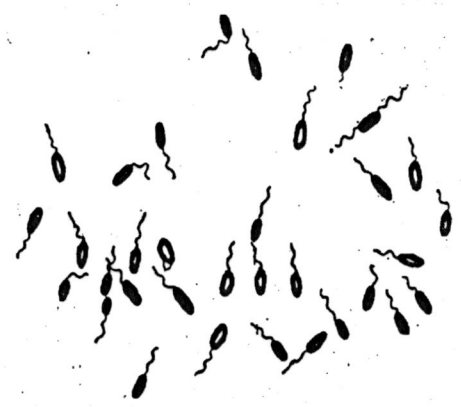

FIG. 22.—Pseudomonas pyocyanea. Showing monotrichous flagellation. After Schmidt and Weis.

(4) Peritrichous — flagella on all sides of the cell (Ex. Bacillus typhosus) (Fig. 25).

The presence of amphitrichous bacteria have been questioned by some. These investigators hold that an amphitrichous bacterium is formed from a monotrichous bacterium which is acquiring a new flagellum preparatory to fission.

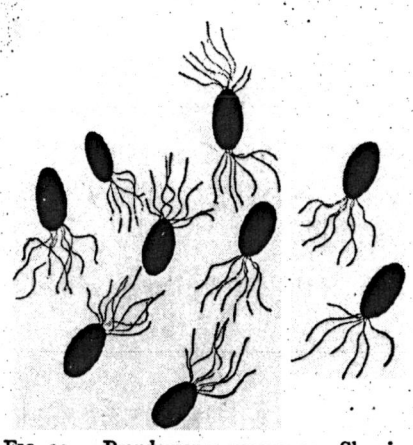

FIG. 23.—Pseudomonas syncyanea. Showing lophotrichous flagellation. After Schmidt and Weis.

In 1894, Migula used the number of flagella on

a bacterium and their mode of attachment as a basis for distinguishing and separating various genera. Fischer, in 1895, used the flagella as means of distinguishing subfamilies.

The flagella are long delicate processes, usually one to twenty times longer than the bacterial cell (1 to 20 ×). They possess a base which is slightly larger than the rest of the process. This base tapers like a cone, with a long filamentous process coming off the apex. The mode of attachment of the flagellum to the bacterial cell is not as yet definitely settled. It is probable that the protoplasm of the bacterial cell is continued out into the flagella and that there is a thin limiting membrane on the outside, similar to, although much thinner than, the cell wall proper. By the use of certain reagents the protoplasm of the flagella has been seen to shrink away from the limiting membrane, and an attachment has been noted of the flagellum to the peripherial zone of protoplasm of the cell. Some writers hold that the flagellum is definitely separated from the cell wall and composed of different material. Some have also held that the flagella

FIG. 24. — Spirillum rubrum. Showing amphotrichous flagellation. After Schmidt and Weis.

FORM AND STRUCTURE OF BACTERIA

are merely appendages of the cell wall and not organs of locomotion. It may be here stated that flagella have never been demonstrated on bacteria devoid of motility and are always

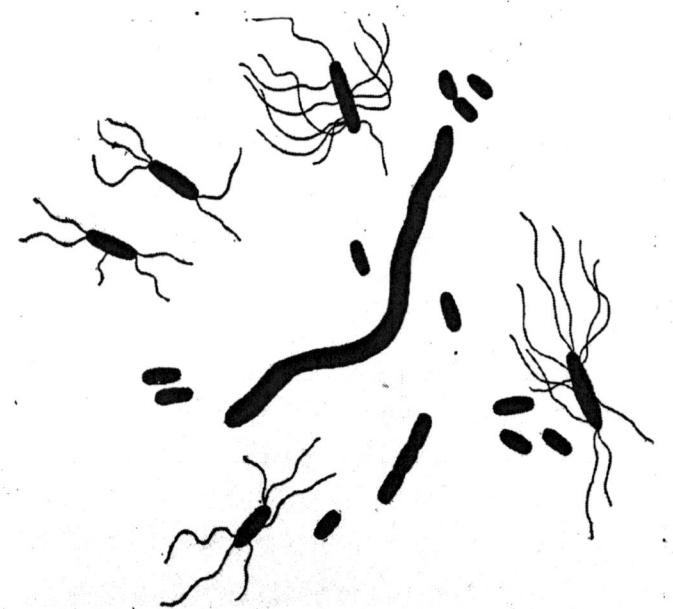

FIG. 25. — B. typhosus. Showing peritrichous flagellation. After Schmidt and Weis.

found on motile bacteria. The protoplasm of the flagellum may be slightly different chemically from the rest of the bacterial cell, for it is a familiar fact that the flagella are very much more liable to heat, chemicals, etc., than the protoplasm of the cell itself. It is possible that the flagella are connected with the cell through pores which connect the internal structures of the two. Under unfavorable conditions the flagella are thrown off, are disintegrated, and completely disappear in a short time.

The flagella on a bacterial cell are very hard to demonstrate. It is only by the most careful technique and the use of special mordants that they can be revealed They cannot be seen definitely in unstained preparations or preparations stained in the ordinary manner. The protoplasm of the flagella does not readily enter into chemical combination with the ordinary bacteriological stains. This points to the fact that its protoplasm is different from that contained within the cell. The flagella may be often revealed by the deposition of stains ($AgNO_3$, etc.) on the outside of the limiting membrane. Many bacteria discard their flagella when they are removed from the medium in which they are growing. Consequently they are very hard to place intact on a slide. They are very sensitive and the flagella are very easily disintegrated during the process of staining. It has been noted that the staining power of a flagellum often varies with the species of bacteria. Mordants are used with the stains in order that the flagella may be demonstrated at all.

As a flagellate bacterium moves it progresses in a definite manner. The mono- and lophotrichous bacteria move with the flagellum or flagella in front like certain infusoria, and rotate these organs in a circular fashion in a direction longitudinal to the long axis of the cell. The cell itself, in certain species, rotates freely when in motion. The peritrichous bacteria move in a longitudinal direction as the other bacteria and in addition may possess an end-over-end motion, tumbling similar to a somersault.

Rapidity of Movement. — Viewed under the microscope the motile bacteria seem to move very swiftly. This idea is, of course, due to the limited field of vision. Fischer estimates the actual average rate of movement under normal conditions of temperature, etc., at ten centimeters in fifteen minutes, or about $\frac{1}{9}$ millimeter per second. It should be noted that the speed is comparatively rapid, taking into consideration the small size of the bacterial cell. The rapidity of movement of a motile bacterium varies with the physiological condition of the cell. The temperature, presence of nutrient material, presence of excretory products, and the general vitality of the cell have much to do with the character of the movement of the cell.

Brownian Movement. — Very frequently when preparations of live bacteria are examined under the microscope they are seen to move backward and forward in an oscillating fashion. They do not progress through the medium. This movement should be carefully differentiated from true locomotion. This phenomenon, which was first described by Brown, is due to the bombardment of molecules in the liquid medium in which the bacteria may be suspended. Particles of India ink show the same sort of movement.

Capsules. — Some species of bacteria secrete a gelatinous substance from the outer layers of the cell protoplasm or the cell wall. When large numbers of bacteria are found together secreting these gelatinous substances in great amount the typical *zoöglœa* is formed. However, the bacteria may occur separately and become surrounded by a thin sheath of a clear, jellylike, highly refractive substance, which is usually

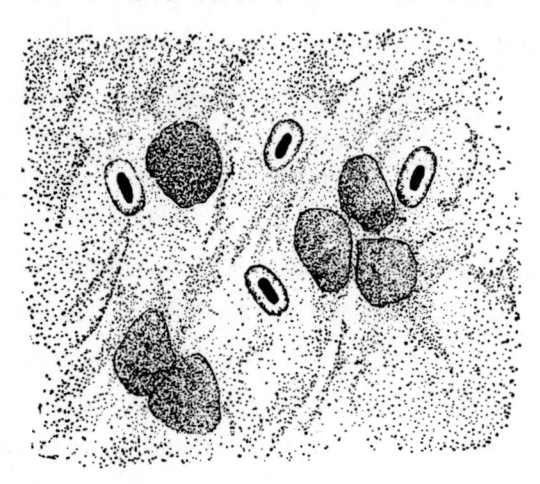

FIG. 26 — Capsules. Bact. pneumonicum (Friedlander). After Weichselbaum.

many times broader than the bacterial cell. To this sheath of gelatinous material the name *capsule* has been applied. Capsule-producing bacteria do not produce capsules under all conditions. The necessary and particular nutrient material must be available for capsule formation. Bacillus capsulatus in milk produces the most typical capsules, while on agar-agar it produces none. Bacterium anthracis on ordinary culture media such as gelatin, agar-agar, beef broth, etc., produces no capsules, while in the blood of an animal infected with anthrax the capsules are very typical. Sometimes several bacterial cells appear to be surrounded by a single capsule, *e.g.* Mic. pneumoniæ. In all probability this appearance is due to the amalgamation of the capsules of the several cells. It is usually necessary to use special stains to demonstrate capsules clearly. Frequently on stained slides clear spaces are seen around the bacterial cell, and these spaces are often confused with capsules. The spaces are artifacts due to the contraction of the gelatinous capsule during the process of drying. Migula says that in all probability all bacteria possess capsules in a rudimentary state.

Sheaths. — Among certain forms of the trichobacteria (Cladothrix, Crenothrix, etc.) there is developed a structure which has a very similar origin to that of a capsule. The outer layers of the cell wall, instead of remaining soft and gelatinous, become hard and form what is called a *sheath*. Phosphate of lime is deposited in the sheaths of some species of bacteria. The sheaths of bacterial cells in a chain of filament frequently become connected together, making the thread of cells very rigid. The cell proper contracts away from the sheath and is free to move. When reproduction takes place the sheaths break open and the individual cells escape. Subsequently the sheath disintegrates (see Fig. 15).

Mass Grouping. — (*a*) Zoöglœa, (*b*) Pellicles, and (*c*) Colonies. Not infrequently bacterial cells are found collected together in aggregate masses. These masses may have no definite shape, and the individual bacteria are held together by a gelatinous secretion. The individual bacteria may be formed into definite chains. The gelatinous material is either secreted by the cell wall or the outer layers of the cell protoplasm. In all probability it originates from the former. The increased absorption of water by the outer layer of the cell wall seems to be responsible for the gelatinous secretion. The term zoöglœa is applied by bacteriologists to these masses of bacteria and gelatinous material, *e.g.* B. vulgatus. This formation is noted on the surface of solid and liquid nutrient substances. The gelatinous material secreted is similar to that which forms the capsules of certain species of bacteria (Fig. 27). It composes a thick covering on the outside of the bacterial chains. This formation is very often seen in the processes of fermentation of Streptococcus mesenterioides in sugar vats. Other clumps of bacteria which are not readily soluble in water and which arise from fusion or imperfect separation of the individual cells are often seen. These masses are called *pseudozoöglœa*. They do not possess the compactness and gelatinization of the true zoöglœa. Zoöglœa and pseudozoöglœa masses compose the so-called slime which collect on various fluids. In nutrient liquids certain bacteria form aggregates producing the appearance of scum on the surface, *e.g.* B. subtilis. These aggregates are sometimes called *pellicles*. The pellicle usually grows until it covers the surface of the liquid. They contain, in addition to the bacteria and

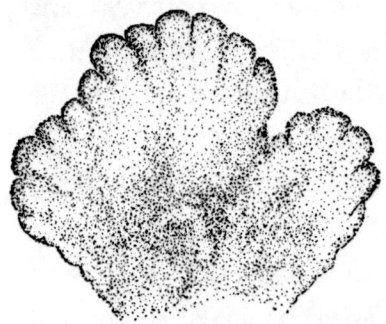

FIG. 27. — Zoöglœa in an aquatic bacterium. The individual cells are thickly aggregated at the periphery, less so in the middle; they are held together by a mucus-like secretion. After Fischer.

FORM AND STRUCTURE OF BACTERIA 39

the gelatinous secretion, some organic material derived from the media. The size of the pellicle varies with the size of the

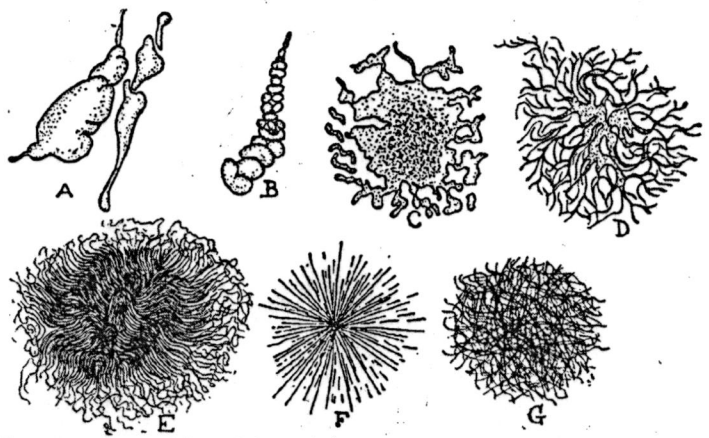

FIG. 28. — Types of bacterial colonies. (*A*) Cochleate (B. coli, abnormal form). (*B*) Conglomerate (B. zopfi). (*C*) Ameboid (B. vulgatus). (*D*) Rhizoid (B. mycoides). (*E*) Curled (Bact. anthracis). (*F*) Myceloid (B. radiatus). (*G*) Filamentous. After Frost.

vessel containing the nutrient fluid. Care should be taken not to confuse these masses of bacteria, *i.e.* zoöglœa, pseudo-zoöglœa, and pellicles with the regular *colonies* of bacteria

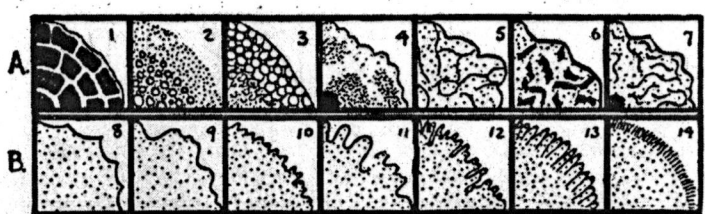

FIG. 29. — Microscopic structure of colonies. (*A*) Colony as a whole. (1) Areolate. (2) Grumose. (3) Moruloid. (4) Clouded. (5) Gyrose. (6) Marmorated. (7) Reticulate. (*B*) Edge of colonies. (8) Repand. (9) Lobate. (10) Erose. (11) Auriculate. (12) Lacerate. (13) Fimbricate. (14) Ciliate. After Frost.

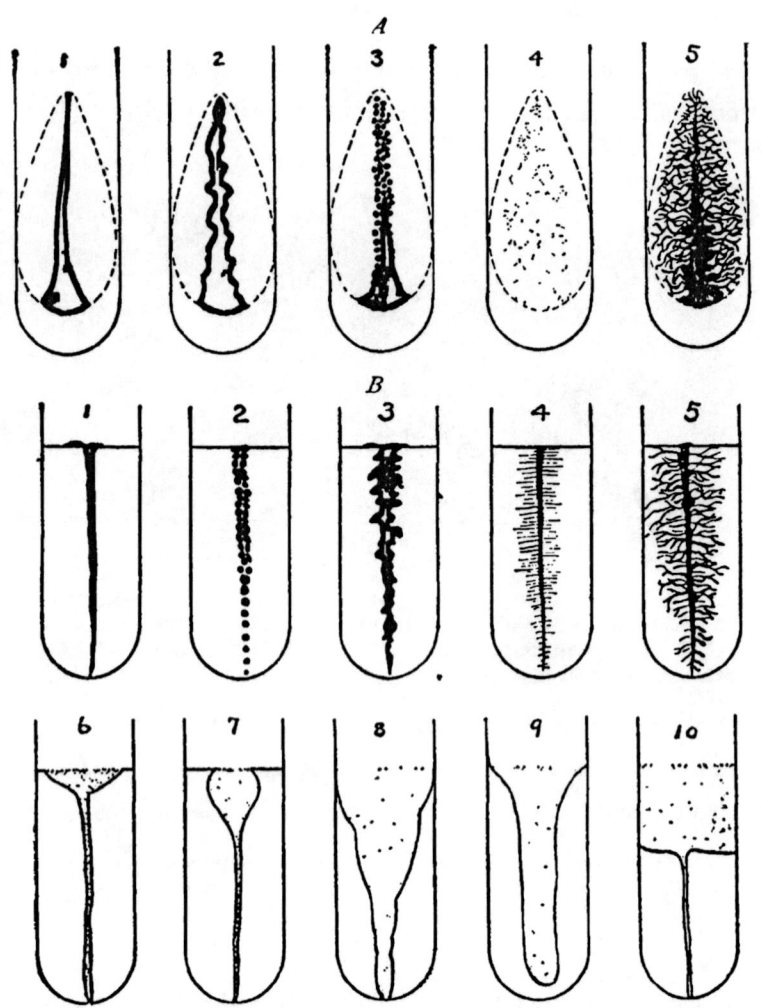

FIG. 30 — (*A*) Types of streak cultures.   (1) Filiform (B coli)   (2) Echinulate (Bact acidi-lactici)   (3) Beaded (Str pyogenes).   (4) Effuse (B vulgatus) 5. Arborescent (B. Mycoides).

(*B*) Types of growth in stab cultures   *Nonliquefying*   (1) Filiform (B coli) (2) Beaded (Str. pyogenes)   (3) Echinate (Bact. acidi-lactici)   (4) Villous (Bact murisepticum).   (5) Arborescent (B. mycoides)   *Liquefying*   (6) Crateriform (B vulgaris, 24 hr).   (7) Napiform (B subtilis, 48 hr).   (8) Infundibuliform (B. prodigiosus).   (9) Saccate (Msp finkleri)   (10) Stratiform (Ps. fluorescens)   After Frost.

developed in nutrient media as a result of reproduction in a definite manner. The type of colony is a characteristic for a definite species and is not an accidental formation. The type of colony is of taxonomic importance; that is, of importance in identifying a definite species (Fig. 28). The edges of the colonies may be regular, smooth, or serrated (Fig. 29). Different descriptive terms are applied to the characteristic fashion in which bacteria grow in colonies. When bacteria are inoculated on the surface of agar tubes or by puncture into gelatin or agar, the various species grow in a very constant and typical manner (Fig. 30).

CHAPTER IV

Reproduction of Bacteria

Introduction. — The process of reproduction among bacteria is exceedingly interesting. If proper food and environment are present, the bacterial cell multiplies at a certain stage of its existence. Reproduction is entirely asexual. The term "reproduction," as it is usually applied, not only includes the production of new individuals but also an increase in the number of individuals. The process is slightly different in the lower and the higher bacteria, and, consequently, reproduction will be considered separately for each class.

Reproduction among the Haplobacteria (Lower Bacteria)

Fission. — The method of reproduction among these forms is by binary division, or *fission*. The cell about to multiply elongates slightly and gradually becomes constricted in the center from all sides in transverse diameter to the long axis of the cell (Fig. 31). The constriction becomes deeper and deeper, carrying in the chitinous or cellulose-like wall, and finally the two parts of the original cell remain attached by only a thin thread. Bacterial cells follow the same laws of cell division as most animal and plant cells. The cell usually increases in size to the normal adult, then divides by fission as the parent did. Not infrequently fission takes place before the

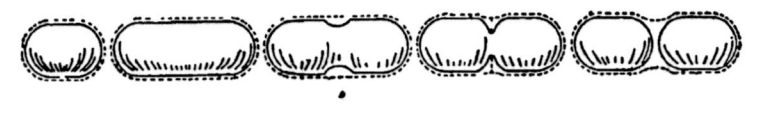

Fig. 31. — Diagram illustrating fission of bacterial cells (bacilli and cocci). After Novy.

adult stage is reached. Involution forms may be produced by this means. Before any constrictions appear in the cell wall the protoplasm within shows evidences of being constricted into two parts. Some writers claim that a membrane forms at the point of division which separates the parent cell into two distinct parts. This in all probability is not always the exact condition, although in some species of bacteria an unstained line does appear in the protoplasm at the point of division. It is claimed by some that this dividing membrane is cellulose, but recent research shows that no such substance as the cellulose of higher plant cells occurs among the lower bacteria. Bacilli and spirilla always divide in a direction transverse to the long axis of the cell. The cocci divide irregularly as regards a definite direction.

Rate of Multiplication. — A bacterium may reach the adult form and divide in from twenty minutes to an hour, varying with the species. Bacteria are very prolific when the requisite conditions of food, temperature, and gaseous environment are at hand. One bacterium dividing once every hour in twenty-four hours would produce if uninhibited 16,777,216 individuals, in forty-eight hours 281,474,710,656 individuals, and in six days the mass produced, if each bacterium weighed on the average of $\frac{1}{10,000,000,000}$ of a milligram, would equal the size of the earth. Uninterrupted division for any period of time beyond or even to twenty-four hours, except in rare cases, is an absolute impossibility. The geometrical progression is not an actual one in the case of bacteria. Long before the cell has multiplied to the extent given in the above figures, the food will have become so reduced, and excretory products will have accumulated to the extent of acting as poisons to the cells themselves and consequently inhibiting fission, so that reproduction will progress much slower than is possible theoretically and will finally cease completely. Not even in an infected body do bacteria multiply uninterruptedly. It is interesting to observe, however, what unlimited powers of reproduction bacteria have, and that we are dealing in the case of these minute plants with a force of almost infinite power.

The power of growth and reproduction of the bacterial cell is due, in all probability, to the fact that the food of bacteria is highly organized and must be in solution and ready for absorption and assimilation. This organic food is derived from the disintegration of complex animal and plant compounds. Green plants usually manufacture their food from simpler substances (CO_2, HO_2, nitrites and nitrates). Animals and fungi use complex organic compounds for food, and before they can be assimilated they must be digested and broken up into somewhat simpler compounds. The food used by most bacteria requires little or no chemical alteration before it can be assimilated by the protoplasm of the cell. Bacteria are not compelled to search about for food as some animals do, but live naturally only in the midst of nutrient material. It should be noted that reproduction in some protozoa (amœba) takes place for a time as rapidly as in the bacteria, but only after the cell has received and assimilated sufficient food. On account of their natural conditions of life bacteria can grow faster and reproduce more rapidly than any other animal or plant cell. There is a great variation among bacteria in regard to the rapidity with which they reproduce. Some species are exceedingly rapid (B. subtilis), and others are comparatively slow (Bact. tuberculosis).

The flagella of the motile bacteria do not in any way interfere with the process of fission among these species. In the lophotrichous bacteria the non-flagellate end of the dividing cell furnishes flagella for one of the new individuals. The other cell uses the old flagellum of the parent. These old flagella may be carried for generations. The contiguous ends of the cells never produce any flagella. In amphitrichous bacteria new flagella are provided by both new individuals. These cells therefore have a new and an old set of locomotive organs. It is held by some that amphitrichous bacteria do not exist, and that the bipolar flagella result during the process of fission of a monotrichous bacterium, the new individual having produced a new flagellum before separating from the original cell. In the peritrichous bacteria as the cells are elongating preparatory to fission, new flagella are developed at the point of constriction between the old flagella. On division being completed, the new flagella come to lie on the end of the cells.

Spore Formation. — Spore formation, according to various writers, is given as a means of multiplication. The formation of the spore is a means of carrying out one phase of the process of reproduction. The term "spore" is applied to the resting stages of plant and animal cells. Obviously, the species must be preserved before reproduction and multiplication can take place. The spore has been likened by some to the seed of plants. The spore and the seed serve to carry the parent cells through unfavorable conditions for definite periods in the life history of the organism. Spores are produced by some bacilli and a few spirilla The first careful study of spores was made by Koch in 1878 in his study of Bacterium anthracis, and by Cohn in his work on Bacillus subtilis. Spore formation usually takes place when the bacterial cell is surrounded by unfavorable conditions, such as exhaustion of the food supply, accumulation of excretory products, abnormal temperatures, etc. It should be noted in this connection that certain protozoan parasites (amœba) become encysted when surrounded by the above-mentioned conditions. A spore will germinate within certain limits of time, when the normal conditions are provided. The first indication of spore formation in a bacterial cell is evidenced

REPRODUCTION OF BACTERIA

by loss of the power of locomotion in motile forms, the formation of small, highly refractile granules within the cell. These granules assume the appearance of globules and coalesce either in the middle, at the end, or very near the end of the cell. The coalesced globule thus formed increases in size and becomes spherical or spheroidal in shape (Fig. 32). The spore never becomes as long as the bacterial cell, but frequently becomes many times broader, thus distending the cell wall. The spore does not always distend the rod. When the spore is greater in diameter than the mother cell and is in the center of the rod, a spindle-shaped appearance may be produced (B. butyricus). If it is at the end of the cell, the common drumstick form is produced (B. tetani). Occasionally, when the spore is located a slight distance from the end of the cell, the appearance of the cell is that of a wedge. This last-mentioned formation is not characteristic for any one species but results rather as a "sport" (Fig. 33). When the spore is fully formed,

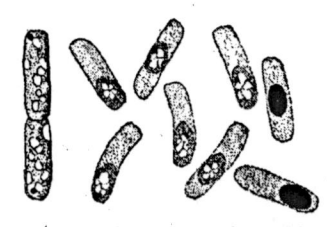

FIG. 32.—Spore formation. After Fischer.

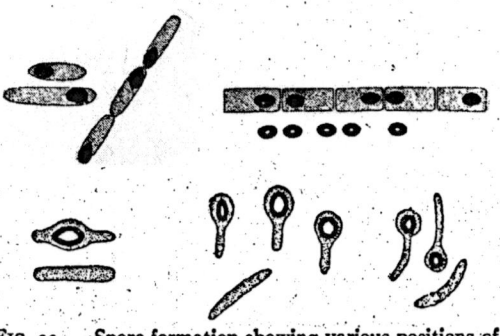

FIG. 33.—Spore formation showing various positions of spores. Original.

the cell wall of the mother cell ruptures and liberates the spore surrounded by a newly secreted and highly resistant membrane. The rest of the original cell undergoes disintegration. When a spore develops into a vegetative form it usually increases in size, loses its high refractive power, and ruptures. The spore may rupture at the end and form a small pore or opening. From this opening the protoplasm grows out and forms the characteristic bacillus or spirillum. The old spore membrane can be often discerned attached to the new vegetative form. Occasionally the spore membrane splits longitudinally and sometimes transversely, so that the young cell has part of the spore on either end or on both sides of it for a short period as it grows in length. In a few species of bacteria there is no rupture of the spore membrane, it being absorbed by the developing vegetative cell. It is probable that the bacterial cell goes into the spore stage as a means of carrying the cell through unfavorable conditions to a time when normal conditions will be present and the cell can reproduce. Some hold the view that sporulation is the highest stage of the life history of certain bacteria. It is necessary for these bacteria to pass through this stage in order to maintain a vigorous species. This condition of affairs has been noted among certain of the algæ. Others believe that it is always necessary for a bacterium to be placed in unfavorable surroundings to form spores. Yet at certain temperatures which are favorable for bacterial growth sporulation occurs. It is possible that the environment may be rapidly changed and not always be perceptible, and this may account for the formation of spores in certain cases where the environment appears normal. Below and above the point where sporulation takes place at a temperature favorable for reproduction no spores are formed, although fission may take place.

Certain species of bacteria may be made to lose the power of spore formation when grown at high temperature (Bact. anthracis). Gaseous environment may also influence the power of a species of bacteria to form spores. Bacterium anthracis in the animal body does not form spores, but when given a large amount of oxygen, on artificial media, it readily forms them.

The spore is a very resistant body. It is resistant to heat, — some species withstanding very high temperatures, — to cold, and to chemicals. Spores, as well as vegetative forms, vary in their powers of resistance with the species. For example, the vegetative form of Bacterium anthracis is killed by one per cent phenol in two minutes, and in the spore stage it requires from one to fifteen days (Koch). Anthrax spores will withstand air drying for years. They are the most resistant spores known. The test of efficiency of all disinfectants is partially based on their ability to destroy anthrax spores. The great resistance of the spore is due to the very compact and impermeable membrane which surrounds it, and also to the fact that its protoplasm contains less water than the vegetative form. The more water there is in a cell the easier it is coagulated. The spore is composed of condensed protoplasm. Ordinary bacteriological stains (anilin dyes) do not stain spores. It requires special methods to stain these highly refractile bodies.

Arthrospores. — In certain vegetative bacterial cells, Cladothrix, Thiothrix, and perhaps a few micrococci which grow in a filamentous form, it is claimed by some writers (Hueppe, *et al.*) that some of the cells increase in size, become refractile, but stain easily and develop a higher power of resistance than the other members of the same group of individuals. They detach themselves from the thread and swim about in the medium surrounding them. These cells are called *arthrospores*.[1] It is claimed that when reproduction takes place these cells are the only ones concerned in the process. There is no new formation within the protoplasm of the vegetative cell, as in most spore-forming bacteria, but the whole of the protoplasm of the cell enters into the formation of the body known as the arthrospore. They do not possess any such increased powers of resistance as do endospores. The majority of bacteriologists at the present do not recognize any such body as the arthrospore (see Fig. 38).

Reproduction among the Trichobacteria (Higher Bacteria)

The higher bacteria are usually filamentous forms, and in a large number of species possess sheaths. The filaments are made up of individuals which are separate but connected terminally with each other. One end of the filament is usually attached to some object. After reaching a certain length the cells on

[1] Not used in the sense proposed by De Bary.

the free end of the filament divide in one, two, or three planes and form reproductive bodies of a specialized type known as gonidia. These gonidia are cast off, acquire flagella in some species, and, for a period, may be motile. They then attach to some object and reproduce a new filament. Gonidia are frequently the same shape as the original cell, although they often assume a rather spherical shape in certain species. At one time gonidia were thought by some to be spores, but they are non-resistant, and do not give any of the staining reactions for spores.

CHAPTER V

MINUTE STRUCTURE OF THE BACTERIAL CELL

Introduction. — Notwithstanding the fact that the bacteria are among the smallest organic bodies known, many facts have been determined in regard to their minute structure Up to the present time, however, our knowledge is very elementary. Little can be learned regarding the minute anatomy of the bacterial cell when in a viable state or in a stained preparation under the ordinary microscope, even when magnified 1000 to 2000 diameters. Much more must be learned in regard to the anatomy and chemistry of the bacteria before we can have a complete understanding of bacteriological processes in general. It is probable that the new ultra-violet microscope when perfected will be of value in working out the structure of bacteria. It has seemed advisable to consider the subject-matter of this chapter under two separate heads, the histology and the chemical structure.

Histology of the Bacterial Cell. — The cells of all species of bacteria are composed of that common organic substance termed protoplasm, cell sap, and a limiting membrane similar to some plant and some animal cells.

Cell Wall. — The protoplasm is said to be naked in a great many animal cells. It may be stated that there is usually a semblance of a cell wall in these cases. In a few instances the cell wall of animal cells approximates the cell wall of the plant in strength. The bacteria in structure stand between the plant and the animal. For example, the cell wall is of a higher order than the animal cell wall, but it is not so highly developed as the cell wall of true plants. It has been positively proved that the bacterial cell possess a limiting cell wall similar to plant cells in some cases and animal cells in others. Many other points go to show that the bacteria belong to an intermediate class as far as structure is concerned. The cell does not possess any clearly defined nucleus or nucleolus, and in this particular differs from the majority of animal and plant cells. Stained by the ordinary bacteriological stains (anilin dyes), no definite structure can be demonstrated on account of the intensity of the stain. Bacteria stain more deeply with the anilin dyes than plant cells.

Protoplasm. — According to some authorities the protoplasm of the bacterial cell is not distributed throughout the whole cell, but composes a layer next to the cell wall. The central part of the cell, in common with plant cells, contains the cell sap, composed largely of water and organic and inorganic substances in solution. The exact condition of affairs, in all probability, is that there is a somewhat denser layer of protoplasm, called *ectoplasm*, next to the cell wall. This layer is not definite and separate from the interior of the cell, thus creating a central cavity as some authors state. Many threads of protoplasmic material run from this outer layer through the interior of the cell, forming as it were a network of protoplasmic threads in the center. The interstices of this network contain the water, inorganic, and organic substances which compose the so-called cell sap. The substances within the ectoplasm compose the *entoplasm*. The thickness of the outer protoplasmic layer, or ectoplasm, varies in the same and different species. On the average it is thicker in the old cells.

By the well-known physical phenomenon of plasmolysis, some very interesting points can be learned in regard to the structure of bacteria. For instance, if a live bacterial cell is placed in a solution of higher density (hypertonic solution) than its cell sap, the solvents (water, etc.) contained therein will pass through the layer of protoplasm next to the cell wall, through the cell wall to join the liquid on the outside, and thus serve to dilute the salts present in the solution. The layer of protoplasm (ectoplasm) constitutes a semipermeable membrane. The cell wall is permeable to most solutes, such as salts, urea, sugars, etc. As a result of the loss of water by the bacterial cell the protoplasm retracts from the cell wall and forms itself into irregular masses within the cell. In certain of the infusoria the protoplasmic layer is attached to the cell wall, and the whole cell assumes an irregular shape. This experiment shows that there is a definite cell wall and that the protoplasm of the cell and the cell wall are distinct from each other. It also serves to explain certain other bodies, such as metachromatic and polar granules, which will be referred to later.

There is a great difference in the way the various species of bacteria are affected by solutions of higher and lower density, or osmotic pressure. There is without doubt a great difference chemically and anatomically between the protoplasm of different species of bacteria, and this accounts for the inability of some species to plasmolyze readily. There is a difference in the permeability of the ectoplasm to the solvents. The ectoplasm in some few species does not prevent the diffusion in and out of the cell of certain particular solutes, while in other bacteria the same solute is unable to pass through the ectoplasmic layer. This is what constitutes a semipermeable membrane, — a membrane permeable to solvents but not to solutes. Old bacteria plasmolyze more easily than young bacteria, and this is probably due to the former having a thicker layer of protoplasm or semipermeable membrane.

The cell sap contains solutes derived from external fluids as well as some generated within. The presence of these solutes within produces a great osmotic pressure against the protoplasmic layer and the cell wall, and there is a constant tendency for the cells to become distended, due to the passage into the cell of solvents, such as water, from the exterior. The pressure inside a bacterial cell may equal two or three atmospheres. It is due to the rigidity of the cell wall that the bacterial cell is able to withstand an internal pressure which would easily rupture the protoplasmic layer which really determines the osmotic pressure. Osmotic pressure, it may be said in passing, depends upon the amount of crystalloids (solutes) in solution Pressure is produced by molecules and ions pounding against the semipermeable membrane. There is a great difference in the way in which various substances diffuse through this or any semipermeable membrane. The osmotic pressure will be directly proportionate to the number of molecules of nonelectrolytes (sugars and other carbohydrates, urea, etc). In the case of the electrolytes (salts) the ions in solution produce the osmotic pressure.

If bacteria are accustomed gradually to the solutions of high osmotic pressure (hypertonic solutions) by passage through fluids of increasing density, there will be no plasmolysis. This shows that the cell is so constituted that the solutes such as salts and crystaloidal nonelectrolytes diffuse slowly through the ectoplasm and become incorporated in the cell sap or entoplasm. The ectoplasm is easily permeated by solvents and in time is permeable to certain solutes.

It is possible to change the contents of a bacterial cell by placing it in a hypotonic solution, that is, a solution of less density and consequently lower osmotic pressure than the cell sap. The classical experiment is to place bacteria which have been accustomed to growing on or in culture media containing salts into a solution of distilled water. The distilled water passes readily through the cell wall and the semipermeable ectoplasm. The cell increases in size consequent to the absorption of water, and if kept under such conditions for any length of time the cell wall will rupture (rhexis) and the protoplasmic and other contents escape into the surrounding liquid (plasmoptysis). A six per cent solution of cane sugar exerts a pressure of 3075 mm. of mercury at 14 degrees C. (sixty pounds to the square inch). Just so, under natural conditions, the form and structure of a bacterial cell may be altered according to the character of the food and the density of the surrounding medium. The phenomena of plasmolysis and plasmoptysis doubtless account for the involution forms among certain species and the so-called pleomorphism of some cells. It may be said in this connection that it is impossible to subject all species of bacteria to the phenomenon of plasmoptysis, due to the fact that their cell wall and ectoplasm are so constituted that salts may diffuse out more readily than in others.

Metachromatic and Polar Granules. — Under certain conditions in some species of bacteria the cells show a peculiar granular appearance when stained with the ordinary anilin dyes. The granules are irregular in size, do not occur in any definite arrangement, and stain darker than or at variance with the surrounding protoplasm (Loeffler's methylene blue stain on Bact. diphtheriæ). These granules are known as *metachromatic granules.* The protoplasm in these cases seems to have a beaded appearance. There have been various staining methods devised to demonstrate these granules. In other species of bacteria there is a concentration of the protoplasm at the poles of the cell. When stained by the various bacteriological stains, these granules of condensed protoplasm stain deeply and are well differentiated from the rest of the cell. These granules are known as *polar granules* (methylene blue stain on B. pestis). Frequently due to the accumulation of the granules in certain parts of the cell the remaining slightly stained protoplasm gives the appearance of vacuoles. These vacuoles appear to contain a clear substance, in all probability cell sap. As to the significance of both metachromatic and polar granules there is still doubt. Obviously, it is necessary to determine whether there is any consistency in their development in certain species of bacteria under any and all conditions. It may be stated that certain bacteria show a slight granular condition of their protoplasm at all times (Bact diphtheriæ), while others do not show such structures with consistency. It is frequently observed when the bacteria are grown under unsatisfactory conditions of temperature, moisture, or food supply. It has been stated that this granular formation within some bacterial cells precedes reproduction. They were supposed by some to be similar to gonidia. They are also known as Babes-Ernst granules. It has not been positively proved that these granules have anything whatever to do with the process of reproduction. Some writers have claimed that they were food products, but this is an erroneous conception. In all probability they are produced artificially in the cell by plasmolysis. As mentioned above, when bacteria are placed in a media of greater density (hypertonic) than that of their entoplasm, the solvents within the cell diffuse out through the semipermeable ectoplasm, and the remaining protoplasm in the cell retracts and collects in irregular particles in various portions of the cell. It is plausible that this condensed protoplasm composes what are called metachromatic and polar granules. Some authors have ascribed to bacteria the power of spontaneous plasmolysis to explain the irregular staining of such bacteria as Bacterium diphtheriæ, Bacterium tuberculosis, and the polar staining of Bacillus pestis (bubonic plague). It should not be overlooked that when staining a preparation of bacteria all the prerequisites for plasmolysis are present. For example, the heating of the preparation before the stain is applied drives the water out of the cell and concentrates the solutes, and consequently causes a retraction of the cell protoplasm from the cell wall, which may collect in granules. It is probable that the formation of polar granules, together with the formation of vacuoles, are either artificially produced, or that they are degenerative changes in the bacterial cell. Definite granules of sulphur have been noted in certain of the higher bacteria (Beggiatoaceæ).

Nucleus. — In regard to the perplexing question as to whether or not a nucleus exists in the bacterial cell, there has been a great deal of investigation. As stated before, there is no definite and circumscribed nucleus in the bacterial cell. When stained with the ordinary nuclear stains (hematoxylin, basic anilin dyes, etc.), the material (chromatin) which takes the stain is distributed throughout the cell. There are also portions of the cell which in some species do not stain (achromatic). Some writers hold the view that the chromatic substance is nuclear material. The nuclear material has, therefore, a general distribution throughout the cell. This is undoubtedly true in the light of present research. Some bacteria, for example certain vibrios, consist almost entirely of chromatin The amount of chromatic material varies a great deal even in the same species under different conditions. It has been suggested that the reason the nuclear material is not aggregated in the regular form of the nucleus may be ascribed to the fact that the bacteria are low in the stage of evolution, and that they divide so rapidly that the nuclear material does not have sufficient time to form itself into the resting stage which the normal nucleus represents. Butschli studied certain large forms of bacteria which contain sulphur granules (Beggiatoaceæ), and he concluded that the large part of the cell was nucleus surrounded by a thin layer of protoplasm. Fischer is inclined to believe that Butschli's preparations were due to plasmolysis. Nakanishi claims he has demonstrated a definite nucleus in the cells of some species of bacteria. This observation has not been confirmed.

Chemical Structure of the Bacterial Cell. — Our knowledge of the exact and complete chemical constitution of the bacterial cell is at present quite as limited as our knowledge of the histological structure. It may be said that bacteria are exceedingly labile, and therefore the ordinary analytical methods cannot be satisfactorily applied to them. It is well known that the chemical constitution of the bacterial cell varies greatly in different species, and in the same species when the bacteria are grown on different varieties of culture media, and on the same media. The chemical constitution also varies with the age of the bacteria. The following from Wells, "Chemical Pathology," quoting Cramer, gives a very good statement of their composition. Cholera vibrios grown on bouillon on analysis showed 65.25 per cent proteid and 25.87 per cent ash. When grown on media free from protein (Uschinsky's medium) they showed 35.75 per cent protein and 13.7 per cent ash. In the same medium 65.63 per cent and 34.37 per cent protein were noted in two strains of cholera vibrios. It cannot be said that any one species of bacteria has a definite chemical structure. However, there are some chemical substances which are found in the same species of bacteria continuously, as, for example, the fats in acid-fast bacteria. The variation in structure is more quantitative than qualitative.

The older analyses, of which there are many, are on the whole incorrect in the light of modern methods of research. The majority of bacteria contain liquids, proteins, water, and salts, such as those of sodium, potassium, magnesium, and phosphorus. Phosphorus in all probability occurs in the largest amounts. According to a recent investigation of Iwanoff the principal constituent of the bacterial cell is a genuine nucleoprotein containing traces of iron and sulphur. Another writer, Nishimura, has reported the finding of certain purin bases, the nucleo-protein end-products, such as guanin, adenin, and xanthin in bacterial cells. Wells says that the nucleoproteids of bacterial cells have been known to split off pentoses similar to higher nucleo-proteins. Certain bacteria have been analyzed and found to be composed of glyconucleoproteins and mucin (*e.g.* B. coli) (Leach). Nencki isolated a nitrogenous body from putrefactive bacteria, which is similar in composition to peptone. Globulins and nucleo-albumens have been reported in the protoplasm of bacteria. The gelatinous material secreted by the bacteria in zoöglœal and pseudozoöglœal formations is very similar in chemical constitution to mucin.

Fats have been found in the protoplasm of a large number of species of bacteria. The fat has been disclosed by staining reactions and by the extraction of the cells with the various fat solvents, such as hot alcohol, chloroform, ether, etc. Lecithin, a phosphorized fat; cholesterin, a monatomic alcohol derived from fatty acids; simple and special bacterial fats, have been isolated. Some lipochromes (coloring matter of fats) are also present. The proportion of material soluble in fat solvents in Bacterium tuberculosis and other acid-fast bacteria is about 20 to 40 per cent of the weight of the bacteria.

With Sudan III, which is a characteristic stain for fat, it has been possible to demonstrate fat only in Bacteria anthracis, Staphylococcus pyogenes var. aureus, Bact. mucosis, and in all the acid-fast bacteria, *i.e.*, Bact. tuberculosis, Bact. lepræ, Bact. smegmatis, Bact. mœlleri (grass bacillus), Bact. butyri (butter bacillus), and others. In other species no fat was demonstrated by Sudan III. Bacteria form the most of their fat when grown on potato or glycerine agar. The amount of the fat in a bacterial cell may be increased by growing the bacteria on a fat-rich medium.

Kresling[1] gives the following analysis of the material after extracting Bacterium tuberculosis with chloroform.

Free fatty acids	14.38 per cent
Neutral fats and fatty acid esters	77.25 per cent
Alcohols obtained from fatty acid esters	39.10 per cent
Lecithin	0.16 per cent
Substances soluble in water	0.73 per cent

The foregoing analysis shows the fatty derivatives which may be present in one species of bacteria.

It has been noted by some chemists that the etherial extracts do not contain the acid-fast substances. It has been claimed that the so-called acid-fast substance is an alcohol having some of the properties of a wax. This subtance was soluble in hot absolute alcohol or ether and insoluble in cold alcohol and ether, thus suggesting its similarity to a wax. Oleïc, isocetinic, and nysistinic, and some saponified lauric acids are present, and it is from them that the fats are formed.

In all probability the insoluble cell wall of bacteria is not composed of pure cellulose. The idea that the wall or limiting-membrane of the cell was composed of cellulose

[1] Quoted from Wells' "Chemical Pathology."

or hemi-cellulose, like most plant cells, has been held for years by a large number of bacteriologists. Recent research has shown that the cell wall in the majority of species is more like that of certain animal cells than of plants. The cell wall is like chitin. It is insoluble and splits into 80 per cent to 90 per cent of a nitrogenous carbohydrate glycosamin (Wells). Chitin is an amino-compound of a carbohydrate It is a polymer of a simple animal carbohydrate as cellulose is a polymer of a simple plant carbohydrate (Wells). Chitin is found in quite a few places, such as on the wings of certain insects, on the coverings of beetles, and in the shells of certain crustaceans, such as the crab and lobster.

No definite carbohydrates have been reported in the bacterial cell, and proven absolutely to be present. Certain substances similar to glycogen have been reported in Bacterium tuberculosis (Levene). In some few bacteria, according to Cramer, when treated with iodine, a substance giving the blue color reaction for starch is noted.

Chlorophyll has been reported in some bacteria. On investigation it has been found that it is not correct to class these organisms as bacteria and that they should be placed among the algæ or Schizophyceæ. Sulphur granules have been noted in certain species of bacteria in the class Beggiatoaceæ.

Pigment granules are noted among some species of bacteria (chromogenic) when certain definite conditions are provided. The chromogenic bacteria and the chemistry of pigments will be considered in a following chapter.

Some bacteria form within their protoplasm complex chemical substances known as toxins, endotoxins, ptomains, and enzymes. The chemistry of these compounds is known only to a limited extent. They will be considered more in detail in subsequent chapters.

Chemical Structure of Spores and Flagella. — Spores are composed of condensed protoplasm. They contain the same chemical substances as the bacterial cell from which they were formed, with the exception that the content of water is lowered much below that of the original cell. Spores are composed of 60 per cent dried substance (Drymont). The water which is present is held in a way to resist drying temperatures below 100° C. The spore wall is chitinous in structure rather than "cellulose-like," and contains in addition some very hygroscopic extractive matter (Wells).

Flagella are composed of condensed protein. Aside from this, as far as is known, their chemical constituents are not unlike those in the vegetative form.

PART III. METHODS USED IN THE STUDY OF BACTERIA

CHAPTER VI

Culture Media

Introduction. — Very little can be determined about the bacteria by microscopical examination alone. It is necessary to cultivate them artificially in order to study them satisfactorily. The reason for this will be seen when one realizes that upwards of two thousand different species of bacteria have been described, some of them man's worst enemies, and all of them belonging to the three simple form types which have been previously described. By microscopical examination we can learn something of their distribution, something of their form and structure, and something of their relation to, or at least their association with, diseases, and such natural processes as fermentation, putrefaction, etc., but nothing more.

The artificial cultivation of bacteria has been developed entirely within the last half century. The first attempts were crude and unsatisfactory, as viewed from our present standpoint, but since the time of Pasteur and Koch great progress has been made. The science of bacteriology begins with this work. The underlying principles of the artificial cultivation of bacteria include the selection of food media, the securing and maintaining its sterility, and the methods of isolation and subculturing.

Character of Food required by Bacteria. — The kind of food required by bacteria varies greatly with the different forms. Some require, for instance, living organic matter; others require and live only on dead organic matter; while still others live only in the absence of organic matter. Attempts have been made to supply a universal medium. This is evidently an impossibility. Media have been devised, however, which furnish a good pabulum for a large number of bacteria. Various decoctions have been used in the past, such as those from fruit, wheat, pea straw, manure, etc.; but the medium most universally used at the present time is that suggested by Loeffler, which is a beef broth or bouillon. Upon this medium most of the bacteria can grow when appropriate additions have been made, with the exception of those bacteria which require living organic matter; that is, the obligate parasites and the bacteria which live only on inorganic food substances.

Composition and Preparation of Various Culture Media. — A large number of different culture media have been devised and are in constant use, but an attempt will be made here to discuss only those that are most commonly used, and such discussions will be only of a general nature. It will be necessary to refer to laboratory guides for the exact formulæ and methods of preparation. Culture media may be roughly divided into those containing albuminous matter, and these may be either liquid, solid, or liquefiable solid media, and nonalbuminous or synthetic media.

Albuminous or Protein Media

Liquid Media

Bouillon. — This medium is the basis of most of the ordinary media used in the laboratory, such as gelatin and agar, and is also largely used as a culture medium itself. It has the following ingredients. The extractions of 500 grams of lean beef, 10 grams of peptone, 5 grams of sodium chloride, neutralized and dissolved in one liter of distilled water. The nutritive value of the various ingredients is a subject that should be briefly considered at this point. The nutritive value of the meat depends almost entirely upon the albuminous substances of which it is composed, but most of these are insoluble and most of them that do go into solution are precipitated on heating, so that very little protein material is furnished by the meat. Its purpose in the medium is largely to furnish extractives, chiefly creatin and xanthin bodies, which are useful to most bacteria. The peptone, which is a soluble albumin, formed from proteins by the action of the gastric juice, is the principal source of nitrogen for the bacteria. The sodium chloride was originally used to aid in the solution of the peptone, but it is now not needed for that purpose and in some laboratories its use is being discarded.

In the preparation of bouillon, one of the most important things to be considered is its neutralization. As a general rule the bacteria require an alkaline rather than an acid reaction, and the medium must, therefore, be made either neutral or very slightly alkaline. The indicators suggested in the various textbooks have been red and blue litmus paper, tumeric paper, and phenolphthalein. Some organic substances are both acid and alkaline to certain indicators — fresh milk, for instance, will turn red litmus paper blue and blue litmus paper red. Other substances, particularly the phosphates, may be neutral to one indicator and acid or alkaline to another. These substances thus give a double or *amphoteric* reaction. It has been determined by Schultz, and others later, that phenolphthalein is least likely to give ambiguous results, and it has largely replaced all other indicators in this work. It must be understood, however, that it reacts to the carbonates, such as carbon dioxide, and media should be neutralized with this indicator only after being boiled and while still hot. It is also true that the alkaline point with phenolphthalein is removed some distance from the neutral point of litmus, so that when a medium is neutralized by means of phenolphthalein it is more alkaline than the bacteria need, and it is necessary on that account, when media is neutralized in this way, to add a certain amount of normal acid to the medium to bring it back to a point most suitable to the bacteria. When a medium is just slightly alkaline to phenolphthalein, it is represented as having a reaction of 0. Any alkaline added in addition to this would be designated by the per cent represented in figures preceded by the minus sign; and media which is acid to phenolphthalein is represented by the per cent of acid preceded by the plus sign. Most of the bacteria, for instance, require a medium from 0 to + 1; while certain bacteria, such as those commonly found in water, reach their maximum of development when the medium is + 1.5. In the preparation of bouillon, as well as that of many other media, it is necessary to clear it, and this is done by adding an egg, or some similar albuminous material, while the medium is cool, at least below the coagulation point of the proteins *i.e.* 60° C., then heated sufficiently to thoroughly coagulate the albuminous substance. This draws the fine particles of the precipitate into larger clumps, or masses, which will be held back by the filter material, and the medium which goes through the filter under these conditions will be perfectly clear.

Bouillon may be modified in various ways by the addition of glycerine (6 per cent) for the Bact. tuberculosis and Bact. mallei; by the addition of dextrose or lactose (1 per cent) for fermentation tests; carbolic acid (.025 per cent) for B. typhosus, etc.

Sugar-Free Bouillon (Smith). — For certain work, such as the detection of indol, a special medium is used from which the muscle sugar has been removed. Since muscle always contains a small amount of sugar (inosit) it is necessary to remove this, and it is done at Smith's suggestion by inoculating a bacterium capable of splitting up this sugar and doing it while the meat is being digested. In this way the sugar is gotten rid of, and the preparation of the medium goes on from this point as in the case of ordinary bouillon.

Dunham's Solution. — Dunham's solution is used at times for the study of bacteria. It simply consists of a 1 per cent peptone solution.

Milk. — The milk of cocoanuts has been used in special instances, but cow's milk is very frequently used for growing bacteria. Fresh milk should be secured and the fat separated, preferably by centrifugalization. Milk is sometimes quite difficult to sterilize on account of the very resistant spores which it may contain, and steaming on four or five consecutive days may be necessary. Litmus is frequently added to milk, which increases the usefulness of this very useful medium.

Among other liquid media used are whey, urine, and beer wort. The latter is used almost exclusively for the growth of yeast.

Solid Media

Potatoes. — Potatoes were first used by Schroeder. He boiled them with their jackets on and then cut them in two with a sterile knife, placed them in a covered dish, and grew bacteria on the cut surface. Esmarch later used slices of potatoes in special glass dishes which he had made; but at the present time they are used almost entirely in test tubes and Petri dishes. Cylinders of the potato, with a sloping front surface, are put in test tubes which are sterilized and used as other test tube media. It is desirable that the color of the potato should not be changed, and to secure this it is best to either boil the potato or, perhaps what is better, to keep the cut potatoes in running water for twelve hours or more before the cylinders are cut out.

Other Vegetables. — Carrots, turnips, and other vegetables are sometimes used for special bacteria in the same way that potatoes are used.

Blood Serum. — This material furnishes a specially valuable medium for certain disease-producing bacteria. Beef, horse, and human serum are the ones commonly used. In any case, the blood is collected, allowed to clot, and then the clear serum is drawn off. This is put into the appropriate vessel and sterilized. The temperature of sterilization is usually low in order to preserve, as much as possible, the transparency of the medium. By sterilization below the coagulation point, or by means of the addition of water, which raises the coagulation point, it is possible to sterilize this medium in a liquid condition, but it is usually solidified or inspissated A special mixture known as Loeffler's blood serum is made by adding one part of dextrose bouillon to three parts of beef blood serum. It is almost universally used for growing the Bact. diphtheriæ in diagnostic laboratories.

Eggs. — Eggs are used at the present time largely for the growth of Bact. tuberculosis. Fresh hens' eggs are broken with greatest care, the contents put in sterile vessels, shaken up and run into sterile test tubes where it is heated and coagulated. Eggs may also be used for other work.

Liquefiable Solid Media

Gelatin. — Gelatin culture medium is made from bouillon by the addition of gelatin. Gelatin is made from connective tissue, extracted either at ordinary pressure or in the digestor (autoclave). Its physical characteristics that are of special interest to the bacteriologist are its melting and solidifying points. It is necessary that a gelatin should be used which in ordinary percentages will not interfere with bacterial growth, and will remain solid at the temperature of a warm room. Chemically its most important feature is its acidity, and the higher grades which have a low acidity, comparatively, should be used. From 10 to 18 per cent of gelatin is added to bouillon in the preparation of this medium. The preparation of gelatin offers no difficulties beyond that of bouillon except that it is necessary to exercise great care in neutralization and to filter it while hot. For the filtration of gelatin and the other liquefiable solid media, wet absorbent cotton can be used to advantage, although it is possible to filter the properly prepared medium through filter paper. It is best sterilized in streaming steam on three consecutive days; but it may be sterilized in an autoclave at a pressure not to exceed ten pounds for fifteen minutes. A fact that must always be borne in mind in preparing gelatin is that its gelatinizing power is injured by prolonged heating during the process of preparation or sterilization, and is lost immediately when heated to 140° C. in the autoclave.

Gelatin is frequently modified by the addition of such substances as dextrose, lactose; and a medium formerly extensively used for the isolation of B. typhosus was a potato-water gelatin containing potassium iodide (Elsner).

Agar. — Agar is a culture medium made by adding a small per cent of the vegetable agar-agar to bouillon. Agar-agar is a seaweed that grows in the Pacific Ocean, and it is known as Bengal isinglass, or Ceylon moss. It occurs in the market as transparent strips, or sticks, and as a white powder. It differs from gelatin in being a carbohydrate simply, and not a protein. It is neutral in reaction and melts at about 99° C. and solidifies at about 40° C. Its chief value in bacteriology comes from its high melting point, and also from the fact that it is not acted upon by ferments which liquefy gelatin, so that it may be used to grow bacteria which need a higher temperature than gelatin would remain solid at and to grow bacteria which would liquefy gelatin. From 1 to 2 per cent of the agar-agar is used. The preparation of agar offers some difficulty to the beginner on account of its difficult solubility and its high solidifying point, which makes it difficult to filter; but if the agar is gotten into a solution first in the water, and the other ingredients added later, it may be prepared very readily and even filtered through filter paper at the ordinary room temperature. For filtration, however, absorbent cotton is frequently used and the process is sometimes hastened by the use of air suction.

Agar is variously modified by the addition of sugars, glycerine, etc. A very common modification is that of Wurtz, where both lactose and litmus are added.

Nonalbuminous (Synthesized) Media. — The albuminous media have a very indefinite composition, and it is quite impossible to make two batches of media exactly alike. This is very unfortunate because certain changes in the characteristics of bacteria are caused by even slight changes in the composition of the medium; and it is sometimes difficult to determine whether slight differences that are recognized in cultures are due to inherent differences in the organism or to differences in the culture media. It would be very desirable, therefore, to have a culture medium of definite composition which could be exactly reproduced from time to time. Attempts have been made to produce such media by the use of chemically pure substances in which the nitrogen was furnished in a comparatively low form, as, for instance, sodium asparaginate. Dujardin showed that fungi could grow in nonalbuminous substances as early as 1841. Later Pasteur used them in his yeast work; and in 1893 Uschinsky showed that most pathogenic bacteria would grow on such media. Uschinsky's medium, which may be given as an illustration of these media, had the following composition: —

Water	1000
Glycerine	30 to 40
Sodium chloride	5 to 7
Calcium chloride	0.1
Magnesium sulphate	0.2 to 0.4

Bipotassium phosphate . . . . 2 to 2 5
Ammonium lactate   . . . . 6 to 7
Sodium asparaginate 3 4

This medium has been used for special purposes, but for many forms it has not been found as valuable as Uschinsky thought. Brieger and others have found it useful in studying the production of ptomains and toxins. On the whole, the use of synthetic media in the past has been disappointing. It is to be hoped that in some of Emil Fischer's polypeptieds, substances will be found which will meet the demands of the bacteria.

A solid, synthesized medium has been used to a limited extent. It consists of a nutrient solution to which water glass or a sodium silicate jelly is added; in this way a solid, transparent medium is formed, and upon this the nitrifying bacteria, which develop only on nonalbuminous media, have been grown.

CHAPTER VII

STERILIZATION

Introduction. — By sterilization is meant the process by which the vitality of all the microörganisms in or upon an object are destroyed, and an object which is entirely free from all living microörganisms and their spores is described as sterile.

Sterilization has come to be confounded with disinfection. By disinfection is meant a process which insures the destruction of those living forms which have the power of producing an infection, or disease, and may or may not be complete in the sense of sterilization.

In the laboratory it is customary to speak of sterilization as the process which frees a substance from bacteria, but does not change its composition or interfere with its nutritive quality. That is, it renders it germ-free but not barren. This is usually accomplished by a physical agent. Disinfection has come to imply a change in composition, due to the fact that chemicals are usually employed in the process. While the above terms are not strictly correct, their use is convenient. Both sterilization and disinfection may be accomplished by either physical or chemical agents.

Sterilization by Physical Agents

Filtration. — It is possible to sterilize fluids by means of filtration. By this means the bacteria are actually removed. Practically the only means of producing a germ-free filtrate is by means of unglazed porcelain. This has been used especially where it is desired to sterilize substances that would be changed when subjected to the action of heat or chemicals. Filtration is used largely to free the bacteria from their soluble products of growth, *e.g.* their toxins. There are two systems of porcelain filters, one is the Pasteur-Chamberlain, the other the Berkefeld system. The Pasteur system is the most reliable, but it is very slow. The Berkefeld is much more rapid, but it is, consequently, not so reliable. With either system great care is necessary with their use and frequent sterilization of them is necessary since the bacteria frequently grow through their walls after they have been in use for a short time.

Sunlight has good disinfecting or sterilizing properties which were first called attention to by Downs and Blunt in 1877, and since then many experiments have been performed. While it has the power of destroying bacteria when they are exposed to it for a few minutes or a few hours, its power of destroying them cannot be depended upon, and it is of no practical importance in this connection.

Cold. — Cold is ordinarily thought to be very effective in destroying bacteria, but in reality it is of very little value.

Frisch, in 1877, exposed both bacilli and micrococci to minus 87° C., produced by the evaporation of liquid carbon dioxide. All such bacteria grew when brought under favorable conditions.

A number of later experiments showed that while freezing kills a certain number of the bacteria it does not kill all of them by any means, and many forms may remain alive for months in frozen water. This is true also of disease-producing bacteria.

Dry Heat. — In 1854, Schultz and Schwann first showed the real value of dry heat in destroying bacteria in their experiments upon spontaneous generation (see Chap. II).

Direct Flame. — This is constantly used in the laboratory for sterilizing the platinum needles, but its use is almost entirely limited to this and to the destruction of worthless but infectious material, such as the carcasses of infected animals. In this case, a special apparatus is necessary, known as the incinerator.

High Dry Heat. — Dry heat at a temperature of 150° C. is constantly used in the laboratory for the sterilization of such materials as glassware, cotton batting, etc. It has been shown that this temperature is sufficient to kill all forms of life, and may be depended upon as a means of producing perfect sterilization, providing the heat can readily reach all parts of the objects to be sterilized. The heat is supplied in an oven or a hot-air sterilizer. This is sometimes provided with a thermometer, but usually this is not necessary, since incipient charring of cotton occurs at about this temperature; and it is thus only necessary to run the sterilizer until cotton in the flask or test tubes, or cotton placed in for this special purpose, is slightly browned.

This method of sterilization has a very limited use, since it cannot, evidently, be used for sterilizing liquids; and because of the charring of vegetable and animal matter at the above temperature, this method cannot be used to sterilize substances made of these and similar materials.

Moist Heat. — Steam for the purpose of sterilization has been used since the time of Schultz and Schwann's experiment, and is applied in the form of either streaming steam or as steam under pressure.

Streaming Steam. — The temperature of streaming steam depends, of course, upon the barometric pressure, but approximates 100° C. It is much more efficient than dry heat at the same temperature. This is probably due to the fact that the walls, or membranes, of the bacteria become moistened and swelled by the steam and thus permit the more ready entrance of the heat to the interior of the cell. By means of streaming steam materials may be sterilized without injury which would not stand dry heat. It is, however, practically impossible to kill bacteria when they are in the spore condition by this means, for it has been found that an exposure of sixteen hours is necessary to kill certain spore bacteria found in the soil. A method which overcomes the difficulty of long exposure was suggested by Tyndall and is known as the intermittent method of sterilization, as the discontinuous method, and sometimes as Tyndallization.

In this method culture media are subjected to a sterilization of from ten to twenty minutes on one day, allowed to stand twenty-four hours and heated again, then allowed to stand another twenty-four hours, and heated a third time. This method almost invariably produces complete sterilization, providing, of course, the material has reached the proper temperature throughout. Its efficiency depends upon two things: first, the fact that streaming steam applied for ten to twenty minutes kills all germ life not in the spore stage; and, second, standing twenty-four hours allows the spores, which were not killed on the first application of steam, opportunity for germination, so that on a second exposure the young bacteria are killed. The third exposure for ten to twenty minutes makes it almost certain that all spores have germinated and have been killed. Evidently this method is not applicable to all materials, since an essential feature is the opportunity for the germination of the spores. It would be impossible to sterilize empty glassware, instruments, bandages, etc., by this method, since there is no opportunity on these materials for the growth of the bacteria in the intervals between heatings.

This method of sterilization is carried out in a steamer, of which there are a number of different types. All that is necessary is a vessel which will hold water, which has a shelf above the water, and a fairly tight cover. An excellent form, almost universally used in this country, is the Arnold steam sterilizer (Fig. 34). This has the advantage of being practically automatic, since the steam which is produced is condensed and reheated.

Steam under Pressure. — Steam under pressure has been used by the French school for a good while and is now coming into general use. Here a temperature of 105 to 120° C. is maintained for fifteen minutes, the latter temperature is destructive of all forms of germ life and may be depended upon as a certain means of sterilization. This method of sterilization is made possible by the use of a special piece of apparatus known as the autoclave, which is essentially a copper vessel that can be hermetically sealed, provided with a thermometer and steam gauge. In practice it is not found necessary to use a thermometer, since the temperature has a definite ratio to the pressure, providing, however, that the atmosphere within the autoclave is saturated with water, and this can be accomplished by leaving a pet-cock open until steam escapes freely.

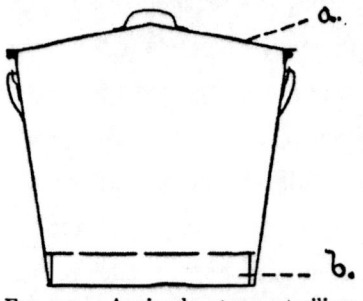

Fig. 34. — A simple steam sterilizer consisting of a galvanized iron pail. *a* is the cover and *b* a false bottom.

On account of the quickness with which materials can be sterilized in the autoclave, this method is becoming deservedly popular. At first it was thought that the high temperature injured the culture media, but it has been found that the

STERILIZATION

ordinary culture media are uninjured by the exposure necessary for sterilization. When sugar media are heated in the autoclave, they are frequently darkened because of a change produced in the sugar by the high heat. This change is known as caramelization. A committee of the American Public Health Association has, however, recently agreed that the autoclave may be used for the sterilization of these media, providing the temperature does not get above 120° C., steam pressure fifteen pounds, and the exposure is not longer than fifteen minutes.

An exceedingly convenient form of autoclave is that manufactured by Bramhall and Dean, and shown in Figure 35.

The intermittent method of sterilization has been used for sterilizing blood and other protein material by using a temperature below the coagulation point of the material to be sterilized, *e.g.* 55 to 60° C. It is necessary, however, to make

FIG. 35.—Autoclave for use with steam under pressure.

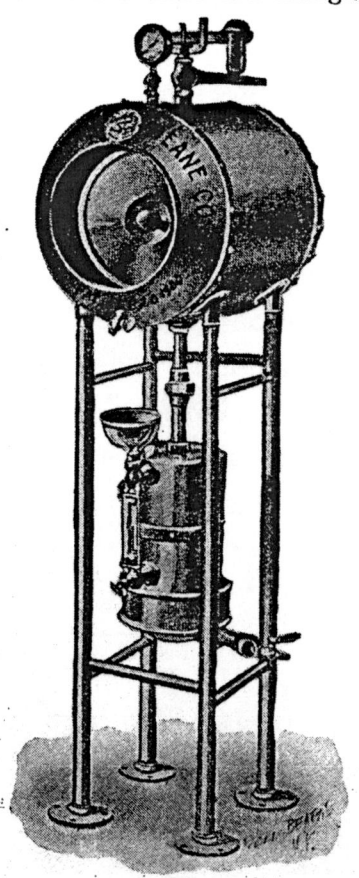

more than three exposures, and to maintain the temperature for a period of time considerably above twenty minutes (one hour or more).

Disinfection. — Chemical substances are used in the laboratory for the purpose of destroying old cultures, for washing the desks, and covering up infectious matter accidentally spilled, washing the hands, etc. The chemicals usually used are carbolic acid (3 to 5 per cent solution), corrosive sublimate (1 to 1000). The value of these is discussed in a later chapter (see Chap XI).

A few disinfectants have been used for sterilizing culture media, such as chloroform and hydrogen peroxide. These chemical substances are later either driven off by heat, or are rendered harmless by the natural changes which go on, so that the nutritive properties of the substances are not destroyed.

CHAPTER VIII

Culture Methods and Apparatus

Introduction. — The artificial cultivation of bacteria marks the beginning of the science of bacteriology. Little was done with the bacteria or known about them until it was possible to cultivate them artificially. The methods of cultivation were difficult and rather slowly developed. Since bacteria occur always in nature in a mixed culture, practically no progress was made until methods of isolation were devised. The picking up of the single organism was so difficult a task that it was first done by Barber within the last few years. A considerable number of different people have taken part in the development of our present methods, but it is really to Robert Koch that chief credit is due, and his plate culture method of isolation really marks the beginning of accurate work in this line. When a single organism is planted on a solid culture medium, the resulting mass of growth is called a colony and is evidently made up of the descendants of a single cell. When a colony is obtained, we have a material for making subcultures, microscopical examinations, animal inoculations, etc. Cultures made from a single colony are called pure cultures, and in studying any organism the first requisite is to get a pure culture. When this is obtained, the study of it can proceed with certainty. In the early days of bacteriology, mixed cultures were frequently confused with pure cultures, and curious and very erroneous ideas were obtained which it has taken many years to correct.

Methods of Isolation

Fractional Methods. — Pasteur and Cohn, working on the problem of artificial cultivation, worked on the supposition that various species of microorganisms, occurring in a mixture, will multiply unequally in any given culture medium according to their different natures. According to this method, one species will attain the ascendency and can be removed and obtained in pure culture. While this idea is partially true, it is almost always the case that the other kinds of microorganisms in the mixture are not dead but simply inactive, and are likely to be transferred with the others and under different conditions may gain the ascendency. Klebs used much the same method, transferring the most luxuriant growths from culture to culture until the pure culture was obtained. These methods are used only to a very limited extent at the present time, and if we had to depend upon them, our knowledge of bacteria would be limited and our idea of their life history erroneous.

Physiological Methods. — The physiological differences in bacteria have been made use of in a number of special methods. Roberts, in 1874, and Cohn, in 1876, isolated certain spore-bearing bacilli by heating the culture before incubating it to nearly or quite the boiling point of water. By this method it is possible to isolate in pure culture such bacteria as the hay bacillus and the potato bacillus. Gayon and Dupetit devised a culture tube to take advantage of the fact that certain bacteria were much more motile than others. These tubes were provided with a long glass spiral through which the bacteria were obliged to travel. The most motile forms would get through the tube first and could be removed before the slower forms arrived. Parietti used a disinfectant to inhibit the growth of certain bacteria without interfering with the growth of others, and by means of a weak solution of carbolic acid and hydrochloric acid in water he found it possible to separate B. coli from other bacteria, and he even claimed that he could separate this bacillus from B. typhosus. These methods are occasionally used at the present time, but the difficulties are the same as those indicated under the head of Fractional Methods, *i.e.* it is necessary to start from an unknown mixture, and it is, therefore, impossible to know the results. The weaker species may not be destroyed, so that after the stronger species begin to degenerate the others get a chance to multiply; and then, again, two or more species may thrive equally well.

The Dilution Methods. — In these methods the principle involved is to dilute material with a sterile liquid, as water, to such an extent that a single unit of the mixture contains not more than one bacterial cell. Lister, in 1878, obtained a pure culture of the lactic acid bacteria. This he did by counting under the microscope the number of bacteria in a drop of milk. He then added sufficient sterile water so that any particular drop of the mixture would contain not over a single organism. He then added a drop of this mixture to each of five sterile test tubes of milk. Only one of these tubes coagulated, and he naturally inferred that his object was attained and that he had in that one tube of milk a pure culture of the lactic acid bacteria. Naegeli and Fritz afterwards used this method. Pasteur applied these principles to the study of yeast, but he diluted his yeast with air rather than with water. Dry yeast was mixed with powdered gypsum, and this mixture was thrown into the air. As the fine dust of the mixture settled, it fell into flasks about the room containing a suitable culture medium and from which the cotton plugs had been removed. Hanson diluted yeast with water and distributed the mixture in flasks. He took a step forward, however, by allowing them to remain undisturbed for a few days, and then rejected as impure those having more than a single speck in a bottle. This method of dilution was carried to the extreme by the French school. While it is possible to get a pure culture in this way, it is quite impossible to isolate all the bacteria occurring in a mixture whose content is known.

Use of Liquefiable Solid Media. — This was suggested by the use of potato as a culture medium. Schroeder, in 1872, noticed that the growth which occurs on a cooked potato when it is exposed to the air is due to bacteria. He also used potatoes to cultivate the color-producing bacteria. Koch later used this medium for isolating bacteria, and it was this work that suggested to him his gelatin plate method which made him, as well as the science which he founded, famous. He tried nine different substances before he hit upon the use of gelatin. Gelatin is used simply to give solidity, and not for any nutritive value. Klebs and Breffeld had previously used it in object glass preparations to prevent evaporation while studying the fungi, but they did not use it as an isolating medium. The method is as follows. The sterilized gelatin is melted, and while it is still warm and in a fluid state it is inoculated with the mixture of bacteria, properly diluted. The medium is then poured on to a glass plate, previously sterilized, and placed in a dish or under a bell jar to protect it from contamination. These glass plates were frequently placed one above the other on glass benches and stored in a moist chamber. For a good many years the original glass plate of Koch has not been used, but in its place the Petri dish, which consists of a flat-bottomed glass dish with a similar glass cover (Fig. 36). Esmarch suggested the use of what is known as Esmarch roll. In this case the gelatin instead of being poured out of the tube is rolled in a thin layer on the interior of the tube. For detailed descriptions of these processes the reader is referred to laboratory guides.

The gelatin plate has a limited use on account of the fact that many of the disease-producing bacteria grow readily only at temperatures above that at which gelatin will remain

90 METHODS USED IN THE STUDY OF BACTERIA

solid, and also because many bacteria digest the gelatin and the colonies run together. It was, therefore, a considerable step in advance when agar-agar replaced gelatin. The high

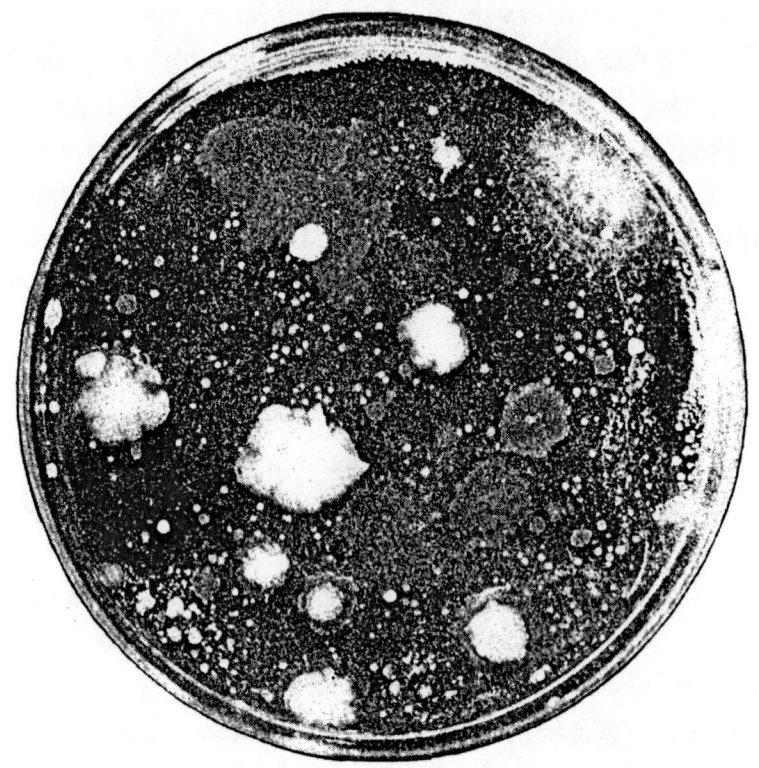

Fig. 36. — Plate culture. Light areas represent colonies from which pure cultures can be obtained. After Lipman.

melting point of this material makes it possible to use it at any temperature suitable for the growth of bacteria. It has, however, certain disadvantages, among which should be mentioned the fact that certain bacteria grow much less characteristically on it than on gelatin, and also because the water of condensation which gathers on the medium permits certain bacteria to overgrow the others and cause confusion.

In the plate method the single bacteria are separated and imbedded in the solid medium which is suitable for their growth, and they soon produce, as a result, a growth or colony varying in size from a pinhead to a centimeter, according to the nature of the bacterium and the conditions under which it is grown. It is taken for granted in this method that each colony grows from a single individual, originally imbedded in the medium. This may or may not be true. Among the bacteria it generally is true, but several yeasts may cling together and form a colony, the individuals of which are of more than one species or variety. To overcome this difficulty Hanson introduced his pure culture method, which consists of a gelatin or agar plate made on a cover-glass which can be placed under the microscope and examined. The cover-glass is marked off into squares which are numbered, and a record is made of the cells occurring in the various squares, and only those colonies are used for subculturing which are derived from a single cell.

Subcultures. — Test tube cultures are usually used in making subcultures because of the convenience in handling and also because of the slight danger from contamination. The gelatin stab culture is frequently used. In this, the platinum needle which has been charged with the particular bacteria is plunged to the depth of the gelatin in the test tube, so that the bacteria are left all along the line of the stab. These cultures are of the greatest value since minute differences in culture characters are revealed. Agar, potato, blood serum, and, occasionally, gelatin are prepared with a sloped surface, and cultures are made on the surface of these known as streak cultures, in which the bacteria are sown on a streak made by the platinum needle by drawing it the full length of the sloped (see Fig. 30) surface. Fluid cultures in bouillon, Dunham's solution, milk, etc., are frequently used. Bacteria are sometimes grown in mass cultures for special purposes, particularly in bouillon for the production of the toxins. A great many attempts have been made to make permanent preparations of bacterial cultures. The attempts, however, have been largely unsuccessful since the cultures fade in color and otherwise change in a relatively short time.

CHAPTER IX

MICROSCOPICAL EXAMINATION OF BACTERIA

History of the Microscope. — The principle of the lens has been understood from the earliest time. Magnifying glasses of rock crystal have been found in the ruins of Nimrod. Aristophanes, 400 B.C., speaks of " burning spheres " which were sold in the shops of Athens; and Seneca, in the middle of the first century, speaks of the magnifying power of glass globes filled with water. It was not, however, until the seventeenth century that powerful magnifying lenses were used for scientific purposes. Leeuwenhoek's work with the simple lens has already been referred to. The first compound microscope was probably made by Hans and Zacharias Janssen of Middleburg, Holland, in 1590. In the compound microscope, as is well known, we observe not the object but an image of the object. Such a microscope consists of two systems of lenses, one with a short and the other with a long focus. These are the essential parts of the microscope. There are certain mechanical appliances necessary to keep the lenses in position, to afford steadiness, proper illumination, etc. The instrument without the optical parts is called the stand. The lens nearest the object is known as the objective, while the lens nearest the observer's eye is known as the eye-piece or ocular. Two of the most serious defects of lenses are what are known as spherical and chromatic aberration. An oil-immersion lens and an Abbé substage condenser are essential parts of a bacteriological microscope.

The Examination of Bacteria. — Bacteria may be examined under the microscope in a living condition or stained. They are examined in a living condition in what are known as hanging drop preparations. These are prepared by taking a drop of the fluid culture, or an emulsion of the bacteria, and putting it on a cover-glass. This cover-glass is then inverted over the cavity in a hollow ground glass slide. The edge of this cavity is oiled so as to prevent evaporation. The bacteria in the hanging drop are thus furnished with opportunity to move about, or to remain in a natural condition. This preparation enables the observer to determine whether or not there is vital movement, and also to detect other subtle peculiarities, so that this preparation is one of great importance. The beginner frequently finds difficulty in making it because of the fact that the bacteria may be some distance from the top of the cover-glass and thus the working distance of the lens is very slight, also because of the difficulty in regulating the amount of light, since these bacteria are so nearly transparent that a little too much light renders them invisible.

Bacteria are also examined in the stained condition by what is known as a cover-glass preparation. Staining methods were not introduced until the latter part of the last century, but since their introduction they have served a very useful purpose. Among the advantages to be gained by staining bacteria are: it brings out the minute variations in form and size that would escape unnoticed in the unstained preparation; it facilitates the differentiation of bacteria from their surroundings, *e.g.* bacteria from tissue; and in some cases certain stains act as differential agents, aiding in the identification of species. Carmine, from the cardinal insect, was introduced in 1850. Hematoxylin (campeachy, or logwood) was used with great success in histology, but neither of the above stains are applicable to bacteria since they give with these forms only a faint tinge. They are chiefly used in bacteriology now as contrast stains. Weigert, in 1877, introduced the anilin dyes. These are derivative of the coal-tar product anilin, $C_6H_5NH_2$. Ehrlich first divided these anilin dyes into two groups, according as the staining action depended on the basic or acid portion of the molecule. For example, fuchsin, the acetate of rosanilin (triamidotriphenylcarbinol, $C_{20}H_{19}N_3C_2H_4O_2$) derives its staining action from rosanilin and is therefore basic. Ammonium picrate derives its staining action from the picric acid part of the molecule and is therefore acid. Basic stains, especially active toward nuclear chromatin, are the only ones used for the staining of bacteria. The acid stains are especially valuable for the protoplasm of the animal or plant cell. The anilin dyes have all the colors of the rainbow. Some of the most important are: —

Violet
  Methyl-violet (Hoffman's violet, dahlia)
  Gentian-violet (benzyl-violet, Pyoktanin)
Blue
  Methylene blue (phenylene blue)
  Victoria blue
  Thionin blue
Red
  Basic fuchsin (basic rubin, magenta)
  Safranin (fuchsin, Girofle)
Brown
  Bismarck brown (vesuvin, phenylene brown)

These dyes are usually used in a weak aqueous solution, and in preparing the bacteria for microscopical examination they are spread in a thin film on a grease-free cover-glass, fixed by heat, stained, washed in water, and mounted in Canada balsam, the exact details for which must be gotten from a laboratory guide. Instead of spreading the bacteria promiscuously over the surface of a cover-glass, a cover-glass may be lowered on to the culture and an impression preparation made, which is fixed and stained as usual. This is a difficult preparation to make, but when properly made gives the relation which individuals bear to one another in the colony. In staining it is necessary for certain purposes to add substances that are known as mordants. Anilin oil, weak alkalies, carbolic acid, and tannic acid are the mordants most frequently used. These mordants hasten the action of the dyes, and are necessary with certain bacteria, and are frequently used even for general purposes. Special stains have been devised for special purposes. Loeffler's alkaline methylene blue is used for staining the Bact. diphtheriæ, Ziehl's carbol fuchsin for the Bact. tuberculosis, and many other special stains are used for special purposes. Processes for double staining have been devised, *e.g.* those for differentiating a spore from the mother cell, the metachromatic bodies from the rest of the protoplasm, the capsule from the cell, etc. Certain selective stains are also used. In particular, Gram's stain, which consists, essentially, of treating the bacteria with a particular dye, *i.e.* anilin oil gentian violet; with Gram's iodine solution (iodine and potassium iodide); then washing in alcohol. With some bacteria the dye and the iodine solution form a compound with the protoplasm of the cell which is insoluble in alcohol. Such bacteria, when put through this process, retain the violet color. Other bacteria, when treated with the stain and the iodine solution, fail to effect a compound with the protoplasm insoluble in alcohol (iodine-pararosanilin-protein). Such bacteria, when treated by this process, are colorless; or, if a counter stain has been used, are of an entirely different color. By means of Gram's stain it is possible to differentiate bacteria that are morphologically similar, and this stain is one of the bacteriologists' most valuable assets.

Most pathogenic *micrococci* retain the violet color when treated by this method and are, therefore, said to be positive to Gram. Many of the disease-producing *bacilli* do not take the Gram stain, are negative to it, while others are positive.

H

Among the well-known disease-producing bacteria that are positive to Gram should be mentioned Bact. anthracis, Bact. pneumoniæ, Bact. tuberculosis, Bact diphtheriæ, and Bacillus tetanus. Among the common disease-producing bacteria negative to Gram should be mentioned B. typhosus, B. feseri (malignant œdema), Bact. mallei (glanders), Micrococcus gonorrheæ, and Spirillum recurrens.

Some species of bacteria bear the name of "acid-fast" bacteria (bacteria of tuberculosis, leprosy, etc.). The protoplasm of these bacteria holds the dye even when treated with strong decolorizing agents, such as mineral acids and alcohols. It requires some time for the protoplasm of the bacteria to take up the stain, but once combined, as with the spore, decolorization is difficult. It is claimed that the high content of fat accounts for the staining properties of these organisms The acid-fastness of Bacterium tuberculosis is due to a high molecular alcohol which has not been worked out thoroughly. It is very similar to a wax according to some writers. It is said to be soluble in boiling absolute alcohol. Some bacteria not normally acid-fast may be made so by growing them on media containing a large amount of fat.

A special stain has been devised for the flagella. In a considerable number of such stains, the mordant is tannic acid and an iron salt. The process of staining flagella is one of the most difficult staining processes that the bacteriologist has to master, and although the methods have been greatly simplified in recent years they still call for great skill and persistence.

The Principles involved in Staining. — The development of the technique of staining has been largely empirical, and at the present time only the most general of the principles involved are understood. In fact, it is not known whether the theory of staining rests upon a chemical or a physical basis. There is some evidence, as will be seen, to show that the principle involved in staining is merely a physical one. There is other evidence that, at least in certain cases, the reaction between the dye and protoplasm may be a chemical one. In a general way it seems true that the staining of the protoplasm is related to the question of diffusion, and those conditions which aid diffusion aid also in staining. In ordinary routine work, the dried bacterial cells are stained with an aqueous solution of the dye, and concentrated alcoholic solutions are not satisfactory for staining dried bacteria. There is diffusion between the dried bacterial cell and the watery solution, and none in the case of dried bacteria and alcohol. If the bacteria are first wet, then they will stain with the alcoholic solutions. The majority of bacteria stain readily with the ordinary aqueous solution of the dyes. To stain certain of them, however, it is necessary to resort to special means. Some of the bacteria, as we have seen, have certain fatty or waxy substances in their cell walls, which render their staining by watery solution of the dyes difficult or well-nigh impossible. When they are once stained, however, it is difficult to destain them. For this purpose even the mineral acids may be used. These bacilli are known as the acid-fast bacilli. In order to stain them it is necessary to add mordants to the stain. The principle involved here is the same as that used in dyeing cloth. For staining purposes the mordants usually used are the iron salts, weak alkalies, carbolic acid, anilin oil, and tannin. These mordants enable one to stain even the most resistant bacteria. When they are once stained it is possible to remove the stain from other objects in the specimen, less acid-fast than themselves, by means of some decolorizing agent, such as the mineral acids, organic acids, alcohols, etc. In this way it is possible to secure double stains, in which one kind of bacteria is stained one color and other bacteria another color. Such a double stain is used for the differential diagnosis of certain bacteria. The bacillus of tuberculosis, for instance, is stained in sputum by using a double stain, by means of which the Bact. tuberculosis is colored a deep crimson, while the rest of the preparation is blue or green in color. The Bact. tuberculosis has this acid-fast property in common with a number of other bacteria, but it is usually possible, by means of slight variations in the technique, or by some other means, to differentiate this germ from the other acid-fast bacilli. Depending upon principles similar to those noted above, a double stain for endospores has been devised and is frequently used.

There are certain other stains which may or may not indicate that the process of staining is a chemical one, but they do indicate at any rate that there is some differentiation in structure in the various parts of the cell. Some bacteria when stained with a weak solution of methylene blue give the bipolar stain. Other bacteria when stained with methylene blue, or similar stains, present granules of various sizes within the cell protoplasm, usually in a polar or equatorial position. These peculiar staining reactions may indicate a variation in the chemical composition of the protoplasm, or the variations may be merely physical ones. In Gram's stain the principle involved is undoubtedly of a chemical nature.

PART IV. TAXONOMY

CHAPTER X

CLASSIFICATION OF BACTERIA

Introduction. — There is considerable confusion at the present time, and there has been for years, in the nomenclature and classification of bacteria. This confusion has largely arisen on account of the fact that the majority of the work on the subject of bacteriology has been done by pathologists and others interested in the results of the vital activity of bacteria rather than their exact position among the plants. Very little systematic work has been done on the bacteria by botanists.

The first observers of bacteria were positive that they were animals and were inclined to believe that they belonged to the infusoria. They have since been placed in the plant kingdom, although they possess many things in common with certain animals.

It may be stated at the outset that there are many classifications of the bacteria. Formerly every author of a textbook on the subject of bacteriology made a new classification. The workers in the various fields also made classifications, as, for example, the botanists, pathologists, agriculturists, chemists, brewers, etc. Until recently no attempt at uniformity has been made. Obviously, any effort at the correlation of the various proposed classifications in a book of this scope would be impossible. Therefore the aim will be to present for due consideration only one classification which will give the clearest idea of the characteristics of the bacteria. As our definite knowledge of the bacteria increase these classifications must necessarily be modified.

It is an established fact that the form, shape, and manner of growth of a definite bacterium may be temporarily modified by the environment which surrounds the organism. The idea that new and well-defined species may be produced by modifications of the environment was held formerly by some bacteriologists. This was the theory of pleomorphism. It has since been proved that the organism which has apparently assumed a new form will return to its original shape when placed in the requisite environment. It was also held for some time rather tenaciously that bacteria had the power of assuming new physiological functions. To this power the term pleogeny was applied. It has been found in this case, as in the former, that the bacterial cell will return to normal when a normal environment is provided (see Chap. III).

There is no doubt but that the last classification of Migula is as accurate and systematic as has been made. This classification has been adopted by the leading American bacteriologists. It seems advantageous, however, to make a slight rearrangement of the classification. A division can be made for sufficient reasons into lower and higher bacteria, or what are termed by Fischer, Haplobacteria and Trichobacteria. Migula divides all bacteria into two orders: the Eubacteria, or true bacteria, and the Thiobacteria, or sulphur bacteria. Under the Eubacteria, Migula places four families, viz.: Coccaceæ, Bacteriaceæ, Spirillaceæ, and Chlamydobacteriaceæ. We believe that a simpler arrangement can be made by placing the families Coccaceæ, Bacteriaceæ, and Spirillaceæ under the suborder of the Haplobacterinæ (Fischer) or lower bacteria, and the Chlamydobacteriaceæ under the suborder Trichobacteriæ (Fischer) or higher bacteria. The various genera in these families as given by Migula are not changed.

There are many species of bacteria which possess definite, while others possess variable, characteristics. It is possible to place them in definite genera and to constitute distinct species. It should be remembered, however, that there is under certain conditions a striking similarity in form and physiological activity among different species of bacteria. For example, certain bacilli are so short that they appear at times to be cocci. It will be easily seen, therefore, that there is always difficulty in the classification of some organisms. The best classification can be made only when all the various species of bacteria are subjected, as nearly as possible, to the same conditions of temperature, light, gaseous environment, food, etc.

Classification of Migula (Modified).—The bacteria are phycochrome-free schizomycetous plants which divide in one, two, or three planes. Reproduction takes place by vegetative multiplication (fission). Resting stages in the form of endospores are produced by many species. Motility is noted in some genera, and this is due to flagella. In Beggiatoa and Spirochæta the organs of locomotion are not definitely known.

I. ORDER: EUBACTERIA (True Bacteria).

The cells are devoid of any nucleus (Zentralkörper) and free from sulphur and bacteriopurpurin, colorless or faintly colored.

I. Suborder: Haplobacterinæ (Lower Bacteria).

I. Family: Coccaceæ (Zopf) Mig.

The cells are globular when in a free state, but in the various stages of division appear somewhat elliptical. A few species in this family are motile. Cell division takes place in all directions of space. Frequently the cells remain attached together, and under these conditions usually show some flattening of the cell at the point of junction with the cell next to it.

Genus: Streptococcus Billroth.

The cells are globular and do not possess any organs of locomotion. Cell division takes place in only one plane. Usually the cells remain united together after division, producing chains or diplococcus forms. No endospores have been noted.

Genus: Micrococcus (Hallier) Cohn.

The cells are globular and do not possess any organs of locomotion. Cell division takes place in two planes at right angles. If the cells remain attached together after cell division, merismopedia plates are formed. The plates give the appearance of a regular flat mass of cells. No endospores have been noted in this genus.

Genus: Sarcina Goodsir.

The cells are globular and do not possess any organs of locomotion. Cell division takes place in three planes, all perpendicular and at right angles to each other. Its cells remain attached after division, cube-like packets are formed The composition of the media sometimes prevents this typical cube formation.

Genus: Planococcus Migula.

The cells are globular. Cell division takes place in two planes at right angles similar to genus Micrococcus. The cells of this genus are motile, possessing one or two long flagella. No endospores are produced in this genus.

Genus: Planosarcina Migula.

The cells are globular. Cell division takes place in three planes as in Sarcina. Cells are motile, having only one flagellum on each. Cells usually remain united in twos and in tetrads and seldom form packets as Sarcina.

II. Family: Bacteriaceæ Migula.

The cells are cylindrical in shape. They vary in length from short, almost spherical bodies to very long rods. Cell division takes places in one direction in a plane perpendicular to the long axis of the cell. Some of the members of this family remain attached together, forming threads, while others separate from each other soon after fission.

Genus: Bacterium Ehrenberg.

The cells are cylindrical, of longer or shorter length. Threads are frequently formed. The cells do not possess any organs of locomotion. Endospores are produced in some few species, but in the majority no such formation occurs. It is possible that endospore formation occurs only under certain environmental conditions.

Genus: Bacillus Cohn.

The cells are cylindrical, of longer or shorter length. The rods are sometimes oval in shape. Cells are motile and possess flagella which are distributed over the entire surface. Endospore formation occurs with marked regularity. The bacteria in this genus are motile only during certain periods of their life. This period varies greatly in length and occurs only in the vegetative stage.

Genus: Pseudomonas Migula.

The cells are cylindrical, of longer or shorter length. The cells are motile and possess polar flagella. These flagella may vary from one to twelve in number. The formation of endospores in this species is claimed by some. If it occurs it is extremely rare. Occasionally certain species in this genus form themselves into threads or chains.

III. Family: Spirillaceæ Migula.

The cells are wound in the form of a spiral or representing the portion of a turn of a spiral. In the latter case, if the cells remain attached together in the form of a thread, a full spiral of several turns is produced. Cell division takes place in only one direction of space, and this is transverse to the long axis of the cell.

Genus: Spirosoma Migula.

The cells are rigid and bent in the form of spirals. The members of this genus are as a general rule quite large. The cells may be free or united together into small gelatinous masses. Some of the cells individually are surrounded by a gelatinous envelope while others are free.

Genus: Microspira Schröter.

The cells are rigid, short, and bent similar to a comma. When the cells are united together, S-shaped threads are formed. The cells are motile, possessing usually one flagellum and rarely two or three flagella. These flagella are about the same length as the cell. No endospores are formed. Some writers make no distinction between Microspira and

Spirillum. The name vibrio has also been applied by some writers to this genus.

Genus: Spirillum Ehrenberg.

The cells are rigid, usually long and forming long, screwlike threads, or, in some cases, only portions of a spiral turn. Cells are motile and possess a tuft of flagella at the pole. The flagella may occur at both ends of the spiral, and they vary greatly in number. Endospore formation has been observed in some species.

Genus: Spirochæta Ehrenberg.

The cells are flexible spirals, very thin and long. No flagella are present. These bacteria move by rotation similar to a screw, and also by lateral motion similar to a snake. The locomotive organs if present are not known. No endospores are produced.

II. Suborder: Trichobacterinæ (Higher Bacteria).

Family: Chlamydobacteriaceæ Migula.

The cells are cylindrical, are united in threads, and surrounded by a sheath. Reproduction takes place by means of motile and nonmotile gonidia. These gonidia arise directly from the vegetative cells and without any resting stage produce new threads of cells.

Genus: Chlamydothrix Migula.

The cells are cylindrical, nonmotile, and arranged in unbranched threads and surrounded by a sheath of varying thickness in different species, being the same diameter at apex and base. Reproduction takes place by means of gonidia, which are round and arise directly from the vegetative cell. This genus is called Leptothrix by Kutzing and Steptothrix by Cohn.

Genus: Crenothrix Cohn.

The cells are united together into filaments which are unbranched. The filaments gradually enlarge toward the free end, thus making a distinction between the apex and base. The sheath which covers the filaments is thick and often becomes infiltrated with the hydroxide of iron after being cast off in water in which there is a large amount of iron. Reproduction takes place by the formation of round gonidia which are formed in the beginning by division perpendicular to the long axis of the cell and later by division in three directions of space. Only one or possibly two species can be placed in this genus.

Genus: Phragmidiothrix Engler.

The cells in the beginning form unbranched threads. Cell division takes place in three directions of space, thus forming within the sheath a mass of cells. Later these cells may burst through, multiply, and form branches after acquiring sheaths. The sheath in this genus is quite thin and can scarcely be seen.

Genus: Sphærotilus Kutzing, 1833 (Cladothrix Cohn).

The cells are cylindrical and the threads are surrounded by sheaths. Dichotomous branching is present, and there is no differentiation in size between the apex and base of the thread. Reproduction takes place by means of gonidia which swarm together within the cell. These gonidia burst out of the cells, attach themselves to some object, and grow into new threads. The gonidia are endowed with flagella which are attached toward the end and below the pole.

II. Order Thiobacteria (Sulphur Bacteria).

The cells do not possess any nucleus and contain sulphur. The cells are colorless or pigmented rose, violet, or red by bacteriopurpurin. The cells are never pigmented green.

I. Family: Beggiatoaceæ Trevisan.

Filamentous bacteria which do not contain bacteriopurpurin. The cells contain sulphur granules. Reproduction takes place in one direction of space.

Genus: Thiothrix Winogradsky.

The cells are nonmotile and the threads are attached to some object. The threads are surrounded by a delicate sheath and the cells contain sulphur granules. Gonidia are produced at the end of the threads. These gonidia are motile and finally attach themselves to some object, and, according to some authors, bend at right angles in the middle and grow into new threads.

Genus: Beggiatoa Trevisan.

The threads are not surrounded by a sheath and are formed of flat cells. The cells are not attached. This genus moves by means of an undulating membrane similar to Oscillaria. As the organism moves, it rotates on its long axis and swings its free ends. Gonidia are unknown, and reproduction takes place by a division and separation of the threads.

II. Family: Rhodobacteriaceæ (Winogradsky's classification, Artificial).

The cells contain bacteriopurpurin and on this account may be red, rose, or violet. Sulphur granules may also be included within the cells.

I Subfamily: Thiocapsaceæ.

The cells are united into colonies. Cell division takes place in three directions of space.

Genus: Thiocystis Winogradsky.

The colonies are small, compact, and enveloped either singly or in groups by a gelatinous cyst. The colonies are also capable of breaking up and the cells moving about.

Genus: Thiocapsa Winogradsky.

The cells are globular in shape and spread out on a substratum in flat colonies. These colonies are surrounded by a common gelatinous secretion similar to a capsule. The cells are nonmotile.

Genus: Thiosarcina Winogradsky.

The colonies form packets similar to the genus Sarcina of the Eubacteria. The cells are nonmotile.

II Subfamily Lamprocystaceæ.

The cells are formed into families. Cell division takes place first in three, then in two directions of space.

Genus: Lamprocystis Schröter.

The cells in the beginning are solid, then hollow, becoming perforated like a net. They separate into small groups and become motile.

III Subfamily Thiopediaceæ.

The cells are united into colonies. Cell division takes place in two directions of space.

Genus: Thiopedia Winogradsky.

The families are formed similar to tubes and are composed of cells arranged in fours and capable of motility.

IV Subfamily Amœbobacteriaceæ.

The cells are united into colonies. Cell division takes place in one direction of space.

Genus: Amœbacter Winogradsky.

The cells are united into colonies, and after division in one direction of space remain attached together by threads of protoplasm. The colonies possess amœboid motility. The cells change form by contraction and the spreading out of the protoplasm.

Genus: Thiothece Winogradsky.

The colonies are inclosed by a thick, gelatinous cyst. The cells are capable of moving and are very loosely surrounded by a common gelatin.

Genus: Thiodictyon Winogradsky.

The colonies are solid, nonmotile, and consist of small cells which are pressed together.

V Subfamily Chromotiaceæ.

The cells are free and capable at all times of motility.

Genus: Chromatium Perty.

The cells are moderately thick, elliptical, or cylindric-elliptical in shape.

Genus: Rhabdochromatium Winogradsky.

The cells are free, rod-shaped, or spindle form. They possess flagella on the poles and are motile at all times.

Genus: Thiospirillum.

The cells are free, continually motile, and spirally twisted.

CHAPTER XI

THE RELATIONSHIP OF BACTERIA

Introduction. — The boundary between the animal and vegetable kingdoms, if such there be, is not definite. There has been much confusion in regard to the accurate differentiation of these kingdoms since the time of the first records of microscopic life. The indications are that it will be some time before scientists will definitely settle this problem and be able to state in certain instances that a particular low form of life is a plant or an animal. We refer, obviously, to those animal and plant forms which are of the simplest structure and which closely resemble each other physiologically and morphologically. In all probability, according to recent investigations, this problem will be greatly elucidated by the chemists who, on the perfection of their technique, will find that the main differences between plants and animals are those of chemical structure.

The terms "animal" and "plant" were devised years ago before the single-celled forms of life which possess similarities to both groups were known. It is in a measure senseless to try to apply these terms to organisms for which they were never intended. The terms, as have been stated by various writers, were intended to apply to such contrasts as oak trees and elephants, and were never to be applied to minute plants and animals. There are certain things which are common to plants and animals down to the very simple forms. There is undoubtedly a gradual transition from one form to the other, and consequently no dividing line can be made between the two. The two groups gradually approach each other in their structure and physiological processes, and finally coalesce.

Conceive then a group of microörganisms at the point where the plant and animal kingdoms unite; a group which includes animals and plants of the simplest anatomical structure, a group in which differentiation into one or the other of the organic kingdoms is difficult and based upon what little is known about their chemistry, anatomy, and physiology. This group would include certain of the protozoa among the animals and certain of the algæ and fungi among the plants. We can make no definite boundary for this group. Haeckel has applied the name " protista " to this group of simple forms of life.

Bacteria Defined. — To this arbitrary group of simple-celled forms the class of microörganisms, which are designated as bacteria, belong. The bacteria are the smallest of all known living organic bodies. The size, of course, varies with the species, but is fairly constant within the limit of the same species.

It has been decided by careful scientific investigations that the bacteria, taking the whole class of organisms into consideration, show more points of resemblance to the plants than to the animals. They have been found to resemble certain of the lower plants very closely. The bacteria are now defined to be *microscopic, unicellular, nonnucleated plants, devoid of chlorophyll and reproducing by direct fission. In some orders the formation of special reproductive cells known as gonidia occur.* Some authors have stated that reproduction also takes place by the formation of endospores. This proposition has been discussed in another chapter.

Bacteria are the most widely distributed and most numerous of all living organisms. The surface of the earth and the soil to an average of four feet contain bacteria. The waters on the surface of the earth contain innumerable bacteria. The air, with the possible exception of that over large bodies of water and in high altitudes, contain varying numbers of bacteria and many species. No family of plants compares with the bacteria in importance.

Points of Resemblance to Other Forms of Life. — The following facts will serve to give an idea of the general points of resemblance of the bacteria to the low plants and animals. It will be seen that they resemble the known plants more closely than the animals, and, consequently, are placed in the lowest order of this kindgom.

1. In some species of bacteria a thin, limiting membrane, which is related to cellulose or hemicellulose, chemically, is present, and in this particular they resemble plant cells. However, recent investigations have shown that the cell wall

in a great many of the lower bacteria resembles, as much if not more, the chitin of certain animal cell walls than it does the cellulose of plants.

2. The form or shape of the bacterial cell is very similar to some of the low plants, such as the blue-green algæ. The bacteria in some cases form filaments, as plants of a low order do.

3. There is a similarity between certain of the low plant forms, such as the fungi and the bacteria, in their physiological processes, as, for example, the assimilation of nutritive products and reproduction. They also resemble certain of the protozoa in the latter process.

4. The food supply of the bacteria is composed of complex organic material built up by higher plants and animals, except in the case of some soil bacteria, which are able to absorb the free nitrogen of the air and use it for nutritive purposes, or derive nitrogen from nitrites or nitrates. This organic material must be in solution in order that it may be absorbed through the cell wall. Inorganic salts are frequently present and seem necessary for protoplasmic nutrition and to assist in keeping up the osmotic pressure of the cell, as is the case in higher plants. Most plants use very simple substances for food.

5. Certain recognized species of bacteria have the power of deriving their nitrogen from the disintegration of ammonia (NH_3) compounds. In this respect they resemble some plants and differ from all animals.

6. Some species of bacteria possess the power of breaking up carbon dioxide (CO_2) into carbon (C) and oxygen (O) without the aid of chlorophyll and sunlight, which are used by higher plants. In some cases the carbon and oxygen are derived from carbonates. They differ from all plants and animals in this respect.

7. Certain bacteria of the soil take up free nitrogen of the air, and in this they resemble some few species of fungi and differ from all animals.

8. A large number of species of bacteria possess organs of locomotion called flagella or cilia, and in this respect they resemble certain animal forms among the protozoa.

9. Bacterial cells possess no definite nucleus as most animal and plant cells do. The cell protoplasm is undifferentiated and the chromatic material distributed throughout all the parts of the cell.

10. Bacterial cells, like all higher plants, do not produce any nitrogen-containing excretions.

Relationship to Plants. — Vegetation on the earth may be divided into four divisions, which are quite distinct.

1. Thallophyta	Algæ, fungi, etc.
2. Bryophyta	Mosses.
3. Pteridophyta	Ferns.
4. Spermatophyta	Seed plants.

The first three divisions compose the Cryptogamia, or non-flowering plants.

The microörganisms known as bacteria belong to the

Thallophyta. The Thallophyta compose a multitude of plants which are very primitive and simple in form This group of plants are devoid of fibro-vascular bundles, roots, stems, and leaves. The cell body produced is called a thallus. The individual cells carry on their metabolic processes independently.

The Thallophyta are subdivided, according to some botanists, into the following groups: —

1. Myxomycetes . . . . Slime molds.
2. Schizophyta . . . . Bacteria, blue-green algæ, etc.
3. Diatomeæ . . . . Diatoms
4. Euphyceæ . . . . True algæ
5. Eumycetes . . . . True fungi

A great many authorities divide the Thallophyta into only two groups — the fungi and the algæ.

Relationship to Eumycetes. — The Eumycetes, or fungi, are closely related to the bacteria in some particulars. Bacteria have been called Schizomycetes, or fission fungi. Physiologically the bacteria, except certain of the soil forms, agree with the fungi in a great many details. Both are metatrophic and paratrophic (Chap. XIV), and therefore require organic material which has been built up by higher plants and animals. The bacteria and the fungi do not resemble each other morphologically. The fungi include the molds, mushrooms, mildews, etc. These plants, like the bacteria, are devoid of chlorophyll and require organic food in solution, and are not able to build up carbohydrates as higher plants do. They are commonly found together with saprogenic bacteria on decaying animal and vegetable material. The fungi cells are granular, nonnucleated, and the protoplasm watery and colorless. They are usually found collected together into filaments called hyphæ. Interwoven hyphæ are collectively called a mycelium. The fungi, no matter what species, can be separated into two distinct parts, the mycelium or vegetative part, and the fruiting head or spore-bearing, reproductive part. No such separation occurs in the lower bacteria. In the higher bacterial forms, when reproduction takes place, all the cells in the filament which are destined to reproduce form *gonidia*, and the vegetative state for these cells ceases to exist. This is also true in a measure in reproduction among the Myxomycetes, or slime molds.

The fungi are related to the algæ through a common ancestry. There is a group among the algæ, or closely related to them, which is called the Phycomycetæ, or algo-fungi. Some botanists hold the view, on seemingly a good basis, that the fungi are modified algæ which have lost their chlorophyll and acquired saprophytic habits.

The yeasts or Saccharomycetes are certainly very closely related to the bacteria. They are unicellular plants which do not ordinarily produce filaments and are devoid of chlorophyll. While having many physiological processes in common, they differ from the bacteria in the method of reproduction, the bacteria reproducing by fission and the yeasts by budding.

Some of the yeasts and molds possess the power of producing disease conditions in the human body.

Relationship to Cyanophyceæ. — The bacteria — taking the whole group into consideration — are without doubt more closely related to the Cyanophyceæ, or blue-green algæ, than to any other plants. The blue-green algæ are single-celled plants which usually form themselves into threads or filaments, and reproduce in the main by fission, similar to bacteria (Fig. 37). The filaments branch and there is a specificity of function among the various cells. They are very closely related to the Chlamydobacteriaceæ and the Thiobacteria. Some forms also resemble the lower bacteria in shape. They are, as before stated, filamentous, and many species possess sheaths. The blue-green algæ compose the remaining portion of the connecting link between the bacteria and the chlorophyll-bearing plants. In addition to their similarity in form they secrete a gelatinous substance from their cell walls similar to some species of bacteria. Some forms (Oscillariæ) are motile. They differ from the bacteria and show an advance over them in the possession of a primitive nucleus and chlorophyll in the outer layers of their protoplasm. The bluish green coloring matter is

FIG. 37. — Anabena rariabilis. Cyanophyte. After Schmidt and Weis.

carried in special hollow chromatophores. This chlorophyll does not seem to be as complex as that of higher plants. Certain bacteria, for example, Bacterium viride Van Teigman, contain a slight amount of green coloring matter similar to the chlorophyll of the blue-green algæ. They are on the whole more highly differentiated than the bacteria. Besides reproducing by fission the Cyanophyceæ at certain periods may reproduce by forming gonidia similar to the higher bacteria.

It should be remembered that there is no genetic relationship between the bacteria and the Cyanophyceæ. They are, however, related through a common ancestor.

Relationship to Euphyceæ. — The Euphyceæ, or true algæ, vary in size and structure from simple microscopic, unicellular forms to highly developed and complex bodies. The Euphyceæ are not related except by a common stock to the Cyanophyceæ, or blue-green algæ. Certain of the unicellular forms resemble the bacteria in their morphology, but differ from them in that they reproduce by zoöspore formation, in the possession of chlorophyll and chromogenic plastids, and also in the character of the cell wall. The similarity of the bacteria and the Euphyceæ is only superficial. The two groups cannot be shown to be related directly.

Relationship to Myxomycetes or Slime Molds. These low forms of life are most frequently found upon decaying logs, leaves, etc. At certain periods they suggest a relationship with some of the single-celled animals and the fungi. Some biologists class them as animals. Structures called sporangia, containing minute microscopic spores which are provided with a cell wall, a nucleus, protoplasm, and capable of generating a new body, are present. These bodies are only slightly resistant and are specific reproductive cells. They do not serve to carry the organism over unfavorable periods as the endospores of bacteria do. Reproduction among the bacteria is a much simpler process than it is in the slime molds. The Myxomycetes do not resemble the bacteria closely

Relationship to Myxobacteriaceæ. — The myxobacteria are rodlike organisms which are motile and multiply by fission. They secrete a firm gelatinous base and often form aggregates of several cells. The formation of these aggregations of cells usually precedes a stage in which the rods become encysted and go into the resting stage or become encysted and form spores. The cells undergo elongation and constriction in the center before division and never remain attached together in chains. The organism moves in a gliding fashion not unlike Beggiatoa. Locomotor organs are unknown. The masses of the cells are reddish in appearance. Myxobacteria are common in moist places, as on decaying wood or on fungi. Their optimum temperature is about 30° C. This group of microorganisms connects the higher or Thiobacteria and the Cyanophyceæ or blue-green algæ and the Myxomycetes or slime molds. This group (Myxobacteria) is sometimes made to constitute a third order under the bacteria.

Relationship to Protozoa. — Bacteria also possess some points of resemblance to certain single-celled animals belonging to the protozoa. There is a species, Polytomauvella, belonging to the order of Flagellata, which is ovoid or bacillus-like in shape and which possesses polar flagella. The number of these flagella is quite definite for the species. There are other species which possess a tuft of flagella at the poles similar to the lophotrichous and amphitrichous bacteria. Still other forms possess a pulsating vacuole which suggests a resemblance to a structure of that nature in Beggiatoa. The cell wall in certain species of bacteria is very similar to the cell wall of certain Sporozoa which belong to the protozoa (Fig. 38).

FIG. 38. — Dimorpha radiata. Showing nucleus, contractile vacuole, etc. (Protozoon.) After Schmidt and Weis.

The process of encystment, which takes place when some of these forms of protozoa come in contact with unfavorable surroundings, closely resembles the formation of endospores by some species of bacteria. In distinct contrast to the bacteria, the protozoa, and particularly the flagellata, possess a well-defined nucleus. Some of the protozoa are quite similar to the fungi and particularly the yeasts, as, for example, Trichomonas intestinalis and Trichomonas vaginalis.

The Myxomycetes, or slime molds, bear many points of

resemblance to the protozoa, and also an equal number of points of resemblance to the myxobacteria.

The bacteria show the most marked similarities to the Cyanophyta, or blue-green algæ, and the Flagellata among the protozoa. They should be considered as a separate group, possessing many points of resemblance to the various low forms of plant and animal life.

PART V. GENERAL PHYSIOLOGY

CHAPTER XII

Relation to Environment

Introduction. — By physiology is meant the science of function. In Part IV we learned about what bacteria are, and in Part V we are to learn what bacteria do. In considering the morphology of bacteria, one of the striking facts brought out was the simplicity of form. Bacteria are reduced to almost the limit of simplicity so far as form and structure are concerned. Generally speaking, structure and function are related. The organisms which have the most complex functions are those which have the most complicated forms. But in the bacteria there is a striking exception to this general rule. The bacteria are very simple so far as their form is concerned, but their functions are very complex, and it is one of the wonders of biology how such a complicated physiology has developed on so simple a morphology.

Functions. — In the subject of physiology we have to consider not only the functions of bacteria, that is, what they do, but we have also to consider the effect which the environment has upon the organism and the modifications which these external conditions have on the functions.

External Conditions. — The external conditions may be without effect on the bacteria, or they may stimulate activity, that is, they may have a tonic effect, or, on the other hand, they may have a repressive effect, and it is the purpose in this connection to consider the most important of the external conditions and determine whether their action is stimulative or repressive, and find out if possible the conditions which are best adapted for the growth of the bacteria or conditions which will lead to their destruction most quickly.

Food. — All forms of life must have food, and the bacteria are no exceptions. Like other forms of life, also, they may be able to get along with a very small amount, that is, on a maintenance ration, or they may do a great deal better on a different or larger amount, that is, on a growing ration. As to the actual amount which is needed by the bacteria it is to be noted that the bacteria are divided into two classes. One class are accustomed to live upon the body of animals or plants, and are known as *parasites*. These require a considerable amount of food. The other class live on dead organic matter, and are known as the *saprophytes*. Some of these may subsist on a surprisingly small amount of organic food. Meade Bolton some years ago called attention to the fact that certain water bacteria were able to live and grow with great rapidity in double-distilled water where the only source of organic matter was the dirt on the sides of the vessels, which he was unable to remove by the most careful methods of cleaning. This is one extreme. Many of the bacteria, however, require a considerable amount of food substance. On the other hand, the excess of food is not without its effect. It is impossible for many of the bacteria to live in foods that are too concentrated. Reference has already been made to the fact that when the bacterial cell is surrounded by a substance that has greater osmotic pressure than the protoplasm of the cell the cell is plasmolyzed. Bacteria are, of course, unable to grow under these conditions. If, then, their food substance is too concentrated, they are unable to make use of it, and this fact is taken advantage of in the preservation of a number of food substances. Condensed milk, for instance, keeps because the bacteria in it are unable to make use of the food which is present there in a too concentrated form. The same thing is true of sirups. At times chemical substances are added which increase the osmotic pressure, as is true in the case of brine.

Chemical Composition of Food. — Food must contain certain chemical elements. Those which are necessary are carbon, oxygen, hydrogen, nitrogen, phosphorus, sulphur, iron, and calcium. No substance is valuable as a food which does not furnish the necessary chemical elements. It is true that not all substances furnishing the necessary elements are necessarily good food substances. It is said that one man's food is another man's poison. So among bacteria; one substance may serve as a medium for the development for one kind of bacteria and be absolutely prohibitive to the growth of another.

Water. — Bacteria require water for growth. They may in

fact be considered as aquatic plants. The reason for this is perfectly evident. They secure their food through absorption, and it is absolutely necessary that they be surrounded by moisture. It is true that bacteria may grow upon solid media, but they can only do so when they are surrounded by, at least, a film of moisture. If they become completely dried, they are unable to feed. They are, however, able to maintain their existence for some time in a desiccated condition, but are not able to grow when in this state. So far as the ability of a microörganism to withstand desiccation is concerned, different kinds of bacteria vary greatly. The spores are able to withstand an almost unlimited amount of desiccation. It is for this reason, largely, that they are so valuable to the bacteria. The vegetative cell is not without this power, however, but the different kinds vary greatly in their ability to withstand complete drying. For example, such an organism as the Msp. comma of Asiatic cholera can withstand drying for only a few hours, or a few days at most. The same is true also of the M. pneumoniæ and Bact. influenzæ; but other vegetative cells, such as the Bact. diphtheriæ, may withstand the effect of desiccation for many days, in some cases as long as 194 days. Reference was made in a preceding paragraph to the effect of the density of the medium on the bacteria, and it will be recalled that when the culture medium is less dense than the protoplasm of the cell, the cell is in a state of turgescence; that when the culture medium is more dense than the protoplasm, the cell is plasmolyzed. It is true also that the density of culture medium may have its tonic effect on the bacteria. Certain bacteria that are accustomed to a considerable concentration will be affected by a diminution in the degree of concentration, and some forms will move towards or away from a different concentration from that to which they are accustomed.

Oxygen. — It is a general law of physiology that all life must breathe. In 1861 Pasteur discovered a microorganism which grew best in the absence of the free oxygen of the air, and since that time we have come to divide bacteria into two classes, so far as their relation to the free oxygen of the air is concerned. One class, known as the *aërobes*, lives in the free oxygen of the air and are comparable, in their oxygen requirements, to ordinary forms of life. The other class, known as the *anaërobes*, grows best in the absence of free oxygen, and some of them grow only when free oxygen is removed. It is not to be understood, however, that these anaërobic microorganisms are an exception to the general rule that all life must breathe. These forms do breathe. The difference is the source of their oxygen. The anaërobes take their oxygen from organic compounds rather than from the free oxygen of the air. Some of the bacteria can grow under both aërobic and anaërobic conditions; some grow best, for instance, under aërobic conditions, but have the faculty of growing under anaërobic conditions. Some bacteria grow best under anaërobic conditions, but have the faculty of growing under aërobic conditions. So that in reality we have four classes of bacteria here. One class, known as the strict or *obligate aerobes*, can grow only under strict aërobic conditions; the *obligate anaerobes* can grow only under strict anaerobic conditions; the *facultative anaerobes* grow best under aërobic conditions, but have the faculty of growing under anaërobic conditions; and the *facultative aërobes* grow best under anaerobic conditions, but have the faculty of growing under aerobic conditions. Anaërobes are widely distributed in nature. They are found, for example, in the soil constantly and in great numbers. Furthermore, they occur in the upper layers of the soil under conditions where oxygen is constantly present; and it is a matter of speculation as to how the conditions favorable for their development are secured. Upon our artificial culture media they are obligate anaerobes. It is thought by some that perhaps in their natural habitat they are not so particular in their oxygen requirements or, what is quite as likely, they may enter into partnership with certain other forms of life which furnish them anaërobic conditions. But whatever the explanation, it is a well-known fact that these forms are widely distributed and among them some of the disease-producing bacteria, as, for example, B. tetani (lockjaw) and Bact. welchii (gaseous emphysema).

Anaërobic Culture Methods. — In order to cultivate these germs on artificial media it is necessary to employ special methods. A great many different methods have been described but they can all be grouped under the following heads: 1. Replacement of air. In this case air is replaced by some inert gas, as hydrogen or carbon dioxide. For this purpose special apparatus is necessary, and a great variety of forms of apparatus has been devised. 2. Absorption of oxygen. This can be done by means of certain chemical substances, such as an alkaline solution of pyrogallic acid. Here, too, the forms of apparatus are numerous. A very simple form of apparatus is made by pushing the cotton plug of a test tube culture into the tube and then filling up with an alkaline solution of pyrogallic acid and closing the test tube with a rubber stopper. 3. Exhaustion of air. This is done by means of an air pump. Any of the above methods are equally good and, in fact, may frequently be combined to advantage. 4. Exclusion of oxygen. This is accomplished by pouring on top of the culture either more culture media or sterile oil. 5. Growth in the presence of air. This is done either by growing with some other organism that is aërobic or some reducing substance, such as litmus or formic acid.

When Pasteur discovered these organisms, he thought that they were the organisms which carried on fermentation, and he defined fermentation as life without air. This on further study has been found to be without basis of fact, but it is true that a considerable number of fermentations are produced by anaërobic bacteria. Among these may be mentioned the butyric acid fermentation, the fermentation of cellulose, the retting of flax, and putrefaction. Reference has already been made to the fact that these anaërobic bacteria may produce disease.

Temperature. — Temperature has a profound influence upon the lower as well as on the higher forms of life. Every organism becomes habituated or attuned to certain temperatures. If the functions of life become adjusted to this particular temperature, any considerable variation affects these functions. An increase of temperature within certain limits increases the activity of the cell   The power of absorption is increased and the excretions are accelerated, so that the whole life process becomes more active. Variations from this temperature, either above or below, decrease the activity   Beyond a certain limit functional activity ceases and growth stops, and finally certain marked variations render the existence of the organism impossible. The temperature limits within which the life of the bacteria is possible are wide, in a general way extending from the temperature of boiling water down to practically absolute zero. The temperature limits within which functional activities occur are very much narrower and for most forms of life are between zero and a temperature slightly above that of the animal body. In considering the effect of temperature on bacteria, there are several cardinal points which must be taken into consideration. There is the *maximum temperature*, which is the highest temperature at which the bacteria are able to carry on their life processes. The *optimum temperature* is that temperature at which the bacteria grow best. The *minimum temperature* is the lowest temperature at which the bacteria are capable of growing, and the *thermal death point* is that temperature at which bacteria are destroyed. The thermal death point will vary, depending, among other things, upon the time the bacteria are subjected to this temperature. The thermal death point is usually defined as the degree of heat required to kill the bacteria when it is applied for ten minutes in a moist condition. The effect of any given temperature upon a bacterium depends upon its condition, that is, whether it is in a vegetative or a latent stage. When the bacterium is in an actively growing condition it is much more susceptible to external influences than when it is in a latent condition, and attention has already been called to the fact that in the spore state the bacteria are unusually resistant. Another factor of a good deal of importance is the kind of heat that is employed; that is, whether it is moist or dry. Moist heat is much more effective than dry heat at the same temperature.

According as bacteria are affected by heat they are divided into three classes. Those which have a low optimum temperature are known as the *psychrophilic bacteria*. These grow at a temperature only a few degrees above zero. The bacteria which have a medium optimum temperature are known as the *mesophilic bacteria* and are more abundant than any other class. This group may well be divided into two subgroups: one in which the optimum temperature is about that of a summer's day (25° to 30° C.) and includes particularly those bacteria which live on dead organic matter, the saprophytes; and the disease-producing bacteria, or parasites, which have as their optimum temperature that of the body of their host (37° to 40° C.). The third class are those which have a high optimum temperature, frequently ranging from 50° to 70° C and are known as the *thermophilic bacteria.*

When the temperature goes above the maximum or falls below the minimum, the bacteria go into a state which resembles that of death and is spoken of as rigor, either heat rigor or cold rigor. Unless the state of rigor continues too long the bacteria are capable of recovering when brought into normal temperatures. There is no definite change which takes place as the result of exposure to extremes of temperature, but the change is cumulative and may finally be destructive. The zone of heat rigor is much narrower than that of cold rigor, and hence the thermal death point more closely follows the maximum than does the cold death point follow the minimum It is a popular notion that cold is frequently and rapidly destructive to bacterial life, but this idea is not borne out by experiment, for it is found that when bacteria are subjected to cold, either that of ordinary ice or much lower temperatures, they can persist for very long periods of time. A number of years ago Prudden froze B. prodigiosus and found that they were living at the end of thirty-seven days in much reduced numbers, but only on the fifty-first day had they entirely disappeared. Sedgwick, likewise, a number of years ago, found that the B. typhosus when frozen in ice persisted in considerable numbers even for a period of 103 days. From this it is clear that ordinary cold cannot be depended upon to kill bacteria, even those of the most delicate sort. When bacteria are subjected to extremes of cold, such as may now readily be obtained by the use of liquid air, it has been found by Ravenel, McFayden, and others that they may live for long periods of time and, indeed, may be little changed. It is to be understood in all of these cases that some individuals readily succumb but that certain others persist, and this is found to be the case whenever bacteria are brought into unfavorable surroundings. There is great difference in the powers of resistance towards any unfavorable conditions by the different individuals in the same culture.

Compared with other forms of life bacteria are more resistant, as will be seen in the following table: —

Comparative Power of Various Organisms to resist Changes of Temperature

	Heat Degrees C.	Cold Degrees C.
Bacteria, vegetative	60	0
" spore	90	−350
Yeast	53	
Algæ	45–60	
Higher plants	47	
Crustacea	30–36	0
Frogs	40–42	−4 to −10
Man	45	

The temperature of the bacterial cell varies with the temperature of the surroundings in the same way that the temperature of the cold-blooded animal varies. The bacteria are therefore spoken of as *poikolothermic* in contradistinction to those organisms which have a constant temperature, as, for instance, the warm-blooded animals, which are known as *homothermic*. Furthermore, it is found that some of the bacteria are able to grow in a wide temperature range. That is, their minimum temperature is widely separated from their maximum temperature, and their optimum is usually a wide zone. These organisms are spoken of as *eurythermic* Most of the saprophytes belong to this class and are thus distinguished from the class of bacteria which are described as *stenothermic*, which have a narrow temperature range. Such bacteria are the pathogenic or disease-producing ones. Many of these, on account of their parasitic mode of life have become adapted to a particular temperature, and only slight variations from this interfere with their life processes in a very striking way. Such a germ is the Bact. tuberculosis, which has become adapted to a parasitic mode of life and is dependent upon a very narrow temperature range. The psychrophilic bacteria were found by Foster growing in melting ice. Fischer found them in sea water. Many others have found that they exist in soil and milk and various other materials. They grow quite rapidly even at a temperature only slightly above zero. These psychrophilic bacteria are similar to the red snow plants found in the north, and the diatoms that swarm the Arctic Seas so far as their resistance to cold is concerned.

Thermal Death Point. — The determination of the thermal death point is a matter of so much practical importance that it is worth while to consider it at some length here. It is important because it is desirable to apply as low a temperature as possible to various food substances so as not to injure them, and at the same time the temperature must be sufficiently high to destroy all germs capable of producing disease. The temperature necessary to kill bacteria in a general way is not far from 60° C. when this is applied for ten minutes in a moist condition. When spores are present, a temperature of 90° to 100° C. is necessary, and sometimes this must be applied by the intermittent method in order to produce complete sterility. The thermal death point of different organisms vary, depending upon inherent characteristics, as seen in the following table: —

Micrcspira comma	52° C.
Streptococcus pyogenes	54° C.
Bacillus typhosus	56° C.
Bacterium diphtheriæ	58° C.
Micrococcus (species unknown)	76° C.

The thermal death point varies with the reaction of the medium upon which the germ is grown and perhaps also with that of the medium in which the test is made. The same variation among individuals that was noted above in considering the effect of cold upon bacteria is noted here. If a quantitative determination is made of the number of bacteria killed at various temperatures just below the thermal death point, it will be found that within a few degrees the great majority of the individuals in a single culture are killed, and this we may speak of as the *normal thermal death point*. Certain individuals possess a high power of resistance and require a higher degree of heat to kill them. The necessary heat required to kill these is spoken of as the *absolute thermal death point*. There have been two methods widely used for the determination of the thermal death point: one devised by Sternberg, who uses a glass bulb, and the other described by the Committee on Standard Procedures appointed by the American Public Health Association. In both of these methods only the absolute thermal death point is determined, and each method has certain advantages and certain disadvantages. A capillary bent tube method, which was devised in the laboratory of one of us, offers certain advantages over both of the other methods. Death from heat is undoubtedly due to the coagulation of the protoplasm, and the different protoplasms have different points of coagulation. One difference which may account for these variations is the different amount of moisture present. This would tend to explain, especially, the high thermal death point of spores compared with the vegetative cell.

> Egg albumin + 50 per cent water coagulates at 56° C.
> Egg albumin + 25 per cent water coagulates at 74°-80° C.
> Egg albumin + 18 per cent water coagulates at 80°-90° C.
> Egg albumin + 6 per cent water coagulates at 145°C.
> Egg albumin dry coagulates at 160°-170° C.

The Action of Chemicals on Bacteria. — Reference has already been made to the chemical reaction of the media, and the influence which it has upon the development of the bacteria. It was noted that the bacteria preferred a neutral or slightly alkaline medium rather than an acid one, although they will tolerate one that is slightly acid.

Chemicals influence bacteria in much the same way that other external agents do, in that under certain conditions chemical substances are tonic, *i.e.* they have a stimulating effect. Other chemicals, or different concentrations of the same chemical, may produce a repressive action leading, ultimately, if the action is persisted in, to the death of the bacteria.

One of the most striking effects of chemicals on bacteria is the power they have to induce and control locomotion. The fact that bacteria seem to be attracted to certain substances is a matter of long standing observation; for instance, in stagnant water or in putrid solutions it is often seen that the bacteria, and other ciliated organisms, collect in masses around certain particles of the decaying or putrefying substances. With higher animals this would be called instinct. This property is widespread throughout both the plant and animal kingdom, and is very frequently noted among the bacteria. This phenomenon is known as *chemotaxis* or chemotropism.

The phenomenon may be noted under different conditions; for instance, if the chemical substance has a nutritive value, it is sometimes spoken of as *trophotropism* (attraction towards food); if the chemical substance is a gas, it is sometimes called *aërotropism*. The simplest manifestation of this phenomenon is the movement of bacteria towards free oxygen. It has already been noted that bacteria in the hanging-drop preparation frequently collect at the outer edge of the drop. This is due to the chemotaxic influence of the oxygen of the air. That it is the oxygen that attracts can be shown in another way; where an algal cell is in the same solution with bacteria, and is actively evolving oxygen as it manufactures its food, the bacteria in the neighborhood are attracted to it. En-

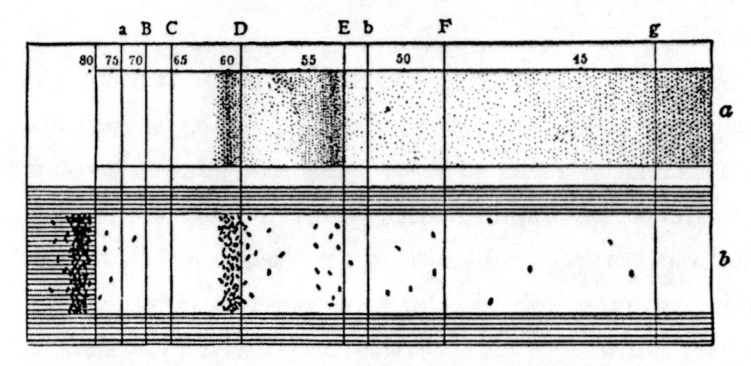

Fig. 39.—a, spectrum of the chromophyll of bacterio-purpurin, showing absorption bands at $\lambda = 0.59\,\mu$ and $\lambda = 0.52\,\mu$. An (invisible) absorption band has been determined by means of the bolometer at $\lambda = 0.85\,\mu$. b, the bacteria are seen aggregated chiefly in the regions of the absorption bands. The accumulation of bacteria in these regions of absorbed energy seems due to the fact that the moving bacteria cannot pass from a region of high energy to one of low without a violent stimulus which impels them back again. (From Engelmann, '83[a].)

gelmann has made use of this property to show the influence of the different colors of the spectrum on a filament of algal cells. The bacteria collect in the zones of greatest absorption, or, in other words, in that part of the filament where oxygen is most rapidly evolving (Fig. 39).

Numerous inorganic salts are capable of producing a chemotaxic influence on bacteria. Some chemical substances produce an attractive effect. Such substances are spoken of as being *positively chemotaxic;* other chemical substances repel the bacteria and are spoken of as *negatively chemotactic.* Pfeiffer found that the salts of the alkalies exert a very positive effect; that the alkaline earths exert a less active influence. Inorganic acids are generally repellent, except phosphoric acid, and the phosphates of the muscle. Organic compounds are frequently attractive. This might readily be expected, because it has been so frequently observed that decomposing organic matter is attractive to bacteria, and this might, in all likelihood, be attributed to organic substances. Many of the organic acids are attractive. Such nitrogen compounds as urea, aspargin, peptone, and meat extract are very attractive. Glycerine is neutral or without effect, while alcohol produces repellent action.

The different concentrations of solutions produce different effects; potassium chloride attracts in dilute solutions but repels in stronger solutions. It is impossible to predict what effect any chemical substance may have on the bacteria on the basis of its chemical constitution. The action is apparently not determined by the elements which enter into the compound, but by the entire compound; for instance, milk sugar produces a positive chemotaxic effect in one per cent solutions, while grape sugar requires a ten per cent solution. It is conceivable that this phenomenon may be of use to the bacteria, for instance, in helping them to select their food; but it appears that food substances are not always positively chemotaxic, and the bacteria have no power, apparently, of differentiating between a substance which is a good food and a poison. As an example, Fischer has cited the fact that a peptone solution to which a little corrosive sublimate has been added exerts a positive chemotaxic influence, and the bacteria rush into the solution only to be destroyed by the presence of the sublimate. It has been thought that this attraction indicated, on the part of the bacteria, a power of selection, and that they were attracted and purposely moved towards these substances. From the work of others, however, it seems likely that this is not the case, but that the bacteria swim about in an aimless fashion, and when they come in contact with these chemotaxic substances are under their influence. They find conditions there more favorable, and hence remain in the zone; but certain bacteria in the solution may fail to get into this zone, and therefore do not come under its influence.

The phenomenon of chemotropism is of general interest throughout biology, and enables us to explain movements of many kinds of life that would otherwise be very difficult to understand. As examples of this we may cite the attractive influence which the female cells have for the male cells among plants and among animals. Overton noted that the bacteria collect around conjugating spirogyra, where the tubes arise. The pollen tube moves down the stamen of flowers, in all probability under the influence of this phenomenon. The spermatozoa of plant and animal cells are attractive to the egg cells because of the excretion, by these egg cells, of certain substances which have a chemotaxic influence on the spermatozoa; and this would explain the phenomenon of fertilization which would be difficult on any other basis.

The white blood corpuscles are susceptible to chemotaxic influences, and certain metamorphoses are due to this. The change from the tadpole stage to the frog stage is brought about because of the chemotaxic influence which certain tissues, undergoing degeneration, have on the white blood corpuscles. The same explanation is used for changes which take place in old age, the degeneration of certain tissues, the loss of pigment in hair, etc. The phenomenon of inflammation is explained on this basis. The invading microörganism exerts a chemotaxic influence on the white blood cells, which cause them to leave the blood vessels and to collect around the invaders, and this phenomenon is really the basis of Metchnikoff's theory of immunity, which is so widely accepted at the present time.

The phenomenon of chemotaxis can be studied under the microscope by a method which was devised by Pfeiffer, and which is carried out as follows: —

Selected capillary glass tubes are placed in watch glasses containing the solution to be tested; they are then placed under a vacuum pump and the air is drawn out so as to completely fill the tubes with the solution. The tubes are then thoroughly rinsed, and the open end of the filled tube is plunged into a hanging drop of the bacteria to be studied. The solution gradually diffuses out, and the bacteria, which at first were evenly distributed throughout the hanging drop, make their way into the tube and collect in it.

Chemical substances may have an entirely different action from that discussed above; namely, a germicidal action. This destructive action is frequently spoken of as an antiseptic or disinfecting action. By an antiseptic is meant a substance which interferes with or prevents the growth of bacteria; while disinfectants are those substances which destroy those bacteria capable of producing infection. All disinfectants, very naturally, possess antiseptic properties, but it does not necessarily follow that all antiseptics possess disinfecting qualities A disinfectant may completely destroy bacteria, and the process may be complete in the sense of sterilization, or it may be incomplete, the chemical being able to destroy only certain cells. A considerable number of the disinfectants, for example, are readily fatal to the vegetative cells, but are unable to kill the spores. The disinfecting action of a substance is influenced by many factors. Some of these factors are resident in the cells themselves and others exist in the external environment. The protoplasmic contents of various bacteria differ to a considerable extent in their resistance to chemical substances. The vegetative cells of some species are twenty times as resistant as are others when acted upon by the same disinfectant and under the same conditions. Then, too, the individuals in the same culture differ in their powers of resistance, some individuals being much more resistant than others.

Certain of the inorganic chemicals are very powerful disinfectants. Many of the chemical elements, such as chlorine, bromine, iodine, and oxygen, are good disinfectants. The heavy metals, such as gold, silver, and mercury, have quite pronounced disinfecting value. Others, such as nickel, zinc, and copper, have only a slight value; while others, as lead and tin, have none. The acids and alkalies do not have a marked germicidal value except when they are used in strong solutions, and then they have a destructive action on metals and fabrics. *Mercuric chloride,* or corrosive sublimate, is one of the most effective of the inorganic salts. This has an antiseptic action in a one-millionth solution, and a disinfectant action in water in a one to five hundred-thousandth solution. This chemical unites with protein matter, and its use as a practical disinfectant is limited on that account. Certain of the *silver salts* are used, particularly in medicine, as antiseptics. *Lime* is of great value as a disinfectant, but when it is air slacked possesses no value. A freshly prepared lime water solution, or a whitewash, makes an excellent disinfectant, and is especially valuable in disinfecting a stable or barn, because it has certain properties in addition to its germicidal ones that are most beneficial, such as absorption of odors, reflection of light, etc. *Chloride of lime* is also an excellent disinfectant. It has recently been shown to be very effective as a disinfectant of sewage effluents. As a gaseous disinfectant *sulphur* has had a very prominent place, and it is popularly believed that the burning of a little sulphur in a room produces a good disinfectant. Sulphur has a good deal of value, but not nearly as much as is ordinarily believed. In order to disinfect a room having a thousand cubic feet of air space (10 by 10 by 10 ft), it is necessary that from three to five pounds of sulphur be burned in it. Furthermore, since burning or oxidizing of sulphur forms sulphur dioxide, and sulphur dioxide is not a good disinfectant, it is not enough merely to burn sulphur. There must be moisture present. Moisture can be obtained by means of steam The active disinfecting agent formed by the union of the sulphur dioxide and the water is sulphurous acid. Sulphurous acid is a good disinfectant but it is also an ideal bleaching agent, and when it is used all of the draperies in a room are destroyed Unless this occurs, the disinfecting process has not been properly carried out, and if it is done, of course the draperies, wall paper, or whatever it may be, are rendered useless. A good deal of misunderstanding, then, has prevailed in the use of sulphur, and it is not popular at the present time for family use. There are conditions, however, under which it works well, and for certain purposes it has no competitor. This is true where it is desirable to kill higher forms of life, such as insects and rodents, and it has very great value for certain lines of work, such as in the disinfection of the holds of infected ships where it is desired to kill rats, mice, and insects.

Formaldehyde is a chemical substance which has come into use as a disinfectant within recent years and has become deservedly popular. It is a gas formed by the incomplete oxidation of methyl alcohol. Although a gas, it is put upon the market as a solution. In its ordinary form the watery solution contains 40 per cent of the gas. For purposes of disinfection formaldehyde may be used either as a gas or a solution. Its uses as a gas will be considered first.

The gas may be produced in the space to be disinfected directly from the methyl alcohol, and for this purpose a number of special lamps have been manufactured. The cheaper ones are unsatisfactory in that they are likely to give an uneven product; the more expensive ones may be quite satisfactory, but both have the disadvantages of leaving a fire burning in a closed room, which is liable to lead to accidents, so that the gas is almost uniformly produced at the present time by regenerating it from the solution. It might naturally be expected that this would be a simple matter, and that all that would be necessary to do would be to evaporate the solution, but when formaldehyde solution evaporates under ordinary conditions it is likely to polymerize; that is, two or more molecules unite to form a very different substance. Some of the polymers, in this case, are solid, so that if an ordinary pan of formaldehyde is evaporated a considerable amount of a white solid is formed, known as paraformaldehyde. In this case the formaldehyde, instead of being given off as a gas, goes into this polymerized form and is lost as a disinfectant. The danger of polymerization is overcome in several ways; one of the means that has been most widely used is the rapid heating of the solution, above the boiling point, in an autoclave, or in special retorts. It has also been found that if glycerine is added in a small amount, namely 10 per cent, that polymerization is prevented.

There are a number of pieces of apparatus on the market, sold at a very reasonable price, which do excellent service as regenerators. Among the lower-priced ones, those having a copper retort, heated by a Primus lamp, are probably the most satisfactory. They are so arranged that they can be run outside of the space to be disinfected The gas produced by them is led into the apartment through a keyhole or other small opening. In this way the operator has the apparatus under his control during the entire operation. The gas can also be regenerated from the paraformaldehyde, or the solid form. In this case the white material, which is put up under different names, is heated over a flame and broken up into the gas. The gas may be regenerated also from the solution when the latter is sprayed in very fine drops on a large surface If the drops are small and sufficiently separated from one another, so that they do not run together and hence evaporate rapidly, little polymerization takes place. These principles are at the basis of what is known as the Chicago Board of Health method of formaldehyde disinfection. This method is useful at times, but the difficulty comes, under ordinary conditions, in getting enough formaldehyde sprayed on to the sheets which are used to produce satisfactory disinfection before it is necessary for the operator to leave the room. In many ways the most satisfactory method of regenerating the gas is to bring it in contact with some chemical substance with which either the water in the solution or a part of the formaldehyde reacts, producing heat and the evolution of gas, which reaction liberates the formaldehyde gas. The substance most frequently used is potassium permanganate. When potassium permanganate and formaldehyde are brought together in the right proportions, there is a violent reaction and the formaldehyde gas is rapidly given off, together with a considerable amount of moisture. A larger amount of formaldehyde is needed to disinfect a given space by this method than those considered above because of the fact that part of it is wasted in the chemical combination, so that this method is somewhat more expensive than others. But, due to the fact that it can be used without any special apparatus, and that practically the materials are universally available and that its efficiency is very high, it is at the present time the method par excellence.

Formaldehyde gas is exceedingly efficient in its germicidal action on bacteria. It has a more or less selective action and does not affect, or at least readily, many other kinds of cells, such as those that compose the tissues of higher plants and animals. It does not kill plants or ordinary animals, such as insects, rats, and mice, in the same concentration required for the destruction of bacteria. This selective action is disadvantageous as well as desirable. On account of this fact sulphur is still used where it is necessary to kill other forms of life than bacteria.

Formaldehyde gas has practically the same specific gravity as air. It therefore readily diffuses throughout the air space.

It has, however, no marked power of penetration, and in order to be effective, all articles to be disinfected must have their surfaces well exposed, and in its practical application it is a point of considerable importance to see that all materials to be disinfected are arranged so that the gas can readily reach them. There is some difference of opinion as to the necessity of moisture. It is usually stated that a considerable amount of moisture is desirable, and this is probably true; but if the amount is sufficient so that it condenses on an object, it can be very readily seen that it might interfere with the absorption of the gas.

The amount of formaldehyde to be used in disinfection is a matter of importance. There is the same danger that not enough may be used as there is in the case of sulphur. In a general way one pint or pound of formaldehyde should be used for every thousand cubic feet of space.

The disadvantages, when compared with sulphur, are first the cost, which is somewhat more, especially where used with potassium permanganate, second, the fact that it does not affect animal life, and therefore is not available for certain kinds of disinfection; and third, the strong odor which frequently persists for some period of time. But the advantages far offset these. The odor which persists after formaldehyde has been used may be neutralized to a considerable extent by the use of ammonia. The ammonia is sprinkled about the room, five parts being used to four parts of the formaldehyde.

Formaldehyde may be used as a liquid disinfectant, and is strongly recommended by many for the purpose of disinfecting sputum, urine, and feces.

In the practical use of formaldehyde for disinfecting a room or an apartment, it is well to remember that first of all the room should be tightly closed, all cracks about the windows and doors should be pasted up with newspaper strips, or a material especially prepared for the purpose, registers, fireplaces, etc., tightly closed, leaving only an exit to be made tight on the outside. All articles in the room needing disinfection should be so arranged that their surfaces are exposed. This means that clothing should be spread out on a line or over chairs, that the bedding should be taken off and likewise spread about, that the pillows and ticks should be removed from the bed and arranged so that the gas can readily reach all parts of them and, if it is thought necessary, an opening made so that the gas can readily get into the interior. Bureau drawers, trunks, etc., must be opened up and articles therein spread out. Where potassium permanganate, or another chemical, is to be used for regenerating the gas, it is necessary to have a large container. Where a considerable amount of work is to be done, it is desirable to have a special piece of apparatus made, such as that suggested by the Illinois State Board of Health. This consists of a tin pail with low straight sides surmounted by a flaring top, the whole to be covered on the outside with asbestos paper and provided with a double tin bottom. Where the amount of work does not warrant getting this apparatus, a good-sized metal pail can be used, but it is best to place this in a metal washtub or on a piece of asbestos of some size. There is by this method considerable danger of spurting, due to the violent chemical action which goes on. It is therefore undesirable to use more than three pounds of permanganate in one receptacle; if more is needed, it is best to have another container. The room or apartments should remain closed at least eight hours; it will then be possible for some one to rush in and open up a window, and then as soon as possible the space should be thoroughly aired, and, if thought necessary, the odor can be neutralized by the use of ammonia.

All disinfection ought to be tested by means of cultures. The test is a very simple one. A standard organism, such as M. pyogenes var. aureus, is spread on sterile squares of cotton cloth, allowed to dry, and put in a sterile test tube. This sterile test tube is placed in the room and the cotton plug removed. After disinfection the test outfit is taken to the laboratory and the cotton cloth is then dropped into culture media. If the media remain sterile, the process of disinfection was satisfactory, otherwise it is to be repeated.

CHAPTER XIII

EFFECT OF EXTERNAL CONDITIONS ON BACTERIA
(*Continued*)

Light. — The relation of protoplasm to light varies with different types of organisms. Light as a form of radiant energy is utilized by certain living forms in building up their food material. In the green plants, for instance, the chlorophyll enables the organism to absorb and use the sun's energy in constructing its food material, and the greatest amount of assimilation occurs in the absorption bands of the chlorophyll. Forms that derive their energy from organic sources do not need light. Colorless plants and animals obtain their energy by breaking down highly complex food substances and are thus independent of the energy of light. Since the bacteria are colorless organisms we would naturally expect that light was not essential to them, and this is true in the main. The majority of bacteria grow best in the dark. A small group of bacteria that will be referred to later obtain their energy much in the same way as the green plants do and are therefore dependent upon sunlight for their energy. The great majority of bacteria, however, prefer darkness rather than light, and for these forms light is not only unnecessary but it may act as a direct poison. The germicidal power of light was first clearly defined and proved experimentally by Downs and Blunt in 1878. This germicidal action of direct sunlight seems to be particularly well marked in the case of those bacteria which produce disease and is therefore a matter of a great deal of

FIG. 40. — Appearance of a gelatine culture of Bacterium anthracis, exposed to the light over only the area *E*, and then incubated for 48 hours. In the area *E* no colonies have developed. (From Ward, '93.)

practical importance. Not only are bacteria readily killed in direct sunlight when they are in a vegetative stage, but Marshall Ward has shown that some of the spores are more quickly killed than are the vegetative cells.

In order to demonstrate the action of direct sunlight on bacteria it is only necessary to seed an agar plate heavily with the organism to be tested. When the agar is thoroughly solidified, the under side of the Petri dish is partially covered with some opaque substance, as black paper. This may be put on in the form of characters, as, for instance, the name of the microörganism used or the year. The Petri dish is then exposed to the action of direct sunlight for some time and is then incubated. If the exposure is sufficient, those parts that have been directly exposed will be clear, while a growth will appear on the protected parts. This action is well illustrated in the accompanying figure. In this experiment it is necessary for the sunlight to pass through the glass, and in doing so a great deal of the energy is lost. The work of Weinzirl was of the greatest importance in this connection, for he showed that it was possible to expose the bacteria without the interposed glass directly to the rays of the sun, and that when this was done the time required to kill the bacteria was very much less than had been formerly supposed. The action of the sunlight in killing the bacteria is remarkable, and frequently an exposure of only a few minutes, five or ten, is sufficient to kill all of the germs. As indicated above, this germicidal action of the sunlight on bacteria is a matter of great hygienic importance, and the life of the disease-producing bacteria outside of the body is rendered very difficult where it is possible for the direct sunlight to get at them. Undoubtedly the destruction of germs takes place in great numbers in nature, particularly in transparent substances, as water. Because of the germicidal action of sunlight, bacteria, in natural waters, are less abundant in the upper layers than at lower levels, more in the morning than at night, and Büchner determined that the light could penetrate water to the depth of a meter or more, and that when bacteria were exposed at various depths they were affected by the sunlight in inverse proportion to the depth below the surface. The effect of the sunlight varies with its intensity, and hence varies with the season of the year, the time of day, and the condition of the sky. In summer the action is several times as pronounced as in winter. A great deal of discussion has occurred regarding the method of the action of sunlight on the bacteria. At first it was thought that perhaps it was due to heat, but it can be readily shown, by interposing a screen, that the action takes place entirely independent of the heat. It has been found that it varies with the kind of light, that is, if white light is broken up into its component parts, certain parts of the spectrum are much more effective than others. If a screen is placed between the sun and the bacteria, which shuts out all but the less refracted rays, such as may be done by the use of a screen of potassium bichromate, it will be found that there is little or no action; that is, these rays are not effective. But if a screen is interposed between the bacteria and the sunlight which allows the more highly refracted rays to pass through, — such a screen, for instance, as one composed of an ammoniacal solution of copper sulphate, — it is found that the maximum effect is obtained. Or, if a spectrum is thrown on a heavily seeded agar plate, it will be found that the greatest effect is in the blue-violet rays, that it diminishes very quickly on both sides, and is practically nothing in the ultra-violet or in the red rays. The exact point where action begins and ends differs with various forms, but generally it begins in the blue end of the green and reaches a maximum in the violet, and diminishes from the violet to the ultra-violet (Fig. 41). The

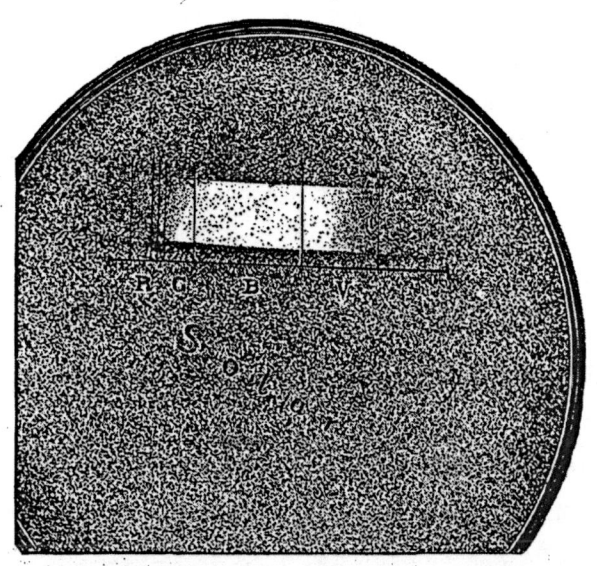

FIG. 41.— Plate of anthrax spores, exposed for 5 hours to the solar spectrum in August, and incubated for 48 hours. The horizontal line shows the length of the spectrum. The vertical lines are not FRAUENHOFER's line, but serve to show the limits of the principal regions of the spectrum. The clearest area is that where fewest spores have developed in the incubation—where, consequently, the bactericidal effect was greatest. (From Ward, '94.)

same kind of action is obtained by electric light, although, of course, the energy is very much less.

Electricity. — A great deal of interest has been manifested in the effect of electricity upon bacteria, and a great many experiments have been performed to determine what this effect is. Aside from the scientific aspect, it has been thought that much practical good might come from the use of electricity as a germicidal agent, but so far the experiments have been disappointing. There is no doubt but that strong currents of electricity would affect bacteria much in the same way that it does other forms of life, but it is very difficult to apply it. If, for instance, a direct current is run through a culture medium, the electrolytic effect on the medium is very marked, and the resulting action on the bacteria is due to the chemicals formed and not to the current itself. An interesting contribution to this subject was made by Zeit in 1901, and his conclusions are as follows: —

"1. A continuous current of 260 to 320 milliamperes passed through bouillon cultures kills bacteria of low thermal death points in ten minutes by the production of heat 98.5° C. The antiseptics produced by electrolysis during this time are not sufficient to prevent the growth of even non-spore-bearing bacteria. The effect is a purely physical one.

"2. A continuous current of forty-eight milliamperes passed through bouillon cultures for from two to three hours does not kill even non-resistant forms of bacteria. The temperature produced by such a current does not rise above 37° C., and the electrolytic products are antiseptic but not germicidal.

"3. A continuous current of 100 milliamperes passed through bouillon cultures for 75 minutes kills all non-resistant forms of bacteria, even if the temperature is artificially kept

EFFECT OF EXTERNAL CONDITIONS ON BACTERIA

below 37° C. The effect is due to the formation of germicidal electrolytic products in the culture. Anthrax spores are killed in two hours. Subtilis spores were still alive after the current was passed for three hours.

" 4. A continuous current passed through bouillon cultures of bacteria produces a strongly acid reaction at the positive pole, due to the liberation of chlorin, which combines with oxygen to form hypochlorous acid. The strongly alkaline reaction of the bouillon culture at the negative pole is due to the formation of sodium hydroxid and the liberation of hydrogen in gas bubbles. With a current of 100 milliamperes for two hours, it required 8.82 milligrams of H_2SO_4 to neutralize 1 c.c. of the culture fluid at the negative pole, and all the most resistant forms of bacteria were destroyed at the positive pole, including anthrax and subtilis spores. At the negative pole anthrax spores were killed also, but subtilis spores remained alive for four hours.

" 5. The continuous current alone, by means of Du Bois-Reymond's method of nonpolarizing electrodes, and exclusion of chemic effects by ions in Kruger's sense, is neither bactericidal nor antiseptic. The apparent antiseptic effect on suspension of bacteria is due to electric osmose. The continuous electric current has no bactericidal nor antiseptic properties, but can destroy bacteria only by its physical effects (heat) or chemic effects (the production of bactericidal substances of electrolysis).

" 6. A magnetic field, either within a helix of wire or between the poles of a powerful electromagnet, has no antiseptic or bactericidal effects whatever.

"7. Alternating currents of a three-inch Ruhmkorff coil passed through bouillon cultures for ten hours favor growth and pigment production.

"8. High frequency, high potential currents — Tesla currents — have neither antiseptic nor bactericidal properties when passed around a bacterial suspension within a solenoid. When exposed to the brush discharges, ozone is produced and kills the bacteria.

"9. Bouillon and hydrocele fluid cultures in test tubes of non-resistant forms of bacteria could not be killed by Rontgen rays after forty-eight hours' exposure at a distance of 20 mm. from the tube.

"10. Suspensions of bacteria in agar plates and exposed for four hours to the rays, according to Rieder's plan, were not killed.

"11. Tubercular sputum exposed to the Röntgen rays for six hours, at a distance of 20 mm. from the tube, caused acute miliary tuberculosis of all the guinea pigs inoculated with it."

Röntgen Rays. — In spite of many experiments and the hopeful view of many, it has been very definitely shown that the Röntgen rays have no bactericidal properties. Bacteria may be exposed to these rays in culture media for practically indefinite periods without being affected. The favorable clinical results which have been obtained in the use of these rays in infectious diseases must be explained upon some other basis. It may possibly be due to the production of certain chemical substances in the tissues, as ozone or hypochlorous acid, or by a stimulation of the cells to renewed activity, or an increased phagocytosis. Some experiments have seemed to indicate that prolonged exposure of cultures to the X-rays may slightly diminish the vitality and virulence of the germs.

Movement. — Bacteria apparently grow better when they are in a state of rest. Experiments show that slight movements are not important in affecting the growth of bacteria, but that more violent movement, such as, for instance, might be obtained by attaching the culture to the piston of a rapidly moving steam engine or a shaking machine, does have an inhibitory action. A practical phase of this subject manifests itself in a discussion of the question of the effect of the movement of a stream on the contained bacteria. It appears from our present knowledge that such movement could not be much of a factor in the purification of a stream.

Pressure. — Ordinary variations in pressure do not affect either the life or the virulence of bacteria, and there is some question whether extremely high pressures affect the cell. Russell, in his work at Naples, found the same species of bacteria both at the surface and in deep-sea dredgings. Others, on the other hand, say that 600 to 700 atmospheres of pressure have an inhibitory effect on putrefactive processes. Roger claims that a pressure of 2000 atmospheres interferes with the virulence of the Bact. anthracis.

Association. — Bacteria are undoubtedly greatly affected by their associates. This association may be with other bacteria or with higher plants and animals. In perhaps the majority of cases no influence is exerted by one organism upon another, but very frequently one species retards the growth of another, that is, there is *antagonism*. This is very frequently seen in cases where a culture medium is inoculated with several different species. One species gets the upper hand and grows for a period to the practical exclusion of all others, then conditions change and another form appears, and so on. That there is a very marked antagonism by some bacteria for others is shown by a number of experiments that have been made which clearly demonstrate that one germ may completely destroy another, probably through the by-products which it produces. Examples of this have been instanced by a number of investigators. The association of organisms at times is advantageous to one or both. The association of the root-nodule bacteria with the leguminous plant is a classical example of *symbiosis*, and it is thought that many bacteria may live in symbiotic relationship with others, especially certain anaërobes and aërobes. Our knowledge of this is very incomplete and fragmentary.

CHAPTER XIV

METABOLISM OF BACTERIA

Introduction. — In previous chapters we have considered the relation of bacteria to their environment. We have now to consider the processes inherent in the bacterial cell, that is, the functions of the cell, and under this will come a discussion of : 1, the general character of the life processes; 2, sources and expenditures of energy; and 3, respiration. The products of metabolism will be left for discussion in a separate chapter.

General Character of Life Processes. — The work of the living cell is determined in part by its environment, but certain functions belong to the cell, and within ordinary limits are not profoundly affected, except as to rate, by external conditions. These general functions are: 1, assimilation; 2, respiration; and 3, growth and movement. To these general functions are to be added the specialized activities of the cell that have been acquired subsequently in the developmental history of the organism. Such special functions are pigment production, fermentation, disease production, etc. All of the life processes of the cell are embraced in the term *metabolism,* which, according to Vines, includes all of the chemical changes which go on in the living protoplasm. The living cell is in a state of unstable equilibrium. Protoplasm is being constantly built up and just as constantly broken down. These two processes, the building up and the tearing down, always go hand in hand. The building up, constructive, or synthetic process is given a special name, *anabolism*. The tearing down, destructive, or analytic process is spoken of as *catabolism*.

Anabolism. — Anabolism includes, according to Vines, all of the chemical processes going on in the cell which lead to the formation of complex substances from simple ones. The cell is constantly absorbing raw material as food, assimilating it, and building it up into protoplasm. The exact way in which assimilation is accomplished is unknown. The requirements of bacteria, so far as their food is concerned, is first that it be soluble, although it is true, as will be pointed out later more specifically, that the bacteria are able to produce substances which dissolve insoluble material and make it possible for them to take up substances that are not soluble. The second requirement is that they have the right kind of food, and the bacteria as a whole can make use of a great many different kinds of food, and may be classified on this basis. Bacteria, with the exception of one group, are unable to make use of the carbon dioxide of the air as a source of carbon. Some bacteria are able to live on dead organic matter; another group require that their food be living organic matter. A classification of bacteria according to their nutritive requirement has been proposed by Fischer, and is as follows: —

I. Prototrophic Bacteria.

Nitrifying bacteria, bacteria of root nodules, sulphur and iron bacteria; occur only in the open in nature, never parasitic, always monotrophic.

II. Metatrophic Bacteria.

Zymogenic, saprogenic, and saprophytic bacteria; occur in the open and upon the external and internal surfaces of the body, sometimes parasitic (facultative parasites), monotrophic, or polytrophic.

III. Paratrophic Bacteria.

Occur only in the tissues and vessels of living organisms, true (obligatory) parasites.

Catabolism. — By catabolism is meant all the chemical processes going on in the cell which lead to the formation of simple substances from complex ones (Vines). The cell protoplasm is constantly being broken down and by-products formed. Anabolism and catabolism are constantly going on in the same cell. If organic matter of the cell is of a higher state than the food from which it was formed, the anabolic process has been greater than the catabolic process, and the organism that builds up organic matter can be properly spoken of as an anabolic organism. If as a result of similar processes in an organism, the end products are lower than those of the food, the organism is said to be catabolic; so that while the anabolic and catabolic processes are concurrent in the same cell the result is either one or the other, and organisms may be classed as anabolic organisms or as catabolic organisms. The anabolic organisms are the green plants and the prototrophic bacteria. The catabolic organisms are the animals, fungi, metatrophic and paratrophic bacteria. These different

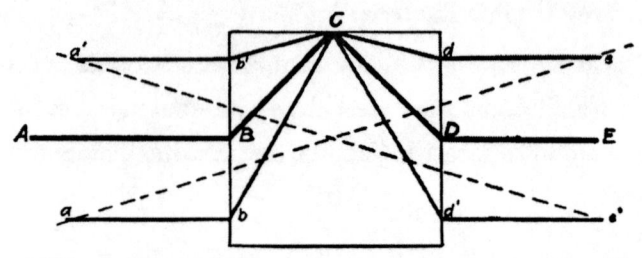

FIG. 42. — Illustrating Metabolism. The square represents a cell. *AB* represents food entering the cell. *BC* represents anabolism. *CD* represents catabolism. *BCD* represents metabolism. *DE* represents the products of metabolism. *ab* represents food of simple composition. *de* represents complex by-products. An organism producing synthetic changes, indicated by the line *ae* is called an anabolic organism. An organism producing the analytic changes, indicated by the line *a'b'Cd'e'* or *a'e'* is called a catabolic organism.

classes of organisms are of mutual aid to each other in the universe. The anabolic organisms build up the food material from simple sources into a form that is available for the catabolic organisms. These, in turn, tear down the complex organic matter and return it to the earth in a simple form ready to be again taken up by the anabolic organisms.

Respiration. — Food is necessary to sustain life but food alone will not enable life to go on. Food consumed represents a source or supply of energy, but this is not available until it is oxidized and the potential energy locked up in the food consumed is transformed into the kinetic energy of work.

Coal represents stored-up energy, but we must transform the latent energy that is imprisoned in the coal into the active energy of motion before it becomes available. This is done by combustion, or oxidation, and by placing the coal under conditions where the affinity of the carbon for oxygen will be satisfied and the kinetic energy will be released in heat. The food consumed by all organisms functions like coal, and the process by which it is oxidized is known as respiration. It was formerly thought that oxygen in a free state was necessary, but it is now known that it is not. The oxygen may be obtained from organic compounds, as in the case of the anaerobes, but the amount of energy obtained when the oxygen is derived in this way is much less than when the free oxygen is used. For example, when 1000 grams of sugar are oxidized to carbon dioxide and water 3939 calories of heat are obtained, but when the same amount of sugar is oxidized to butyric acid, hydrogen, and carbon dioxide, only 414 calories are obtained. As a result of the process of respiration carbon dioxide is universally produced, as well as water. In addition to this, energy is dissipated in the form of heat, light, and motion. In the case of the bacteria the heat formed during the process of respiration is not apparent or easily measured except in certain conditions where a high degree of heat is produced. For instance, in certain fermenting masses the temperature may be raised to 60° or 70° C. and the bacteria have some relation to the spontaneous combustion of hay, cotton waste, etc. Energy is sometimes given off in the form of light, as in phosphorescence. This characteristic is common in various forms of life, particularly in marine animal forms among the photobacteria. These are saprophytes which live in salt water and grow especially on peptones, such as are common in dead fish. They produce light only in the presence of oxygen, and the phenomenon of phosphorescence is intimately associated with respiration. The energy obtained as a result of respiration shows itself also in motion, and a good example of this is frequently seen in hanging-drop preparation, where the aërobic bacteria lose their power of motion when free access to the oxygen of the air is denied them.

CHAPTER XV

Products of Metabolism

Introduction. — Bacteria differ from other plants in general in that their catabolic properties exceed their anabolic. They are preëminently analytical rather than synthetic organisms. In the multiplication of cells a large amount of organic matter is accumulated in the protoplasm, but this is relatively small compared with the disintegrating processes which they are able to inaugurate. It is proposed in this chapter to consider some of the products of metabolism, principally, in order that we may understand something more of the nature of the changes which go on in the bacterial cell, but also because the determination of some of these by-products is a matter of great importance in the differentiation of various bacteria. In considering the products of metabolism, however, it will be difficult to distinguish between those which are produced within the cell and those substances which are formed outside of the cell as a result of the breaking down of the food substance or the abstraction of certain elements therefrom. In certain cases it is impossible to know whether a particular product is actually formed within the cell or whether it is a split product. Very frequently, from the same nutrient medium, a great variety of products is produced by a particular organism. It very frequently happens, however, that one is more prominent than the others, and certain bacteria have come to be known as bacteria which produce certain characteristic by-products, as, for instance, the acetic acid, the lactic acid bacteria; but in all of these cases other products are formed as well. These are only the most striking by-products. The products produced by the bacteria usually inhibit their growth if they are allowed to accumulate Sometimes the by-products are of such a nature that they actually destroy the cells which produce them after a considerable amount of the substance has been produced. The amount of substance which different bacteria are able to tolerate varies with different species. For example, the lactic acid bacterium has its growth inhibited when o 8 per cent of acid is formed The acetic acid bacterium can produce 10 per cent of acetic acid before its growth is prevented, and yeast can produce alcohol to the extent of 15 per cent before its further development is inhibited. By removing the soluble products it is possible for the bacteria to continue their activity. This can be done by neutralizing them with chemical substances, or in some cases by growing the organism in a permeable sack, such as one made of collodion. The by-products here are removed by dialysis, permitting the further growth of the organism, which may continue until all the food substances are used up. In considering the products of metabolism, attention should be called to the difference between the extra-cellular and the intra-cellular products. Many products are formed that are of such a nature that they can pass through the cell wall readily and are excreted. These are known as extra-cellular products and are to be distinguished sharply from the split products which are referred to above. Many of the products of metabolism, however, are of such a nature that they do not readily pass through the cell walls and are liberated only on the death of the cell. These are the intra-cellular products. All cells in their metabolism produce certain by-products, such as carbon dioxide, water, nitrogen, waste products, and energy. But in addition to these, many organisms produce in considerable amount definite by-products by which they are characterized. Many organisms, for instance, produce substances which have the power of reducing other substances. These *reduction substances* are found among the denitifying bacteria where the nitrates are reduced to the nitrites, and also where colored substances are reduced to colorless or leucoproducts. An example of this is seen in the growth of many bacteria in litmus milk. The color of the litmus is frequently lost completely, due to the formation of some reducing substance. Culture media containing methylene blue are also reduced by certain bacteria. Neutral red, when added to culture media, is reduced by certain forms, and this reaction is very useful in the differentiation of various bacteria. It was formerly supposed that this reduction was due to the splitting off of oxygen from the reducible substance, but it is now known that this explanation is not sufficient, since some substances are reduced, as, for example, methylene blue, which do not contain oxygen. In these cases it may be that nascent hydrogen is added. Certain bacteria produce *oxidative changes*. The acetic acid bacteria oxidize ethyl alcohol to acetic acid. The nitrifying bacteria oxidize ammonia and the nitrites to nitrates The sulphur bacteria oxidize sulphuretted hydrogen to sulphur, and the iron bacteria oxidize the ferrous to the ferric salts. *Gases* are frequently produced as the result of the metabolism of bacteria. Among the more common gases are carbon dioxide, hydrogen, nitrogen, methane, and ammonia. These gases are frequently of a good deal of value in differentiating one organism from another. Closely allied bacteria differ greatly in their power to ferment certain substances. One may produce an abundance of gas in a food medium in which a close relative will produce none. The gaseous by-products of bacteria have been carefully studied in a number of cases, but the complete analysis of the gases is a matter of considerable chemical difficulty. An approximate method, however, for determining the amount of gas produced and its formula, is very commonly used in the bacteriological laboratory and is known as the fermentation tube which was introduced for this purpose by Theobald Smith.

Bacteria very frequently produce *acids* as a result of the decomposition of sugar. The acids most commonly produced are lactic, acetic, and butyric. Here, again, the acid production serves as a means of differentiating closely allied bacteria. The method of detecting acid production usually used is to grow the germs in milk containing litmus, or in sugar media to which litmus is added. In this the formation of acid is indicated by the change of the blue litmus to a red color. Many bacteria produce an *alkali* rather than an acid. This is detected in the same way as the acid. Some bacteria are able to produce either an acid or an alkali, depending upon the nature of their food material. When the Bact. diphtheriæ, for example, is grown in a culture medium containing sugar (and all media made from meat contain a small amount unless special means for removing it have been employed), it produces first an acid reaction, and then when the sugar is used up it produces an alkaline reaction in the culture medium. It has been found that when this germ is producing acid it does not form its toxin readily, but when the sugar is removed, then the toxin production goes on much more readily, so that it becomes a matter of a great deal of practical importance in the production of the toxin, to be used for the manufacture of antitoxin, to have the culture medium free from sugar to start with so that the germ may begin its toxin production immediately. A number of by-products of a good deal of importance contain nitrogen. Among the simpler of the *nitrogenous substances* are indol and skatol. *Indol* is very commonly produced by bacteria, and, since it can be detected by a color reaction, it is a product of a good deal of importance in the differentiation of microorganisms. When indol in the presence of a nitrite is treated with sulphuric acid there is developed a pink color. In order to determine then whether or not a particular culture has indol present or not it is only necessary to add a solution of nitrite and some sulphuric acid. It was originally supposed that indol was produced by putrefactive bacteria alone, but now it is known that it is produced by many other bacteria. Sometimes it is produced in very small amounts, and at other times more abundantly Sometimes also certain bacteria produce in addition to the indol a nitrite. In this case it is only necessary to add the sulphuric acid in order to get the characteristic reaction. This reaction is known as the *cholera red reaction*, and was at first supposed to be characteristic of the Msp. comma of Asiatic cholera, but it is now known that a considerable number of bacteria give this cholera red reaction and, in making a determination of the presence of indol, sulphuric acid should be added first and the nitrite afterwards in order to differentiate between the simple production of indol and the production of the nitroso-indol Other nitrogen by-products of great importance produced by bacteria are the enzymes. These are substances that stand midway between living and nonliving matter.

Bacterial Enzymes and their Mechanism of Action — Up to the present time no enzyme has been isolated in a pure state. Consequently, nothing definite is known in regard to the chemistry of these compounds. Enzymes are recognized by the various chemical changes which they produce. They are probably specific substances. Different enzymes have been noted which are able to produce fermentations of saccharose (inverting enzymes); of dextrose, lactose, cellulose (amylolytic enzymes), producing eventually carbon dioxide and water; which coagulate milk similar to rennet (rennet enzymes); which digest protein, producing amino-acids, etc., (proteolytic enzymes); and that split fats into fatty acids and glycerine (steatolytic enzymes).

Colloidal solutions of metals, such as platinum, show many similarities in action to known enzymes. These colloids can be made to produce changes in proteins almost identical with those produced by true enzymes. They are also affected by chemical changes and by temperature in the same way as enzymes.

There are many writers who hold the view that all so-called enzyme action is due to physical changes produced in the various organic substances, and not to any definite chemical reactions. The magnetism in the magnetic bar is in many ways similar to an enzyme. When heated magnetism and enzymes disappear, when treated with acids and alkalies they disappear, and neither can be isolated in a pure state. Arthus thinks that enzymes are not forms of matter, but that they are forms of energy.

Enzymes possess the power of producing chemical changes without entering to any great extent into the reaction. They can produce an oxidation of a sugar compound into carbon dioxide and water, and can break down protein compounds into carbon dioxide, water, and amino-acids. These changes can also be brought about by strong reagents (acids and alkalies), or by superheated steam under pressure, but not with nearly so great ease as by enzymes. Bacterial enzymes are most active when they come directly from living bacterial cells. The filtrates of cultures of bacteria and dead bacteria possess very little enzyme compared with the live cells.

The intra-cellular enzymes are divided into two general classes: oxidizing or hydrating, and reducing or dehydrating, enzymes. Oxidation is accomplished by means of catalytic agents, enzymes, within the bacterial cell. One of the most studied of the oxidizing intra-cellular enzymes is catalase. This enzyme, as well as most of the others, has the power of decomposing hydrogen dioxide and liberating nascent oxygen. Many bacterial cultures contain substances which can decompose hydrogen dioxide (Bact. tuberculosis, Bact. diphtheriæ, M. pyogenes var. aureus). Catalase is distinct and separate from the toxin.

The question of the occurrence of reducing enyzmes of bacterial origin is still an unsettled problem. In all probability they do occur in some species.

It was formerly supposed by some investigators that all the chemical reactions which occurred when animal and vegetable cells were present, were due to the cells themselves as a whole. The reactions have since been proved to be due to the definite chemical substances which we now know as enzymes and which are secreted by the cell protoplasm.

Enzyme action is in no material way different from other chemical reactions. The enzyme reactions are reversible and consequently there is a tendency for an equilibrium to be established by both sides of the equation. Enzymes act like all catalytic agents, thus increasing the speed of the reaction. In some cases it seems that the speed of the reaction increases the amount of enzyme produced. It is not known what the methods of catalysis in enzymes are. It has been noted also that enzymes hasten the synthesis of some compounds. Enzymes may possibly form loose chemical combinations with the substances on which they act and with water, and the resulting compound be unstable and easily broken down and the water remain connected with some of the components of the substance which was acted upon. There is some experimental evidence to show that enzymes may enter into loose chemical combination with the substance attacked. It has also been suggested that the enzymes may increase the ionization. Salt solutions favor enzyme action evidently on account of action of ions.

The action of enzymes is specific. They differ from ordinary chemical reagents in that they attack only specific organic substances. For example, proteolytic enzymes only attack proteins and amylolytic enzymes only carbohydrate compounds.

In some particulars enzymes are related to bacterial toxins. This phase of the subject has been discussed in another chapter.

Enzymes form colloidal solutions which are only slightly dialyzable. On filtration through porcelain 10 to 25 per cent of the enzymes are lost during each filtration. This, of course, indicates that they are composed of molecules of large size.

Enzymes, with few exceptions, are more resistant to outside agents than the cells which produce them. Often dilute solutions of chemicals will kill bacteria, as before stated, but will not destroy the intra-cellular enzymes. Formaldehyde gas (HCOH), however, in very dilute solutions is very destructive to bacteria and their enzymes. The radium rays will also kill some enzymes.

The temperature limits of enzyme action vary between 35° C. and 45° C., no matter from what species of bacteria they are derived. Enzymes, like most toxins, are destroyed at 70° C. when in aqueous solutions. They are not affected by liquid air (−190° C.), or by 100° C. when in a dried state. Bacterial enzymes in a moist condition may be converted into inactive compounds (enzymoids) when subjected to heat at comparatively low temperatures. Sunlight, X-rays, radium rays, markedly inhibit the action of all enzymes except the amylolytic, when they are in aqueous solutions.

Enzyme action is retarded by the accumulation of bacterial metabolic products. In some cases those metabolic products are detrimental to the enzymes themselves. This is true in acetic acid fermentation when alcohol and acetic acid are produced. It can be said, however, that this inhibition is probably due to the establishment of an equilibrium.

Autolytic Bacterial Enzymes. — A large number of bacteria produce proteolytic enzymes which are capable of digesting other bacterial cells, and also capable of digesting themselves (autolysis). Enzymes of this character are called autolytic.

It has been noted that in the growth of some species of bacteria on artificial media that the bacteria increase in numbers for a varying period of time, then gradually decrease. This phenomenon occurs in some cultures of Msp. comma. This fact can only be accounted for by assuming in some cases that the proteolytic enzymes of the cholera bacteria digest themselves (autolytic) and their neighbors (isolytic).

Growth proceeds when the autolytic enzymes are removed. In those diseases due to bacteria which produce endotoxins it is probable that these toxic products are liberated from the bacterial cell by the action of autolytic enzymes, by leucocytic enzymes, and by the proteolytic enzymes of tissue cells in the vicinity of the diseased area (typhoid, tuberculosis, dysentery, cholera, etc.). It would seem from what has been learned from recent investigations that the autolytic enyzmes are very similar to nuclein in structure. Autolysis of Bacterium tuberculosis and allied forms progresses very slowly. In time the endotoxins themselves are digested by the proteolytic enzymes.

Pseudomonas pyocyanea produces a proteolytic enzyme which is heterolytic and furthermore selective in its action. The enzyme produced is decidedly antagonistic to a Bact. anthracis and Bact. diphtheriæ. It prevents growth absolutely if it is produced by a vigorous culture. This enzyme can be easily isolated. It is called pyocyanase.

It is probable that autolysis of bacteria takes place, in the majority of cases, when the bacteria are lacking in some requisite food product. It is the opinion of some investigators that, normally, the proteolytic (autolytic) enzymes are held in check by the synthesis of the protein food materials (Wells). There is also the probability that antienzymes may be generated.

Antienzymes. — Enzymes, like other complex metabolic products of bacteria, produce in the body fluids of immunized animals, antibodies. Antienzymes for proteolytic enzymes can be produced with the greatest ease. Antiamylolytic and other enzymes are difficult to prepare. When combined with the specific enzymes, either *in vivo* or *in vitro*, the antienzyme renders the former inactive. Antienzymes can be produced by the immunization of animals with enzymes which have been subjected to heat at comparatively low temperatures (enzymoids). The antienzymes are really destroyed by a heat of 70° C.

The most important products of metabolism are the poisonous substances which are produced by bacteria. These substances are known as the ptomains, toxins, endotoxins, and the toxic bacterial proteins. These will be discussed in detail in Chapter XXII.

PART VI. BIOLOGY OF SPECIAL-IZED GROUPS

CHAPTER XVI

Prototrophic Bacteria

Introduction. — The prototrophic bacteria comprise those which, from a physiological standpoint, are the most primitive. They obtain their food from inorganic sources and are able to build up these simple substances into their complex protoplasm. It seems probable that such organisms as these must have been the original forms of life on the earth, and that the metatrophic and paratrophic have developed from them, and, in a sense, these must be considered as degenerates.

From this standpoint the prototrophic bacteria occupy a very important place in the developmental history of life on the earth. Many of them at the present time, as well as in the past, are of inestimable service to man. These prototrophic bacteria include the nitrifying, the iron, the sulphur, and the legume, or nitrogen-fixing bacteria.

Nitrifying Bacteria. — The nitrifying bacteria oxidize ammonia to the nitrites and the nitrates. There are several different species which belong to two different classes: those which carry on the first part of the process, that is, oxidize ammonia to nitrites, are known as the *nitroso-bacteria*. The other class are the *nitrifying bacteria* proper (Fig. 43).

The chemical changes brought about by the nitrifying bacteria in the oxidation of ammonia is represented by the following formula: —

$$2 NH_3 + 6 O = 2 HNO_2 + 2 H_2O.$$

And the second stage is represented by the formula: —

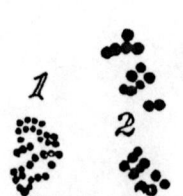

$$2 HNO_2 + 2 O = 2 HNO_3.$$

Fig 43 — Nitrifying bacteria (1) Nitrous ferments, (2) nitric ferments × 2000 After Burri and Stutzer. (Lipman)

The energy obtained by this oxidation process enables these bacteria to make use of the carbon and nitrogen in an inorganic form and thus to synthesize organic matter.

These bacteria not only do not require organic matter for food but, in pure culture at least, the organic material interferes with their development. The process of nitrification is strictly an oxidizing process, and, in order that the process may go on, an abundant oxygen supply must be available. Furthermore, the activity of these organisms is checked by the presence of considerable amounts of the acids, so that if the process continues, bases must be supplied which will unite with the acids to form salts. The nitrification of soils is dependent upon the action of these bacteria, and our knowledge of the life history of these germs is a matter of practical importance when it is applied to soil fertility. Certain phases of this will be referred to in another connection. These bacteria are widely distributed in the

PROTOTROPHIC BACTERIA 185

soil, and the importance of nitrification in Nature's food cycle cannot be overestimated.

Nitrogen-fixing Bacteria. — Nitrogen-fixing bacteria, or legume bacteria, occur in the nodules which are found on the roots of various leguminous plants. Growing in these nodules these bacteria are able to fix the nitrogen of the air into a form which is available for plant use, and while they live in the plant they are not to be regarded as parasites, or even as metatrophic bacteria, but they belong to the group under discussion in this chapter; namely, the prototrophic bacteria. They are bacilli so far as their form is concerned, and there are many different kinds. Whether these different kinds are separate species or merely varieties, is a question that is not fully settled. These germs are not strictly prototrophic, but may be cultivated upon artificial media in which they make use of organic food material. There are different forms associated with the different plants. One peculiarity, however, of all forms is the tendency, at a certain stage in their life history, to assume irregular or

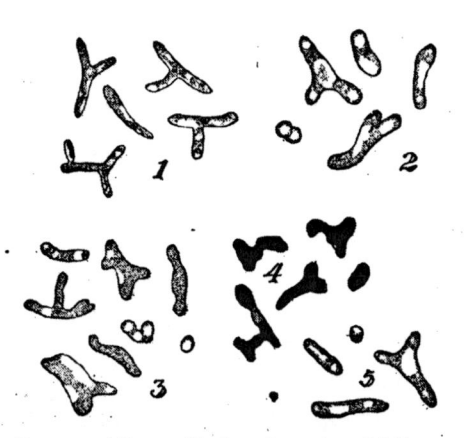

FIG. 44. — Bacteroids from legumes. (1) From Melilotus alba. (2, 3, 5) From Medicago sativa. (4) From Vicia villoso. After Harrison and Barlow. (Lipman.)

bizarre shapes, which are usually known as bacteroids (Fig. 44). These legume bacteria make their way into the roots through the root hairs and induce the formation of tubercles, or nodules. In these the bacteria live and rapidly multiply, and it is here that they take the elemental nitrogen of the air and fix it in a form available for plant use. It has been abundantly shown that the power of these leguminous plants to make use of the nitrogen of the air depends on the activity of these microorganisms. If these legumes are sown in sterile soil and protected from inoculation, they will cease to grow as soon as the nitrogen of the seed has disappeared; whereas, other plants under exactly the same condition, except that they have been infected with pure cultures or soil washings, continue to grow. These legume bacteria are of extreme importance in agricultural pursuits, and will be referred to again in a later chapter. Other bacteria, found in the soil, are able to fix nitrogen when growing independently of legumes or plants.

Sulphur Bacteria. — Many bacteria (putrefactive) are able to produce sulphuretted hydrogen, but the sulphur bacteria proper take this hydrogen sulphide that has been produced by another group and use it as food, oxidizing into sulphuric acid (Fig. 45). These sulphur bacteria belong to two groups, one of which is colorless and the other contains a coloring matter. Thiothrix may be taken as an example of the filamentous forms of the colorless group. The Thiothrix is composed of a thread of cells which is usually attached to some object. This filament of cells is surrounded by a thin sheath. Reproduction takes place by means of gonidia. The gonidia are formed from the terminal cells of the filament and are liberated in the usual way. Certain nonfilamentous forms, such as Beggiatoa, are well known. Both of these forms make use of hydrogen sulphide as a food, oxidizing it to water and elemental sulphur. These sulphur granules are stored in the cell itself. These bacteria do not grow in highly nutritious culture media, but are able to obtain their food from relatively simple substances by means of the energy which is obtained by the oxidation of the sulphuretted hydrogen. Their carbon may be obtained from the air or from small traces of formic or proprionic acids. Nitrogen may be obtained from the air or from ammonia. In the synthesizing of organic material they work independent of the rays of sunlight.

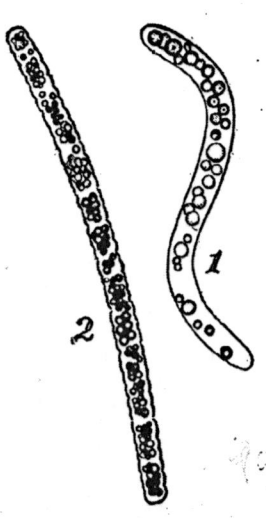

FIG. 45. — Sulphur bacteria: (1) Thiospirillum Winogradskii. (2) Beggiatoa alba. × 2000. After Corsini. (Lipman).

Another group of these sulphur bacteria are colored purple by a coloring matter known as bacteriopurpurin, which acts in a way similar to the chlorophyll of green plants. These bacteria are large micrococci which have the coloring matter evenly distributed throughout the protoplasm. They have a double source of energy, that which is obtained by the use of sulphuretted hydrogen, as in the group described above, and also by means of the bacteriopurpurin which enables them to synthesize organic matter with the energy obtained from the sun's rays.

Iron Bacteria. — The iron bacteria are represented by the organism Crenothrix polyspora, which was described by F. Cohn in 1870. This bacterium consists of a filament of cells attached to some object. The cells in this filament are smaller at the base and increase in diameter higher up. The range in size is from one and a half to five microns. These bacteria occur in tufts and each filament is surrounded by a sheath. The cells at the outer end of the filament break up into gonidia. As ordinarily seen, these bacteria have their sheaths permeated by reddish brown masses of ferric oxide. These bacteria take ferric carbonate and oxidize it to ferric hydroxide, as represented in the following formula: —

$$2\ FeCO_3 + 3\ H_2O + O = Fe_2(OH)_6 + 2\ CO_2.$$

As a result of this oxidation process, energy is obtained which enables these bacteria to synthesize organic material. They obtain their nitrogen from inorganic sources and are not dependent upon organic matter for support. These bacteria grow readily in waters free from organic matter providing the iron salts are present. They are widely distributed in nature and are found in swamps, meadows, and marshes, and are especially likely to grow in deep well waters which are iron bearing. Sometimes their growth is such as to render the water undesirable first for laundry purposes, and later for drinking purposes, although the only objection here is an æsthetic one. Their growth in the water pipes of a city sometimes occurs to such an extent that the flow of water is interfered with. Water calamities of this sort have been experienced by a number of cities, particularly Lille and Berlin.

"There is reason to suppose that the masses of iron ore in northern Minnesota upon the Mesaba range were deposited there by the activity of iron bacteria living in the warm waters of an ancient ocean. We may imagine such a primeval sea, hot like the geysers of the Yellowstone, its waters impregnated with iron and furnishing a splendid field for the peculiar activities of the iron bacteria. Living in such an ocean for thousands of years, as they have done, there is nothing unreasonable in attributing to them the deposits of iron ore which during these latter days are being mined for commercial purposes." (Mac Millan.)

Another representative of this group is Cladothrix odorifera, which is commonly found in the soil and which gives the peculiar odor to the soil such as that which is particularly noticed after a rain storm.

CHAPTER XVII

Chromogenic Bacteria

Introduction. — Some species of bacteria when growing in cultures exhibit various colors. Bacteria of this character are called *chromogenic*.

The majority of bacteria produce no color whatever and appear white or colorless when growing in cultures. They are called *non-chromogenic*.

Range of Color. — The chromogenic bacteria present, in the various species, all the colors of the solar spectrum. The following table gives the colors of the spectrum and an example of a chromogenic bacterium which will normally produce practically the corresponding color in cultures.

Red	Bacillus prodigiosus Flugge
Orange	Sarcina aurantiaca Flugge
Yellow	Micrococcus flavus Flugge
Green	Bacterium viridis Kruse
Blue	Pseudomonas syncyanea Migula
Indigo	Pseudomonas indigofera Voges
Violet	Bacillus violaceous Jordan

There are also species of bacteria which produce all the shades between the various colors of the spectrum.

The color of chromogenic bacteria is due to pigment granules. The position of the pigment granules in relation to the cell is important. It has been found that there is a great variation among different species in this particular.

Location of Pigments. — In the cultures of some species of bacteria the pigment granules can be seen outside the bacteria, between the cells. In cultures of Bacillus prodigiosus, Pseudomonas indigofera, and the large majority of the chromogenic bacteria this condition is noted. Those bacteria which excrete their pigment are called *chromoparous*.

There are other chromogenic bacteria which do not excrete the pigment granules but retain them within the cell protoplasm. These bacteria are called *chromatophorous*. The pigment granules are found to be most abundant in the outer layers of the cell protoplasm. A large number of species among the higher bacteria, as, for example, in the genus Thiocystis among the Beggiatoaceæ, belong to this class of chromogenic organisms. Pigmented protoplasm of this character is also noted in those species of bacteria (Bact. chlorinum) (Bacillus virens, etc.), which are closely related to the Cyanophyta (blue-green algæ), and in which coloring matter similar to chlorophyll is found.

There is still another class of chromogenic bacteria in which, by the aid of the microscope, the pigment granules can be seen to be definitely contained within the cell wall. Chromogenic bacteria of this class are called *parachromatophorous*. Bacillus violaceous is a typical example of a bacterium belonging to this class.

Pigment production in the majority of bacteria is of practically no physiological importance. The pigment granules are usually excreted as rapidly as they are formed. In only those cases where the pigment is combined with the protoplasm of the cell (chromatophorous) is it of any importance. In this case it undoubtedly serves the functions of the chlorophyll in the higher plants. It can, therefore, absorb carbon dioxide (CO_2) and give off oxygen (O) in the presence of sunlight. This fact has been demonstrated in the case of the bacteriopurpurin of the sulphur bacteria. In all chromoparous bacteria, the pigment granules can only be regarded as excretory products of the cell. No connection with the nutritive processes of the cell can be demonstrated. Chromogenesis seems to be an unessential process.

In regard to the conditions under which pigment formation takes place it may be said in the beginning that pigment formation rarely takes place in the absence of oxygen. In cultures it is noted that only the superficial layers of bacteria produce any pigment, those beneath being colorless. Oxygen seems to be a prerequisite in most cases. This point will be again referred to. Pigment formation in most species of bacteria takes place equally well in the light and in the dark. In a few species pigment formation is inhibited by darkness (chromatophorous). Bacillus mycoides var. roseus produces pigment only in the dark. High temperatures usually inhibit pigment formation (37° C. and above). Colored lights have no effect on chromogenesis.

Some pigments are closely related chemically to the lipochromes and others to the ptomains. The reaction and chemical constitution of the media on which bacteria are growing markedly influences chromogenesis in some cases. Acids and alkalies usually produce some change in the pigment when they are applied to it. Occasionally the color may be destroyed, changed to a different color, or to a color which will return to the original when the requisite reaction is restored. E. F. Smith and others give the following examples: The yellow pigment of Bacterium campestre remains unchanged and Bacillus prodigiosus changes from red to carmine in certain acid solutions and yellowish brown in certain alkalies. The blue color of Pseudomonas syncyanea is produced only in acid milk. The blue-green fluorescent color often seen in some chromogenic bacteria is produced only in alkaline media. Some chromogenic bacteria produce alkalies (NH_3, etc.). This depends on the supply of nitrogen and carbon. In gelatin Pseudomonas pyocyanea does not form alkali, but in ammonium succinate it does.

In this last-mentioned group of blue-green fluorescent organisms, of which Pseudomonas fluorescens is a typical example, it is probable that there are two distinct pigments produced. Jordan has studied these pigments carefully and states that there is present a blue pigment, called pyocyanin, which is visible by gaslight and soluble in chloroform, and a green fluorescent pigment, called fluorescin, which is yellowish in gaslight and insoluble in alcohol and chloroform. Bacteria readily lose their power to produce pyocyanin.

Bacterial pigments are secreted as colorless compounds, which, in the majority of cases, are waste products of the bacterial cell. These compounds are of the nature of leucobases, which assume color only when oxidized by the air. The yellow and black pigments are distinct oxidation products. Chromogenic bacteria can be grown under certain conditions, as, for example, at high temperatures, and no pigment will be produced. Non-chromogenic forms can be produced from ordinarily chromogenic forms, etc. There can be no doubt that pigment formation is an unessential metabolic process to the bacterial cell except, as mentioned before, in the chromatophorous bacteria. Very few chromogenic bacteria are pathogenic to animals. Pseudomonas pyocyanea and the various pyogenic micrococci are among the common forms Chromogenic bacteria among the plant pathogens are not uncommon.

Migula has arranged the chromogenic bacteria into three classes, as follows. Those producing —

(1) Pigments soluble in water.

(2) Pigments insoluble in water, soluble in alcohol.

(3) Pigments insoluble in water and alcohol.

Pigments Soluble in Water.—Chromogenic bacteria which produce fluorescent pigments, which are soluble in the culture media and diffuse through it, belong to this class. Pseudomonas pyocyanea, Pseudomonas fluorescens, and Pseudomonas syncyanea are typical organisms of this group. Pseudomonas pyocyanea and Pseudomonas fluorescens, referred to above, produce two pigments; namely, pyocyanin and fluorescin. Ledderhose analyzed pyocyanin and found it to be similar in structure to some of the known ptomains ($C_{14}H_{14}N_2O$). It seems to be drived from the aromatics and closely related to the anthracines. Pyocyanin is non-toxic to animals.

When treated with acids, fluorescin becomes colorless and pyocyanin turns red. Soluble phosphates and sulphates seem to be necessary for the production of fluorescin but not pyocyanin. Pyocyanin can be produced in media devoid of protein.

Both pyocyanin and fluorescin are soluble in water. Pyocyanin is also soluble in chloroform but insoluble in alcohol, and fluorescin is insoluble in both alcohol and chloroform.

Pigments Insoluble in Water, Soluble in Alcohol. — The Micrococcus pyogenes vars. aureus, citreus, flavus, and Bacillus prodigiosus are typical examples of chromogenic bacteria of this class.

It is claimed by those investigators who have studied the pigment granules of this class that they are fat-like in nature and similar to lipochromes. They are soluble in all fat solvents, form dendritic crystals, can be saponified, and on decomposition give the acrolein reaction (C_3H_4O) and fat odors. When concentrated sulphuric acid is added, the lipocyanin reaction occurs and the pigment granules are changed to blue.

Pigments Insoluble in Water and Alcohol. — Very few species of bacteria belong to this class. Wells mentions the

Micrococcus citreus var flavus as a typical example The chemical structure of these insoluble pigments is unknown.

The pigments of chromogenic bacteria have also been classified as diffusible (Ex. Ps. pyocyanea) and nondiffusible (Ex. B. prodigiosus). This classification is of no practical value.

Some species of chromogenic bacteria which attack plants produce a brown stain on the plant at the point of inoculation (Bact. campestre (yellow) on stems and leaves of cucumbers and tomatoes), while other non-chromogenic forms produce the same effect on the plant (Bacterium solancearum on stems and leaves of cucumbers and tomatoes). Plants, under various conditions, show stains which cannot be attributed to any chromogenic bacterium or other microorganism. These stains are oxidation products. For example, when Bacterium vascularum attacks sugar cane very often the plant shows a red stain. It has been noted, however, that fungus growths and insect stings will produce the same color. This coloring of plants has been noted in many species and under various conditions. It is frequently noted in green fruits and flowers.

The subject of the chromogenic bacterial pigments from the various species of bacteria has not been exhaustively studied as yet. Most of the investigations so far have been on the blue-green and fluorescent pigments pyocyanin and fluorescin, which were referred to above.

Historical Allusions. — The red chromogenic bacterium known as Bacillus prodigiosus has a very interesting history.

In the Church of St. Genaro in Naples twice a year a crytsal vial containing a solid substance of a dark color was exposed in the early days under a glass case to the gaze of the people. This was declared by the priests to be the blood of St. Janarius, which could be changed from a solid to a liquid in one night. When General Championet, commanding the French, entered Naples in 1799, the miracle of the liquefaction of the blood was not performed and there was great dissension among the people. The monks declared that the liquefaction was the work of God, and that they could not bring it about. However, General Championet informed them that the miracle must take place at a definite time under penalty of death. The miracle took place as desired, and it was found that the monks possessed a substance which they kept from year to year which when added to gelatinous material would bring about a liquefaction. We now know that, unknown to them, the monks had a culture of Bacillus prodigiosus, which produces a proteolytic enzyme capable of liquefying gelatin. The same bacterium has been noted on bread in damp churches, on oil paintings, etc., and was interpreted to be the blood of Christ.

CHAPTER XVIII

Photogenic Bacteria

Introduction. — There are certain species of saprophytic bacteria which possess the power of throwing off light when the requisite conditions are provided. Bacteria of this character are called *photogenic*.

The power of luminosity, or phosphorescence, is due in all probability to the combustion of various food materials and to cell respiration, just as the phosphorescence of insects is a combustion process. Luminosity itself is of no physiological importance.

Distribution. — The majority of photogenic bacteria are found in salt water and on the fresh and decomposing flesh of marine animals, such as fish. The phosphorescence of the sea is due in a large part to bacteria and also to phosphorescent protozoa.

It has been known for some time that the light often noted emanating from decomposing willows and other trees, and particularly from decaying stumps of trees, is due to a fungus. This fungus is in some cases similar to a mold, and in other cases photogenic bacteria have been found. The much renowned "will-o'-the wisp" phenomenon is caused by saprogenic microörganisms (non-photogenic) which generate inflammable gases, such as phosphoretted hydrogen and methane.

Some vegetables, such as potatoes, beans, etc., on decomposition may give off light and show the presence of phosphorescent bacteria. Decomposing meats, particularly sausages and fish, also may be covered with different species of phosphorescent bacteria.

Food Requirements. — As stated above, all the photogenic bacteria which occur in water are marine. On cultivation of these bacteria it is therefore necessary for the media to contain two to three per cent sodium chloride in addition to other salts, peptone, and some carbon compound such as sugar or glycerine.

Magnesium, potassium and calcium chloride, potassium sulphate, stimulate the production of light by bacteria. Gorham states that he has been able to grow phosphorescent bacteria on purely synthetic media.

Fischer states that the phosphorescence of the sea is due to the growth of saprophytic photogenic bacteria on dead sea animals and the subsequent washing off of these forms in large numbers by the waves.

Hans Molisch in " Leuchtende Pflanzen " reports the isolation of twenty-six species of photogenic bacteria. He states that the flesh of cattle (48 per cent of the samples examined) and salt water fish (100 per cent of the samples examined) on exposure to the air show phosphorescence, and the photogenic bacteria can be isolated. Fresh water fish seldom if ever show any phosphorescence. His experiments showed that horse flesh (65 per cent of samples) and cattle flesh (89 per cent of samples) when placed in three per cent sodium chloride and allowed to stand in the air became phosphorescent and the bacteria could be isolated.

Oxygen Requirements. — Oxygen is absolutely necessary for the production of light by bacteria. Phosphorescence is an oxidation phenomenon Under anaerobic conditions the photogenic bacteria grow slowly but do not produce any light until aerobic conditions are provided. When a highly combustible carbohydrate food is present, phosphorescence is greatly increased.

Fischer calls attention to the well-known fact that phosphorescence is not nearly so marked in smooth sea water as it is in rough, and is most noticeable on the crest of the waves and in the wake of a ship where the water is churned up. When the oxygen of the air comes in contact with the phosphorescent material, as it does when the sea water is disturbed, the light produced is greatly augmented

Temperature Requirements. — The temperature at which light production takes place is subject to great variation. The limits of phosphorescence, according to E. F. Smith, are from $-5°$ C. to $28°$ C. Light production seems to be the most intense from $5°$ C. to $20°$ C. The phosphorescent bacteria of the Baltic Sea and the North Sea flourish best at $18°$ C., but can grow well at $0°$ C., resembling in this respect other inhabitants of the Northern waters.

Isolation. — Phosphorescent bacteria can be obtained for experimental work by placing oyster shells or the flesh of herring and haddocks in a solution of two to three per cent sodium chloride at 5° C. to 10° C. for a few days. The solid material and the liquid become bluish green in color and emit a pale light. The bacteria can be isolated according to the ordinary bacteriological methods, but must be grown in media containing an infusion of fish, etc., and two to three per cent of sodium chloride.

Cultures in gelatin containing the above-mentioned ingredients may become so luminous as to be photographed in their own light after long exposure. Cultures have been reported which produce enough light for a person to see the face of a watch in total darkness.

Of the several varieties of photogenic bacteria, Pseudomonas phosphorescens var. liquefaciens is one of the most common. The optimum temperature of this bacterium is about 16° C. to 18° C., the maximum 28° C., and the minimum −2° C.

Pathogenesis. — E. F. Smith reports one disease of animals which is due to a distinctly photogenic bacterium, and that is the white or sluggish disease of sand fleas on the shores of France and in the vicinity of Woods Hole, Massachusetts. No diseases of plants have been reported as due to photogenic bacteria.

CHAPTER XIX

ZYMOGENIC BACTERIA

Introduction. Definitions. — There are certain species of bacteria which secrete within their cell protoplasm enzymes or ferment-like substances. The amount of enyzme produced by a bacterium is modified by the quality and the amount of the food which it receives. When grown upon a medium containing proteins, the bacteria produce proteolytic enzymes in excess. When grown upon a substance containing carbohydrates, amylolytic enzymes are produced. No enzymes are produced without organic food of some character.

The term "zymogenic" has been applied to those bacteria which produce amylolytic enzymes capable of fermenting carbohydrate compounds. Fermentation, as will be pointed out later, is a distinct enzyme process. As a matter of fact, all processes in which the enzymes of various kinds are concerned are modified fermentations. The first important work on the subject of fermentation was done by Pasteur in 1857.

The zymogenic bacteria in our subsequent discussions will be considered to be those bacteria whose metabolic processes are characterized by the hydrating or oxydizing action of enzymes on carbohydrate compounds.

All animals and plants are composed, in addition to nitrogenous compounds, of a large percentage of carbon compounds. During the life of all animals, carbon in the form of carbon dioxide (CO_2) is expired continually into the air. Part of the carbon dioxide thus expired by animals is taken up by the chlorophyll-bearing plants and higher pigmented algæ, and, by the aid of the kinetic energy of the sunlight, is absorbed, fixed, and subsequently made into complex organic compounds. In the process of plant respiration, a small amount of carbon in the form of carbon dioxide is again returned to the air. The remaining portion of the carbon is not liberated until the plant dies and is disintegrated. There is also a large amount of carbon and nitrogen liberated when the animal dies and is decomposed.

The carbon is liberated from the animal and plant body by the activity of bacteria. It escapes here also in the form of carbon dioxide. The zymogenic bacteria and the saprogenic bacteria, which will be considered later, are responsible for the liberation of these compounds. The nitrogenous compounds are acted upon chiefly by the saprogenic or putrefactive bacteria, while the carbohydrate compounds and organic acids, which are in a measure non-putrefactive, are acted upon by the zymogenic or fermentive bacteria.

The term "fermentation" is used by various writers in a variety of different ways. The term will be used in this discussion to mean the breaking up of complex carbohydrate compounds by the action of the enzymes of microorganisms.

Furthermore, the terms "ferment" and "enzyme" are often used in different senses. Fermentation, according to many writers, is applied to a direct metabolic function of the viable protoplasm of cells which serves them as a source of energy, while enzyme action is not dependent upon living protoplasm of cells and does not furnish any energy to the cells. The above distinctions raise many objections.

Organized and Unorganized Ferments — Many writers make a division of the agents of fermentation into organized ferments and unorganized ferments or enzymes It is stated that organized ferments are living cells, such as bacteria, yeasts, molds, etc, and are only able to produce chemical changes so long as the cells are alive. Enzymes are considered to be chemical substances, the secreted products of cells, and capable of producing marked chemical reactions in organic compounds in the absence of the cells producing them (pepsin, trypsin, ptyalin, etc.). It is claimed, however, that the organized ferment and the enzyme may act in a similar manner in many cases. Fischer says that in both cases the chemical changes produced are specific and are performed without the loss of energy, and that the ferment substances themselves do not enter into the reaction. Fischer also states that enzymes exercise a hydrating influence which causes the substances that are attacked to take up water and form substances of an entirely different chemical constitution.

The action of diastase (amylolytic) on starch, (a), and invertase on cane sugar, (b), may be given as examples.

(a) $C_6H_{10}O_5 + H_2O = C_6H_{12}O_6$ (Dextrose).
(b) $C_{12}H_{22}O_{11} + H_2O = C_6H_{12}O_6 + C_6H_{12}O_6$
(Dextrose and Levulose).

There are no by-products such as carbon dioxide (CO_2) and other gases produced without further oxidation.

Some writers claim that antiseptics stop fermentation by killing the microörganisms while they do not seriously impair the enzymes, but it has been noted that enzymes in dilute solutions are just as susceptible to the action of antiseptics. The latest research on this subject indicates that all the reactions which occur during the fermentation of carbohydrates are enzyme processes.

As a matter of fact, enzymes are secreted by all cells classed by Fischer and others as organized ferments, and it is the enzymes which produce the chemical change. There is abundant experimental evidence to support this statement. Filtrates from cultures of bacteria, and bacteria killed by such agents as thymol, contain enzymes of various chemical constitutions. There is no sufficient basis for the division of ferments into the two classes, organized and unorganized. The chemical processes in both are fundamentally the same.

Fermentation, therefore, is to be regarded as a composite chemical process of oxidation, which is brought about by the hydrating action of the intra-cellular amylolytic enzymes of bacteria and some other microörganisms on carbohydrate compounds.

Various substances are produced during the process of fermentation. Gases may or may not be produced; acids and alcohols and ethers and esters are formed in small quantities. The gases which may be produced during fermentive processes are carbon dioxide, oxygen, hydrogen, nitrogen, and methane or marsh gas. Among the alcohols are methyl, ethyl, butyl, propyl, glycerine, and many higher alcohols.

It should be noted that all fermentation is not due to the enzymes which bacteria produce. A large variety of yeasts and some species of molds are concerned in some fermentive processes. The majority of all alcoholic fermentations are due to yeasts (Saccharomycetes). Some bacteria, such as Bacillus coli, produce small amounts of alcohol.

The fermentations due directly to bacteria will be briefly considered. The fermentive processes are designated by the most important by-product produced. Thus we speak of lactic acid fermentation, acetic acid fermentation, and butyric acid fermentation.

It seems that in the majority of bacterial fermentations there is a specific bacterium or group of bacteria which is prominent in the process.

Lactic Acid Fermentation. — The bacteria concerned in this fermentation are very widely distributed. They are found chiefly in milk, but may also occur in other solutions, as, for example, distillery mash.

There are about one hundred species of bacteria which may cause lactic acid fermentation. They can be grouped as the "lactic acid producers." One of the common species is Bact. acidi lactici, and a very closely related species, B. lactis aerogenes. Msp. comma and the spirilla belonging to the same family, B. prodigiosus and many sarcina found in brewery mashes, possess the power of producing lactic acid.

Lactose or milk sugar ($C_{12}H_{22}O_{11}$) is the ordinary carbohydrate which is acted upon by the lactic acid organisms. In addition to lactose, glucose and cane sugar may be fermented. Starch, maltose, or cellulose are not acted upon directly by the enzymes of the lactic acid bacteria. They may be changed into the foregoing sugars, however, by enzyme action of other bacteria and then be subsequently attacked by the lactic acid bacteria and changed into lactic acid. The following is approximately the chemical reaction which takes place on lactose: —

$$C_{12}H_{22}O_{11} + H_2O = 4\ CH_3CH(OH)COOH\ \text{(lactic acid)}.$$

Lactic acid fermentation is an aërobic process, and the fermentation is immediately inhibited in the absence of oxygen. The maximum acid formation, and, necessarily, the optimum temperature of the lactic acid bacteria, average about 30° C. to 35° C. in the majority of species, and as low as 10° C. and as high as 52° C. in some few varieties.

Lactic acid fermentation can progress only when the acid produced is neutralized by some alkaline substance in solution, such as calcium carbonate, etc. Lactic acid inhibits the growth of most all of the species of bacteria concerned in the process when its concentration reaches about (0.8 per cent) eight tenths to (1 per cent) one per cent.

About eighty per cent (80 per cent) of the fermentable sugar is converted into lactic acid, small amounts of acetic, formic, and succinic acids, carbon dioxide, hydrogen, nitrogen, methane, and alcohols, under favorable conditions A certain amount of lactose and other sugars always remains in solution unfermented.

Acetic Acid Fermentation. — This fermentive or enzyme process, like all others of this group, is in part a distinct oxidation process. The bacterial enzymes act on the carbohydrate sugars and break them down into ethyl alcohol and carbon dioxide. The oxidation of the alcohol results in the formation of aceticaldehyde and later acetic acid. The acetic acid is still further oxidized to carbon dioxide and water.

The following reactions on dextrose will serve to elucidate the process : —

$C_6H_{12}O_6 + H_2O = 2\ CH_3 \cdot CH_2OH + 2\ CO_2 + H_2O$ (ethyl alcohol, carbon dioxide, and water).

$CH_3CH_2OH + O = CH_3 \cdot COH + H_2O$ (ethylaldehyde or aceticaldehyde).

$CH^3COH + O = CH_3 \cdot COOH$ (acetic acid).

$CH_3COOH + 4\ O = 2\ H_2O + 2\ CO_2$ (water and carbon dioxide).

Many alcoholic liquids may be oxidized to form acetic acid, carbon dioxide, and water, or may be oxidized directly into water and carbon dioxide without any acid formation.

Maximum acetic acid fermentation takes place at a temperature of about 35° C. and ceases at 45° C. and 5° C. to −5° C. In a concentration of fourteen per cent (14 per cent) acetic acid inhibits all bacterial growth.

Acetic fermentation is very prominent in the vinegar industries in some countries. The alcoholic liquids, such as cider, wine, etc., are brought in contact with acetic acid bacteria and also with a free supply of oxygen (air), and by this process are oxidized.

Acetic acid is formed in practically all fermentive processes (lactic, butyric, acetic, etc.). The species of bacteria which are able to produce acetic acid are not so numerous as the lactic acid bacteria. Bacillus acetici is a common form. The process is aërobic. The bacteria cannot produce acid in the absence of alcohol. It is probable that the carbon of the alcohol serves as a food.

Butyric Acid Fermentation. — The formation of butyric acid by the enzymes of bacteria is a process which is quite widely distributed. The fermentation is carried on only under strictly anaërobic conditions. At one time it was thought that lactic and butyric fermentations were due to enzymes of the same bacteria (Amylobacter butyricus). It has since been proved that specific bacteria are the cause of the major portion of these fermentations. About twenty different species of butyric acid bacteria have been isolated. Usually in the butyric acid fermentation, as in all of the enzyme processes of this type, hydrogen, carbon dioxide, and traces of fatty acids are produced in addition.

Some of the butyric acid organisms, besides possessing enzymes which will ferment practically all the carbohydrate compounds, will also cause a fermentation of such substances as glycerine, gum arabic, etc. Bacillus orthobutyricus is a bacterium of this type.

Some butyric acid bacteria, for example, Bacillus butyricus, possess in addition to zymogenic enzymes also saprogenic enzymes capable of disintegrating proteins. Consequently, it is not uncommon to find butyric acid in putrefying substances. Butyric acid can also be produced by the splitting of certain protein compounds.

It is quite common for butyric acid bacteria to infect sour milk containing lactic acid and disintegrate this acid and what lactose may be remaining. The following reactions show what takes place when lactose (a) and lactic acid (b) are attacked: —

(a) $C_{12}H_{22}O_{11} + H_2O = 4\,CH_3 \cdot CH(OH)COOH$ (lactic acid).
(b) $2\,CH_3CH(OH)COOH + 2\,O = CH_3 \cdot CH_2CH_2COOH$ (butyric acid) $+ 2\,CO_2 + 2\,H_2O$.

Butyric acid bacterial enzymes are claimed by some writers (Fischer) to be the indirect cause of symptomatic anthrax and malignant œdema, two anaërobic disease processes.

Methane (CH₄) and Mucilaginous Fermentation. — This form of fermentation is due to the action of enzymes, which are secreted by several species of bacteria, on cellulose. Spirillum rugula is one of the bacteria which is concerned in the production of methane (CH₄). It is not an infrequent occurrence for wine, beer, vegetables, and especially milk, to become slimy and appear mucilaginous in character. This condition is due to the bacterial enzymes fermenting carbohydrate compounds. The mucilaginous, gumlike substance (galactan) is very similar to cellulose. The fermented materials absorb a great amount of water and thus form a sticky mass.

The bacterial enzymes invert the cellulose or lactose into dextrose, and this in turn is broken up into methane, carbon dioxide, hydrogen, and fatty acids. The reactions are uncertain after the inversion, but it seems probable that the methane results from the splitting of alcohols which are formed in the process. The following represents the reaction:

$$(C_6H_{10}O_5)_n + {}_nH_2O = 3_nCO_2 + 3_nCH_4 \text{ (methane)}.$$

Methane is one of the principal constituents of petroleum gas (40 per cent). Coal yields as high as 80 or 90 percentage of methane.

Fermentation of the Higher Alcohols, Aromatics, and Fatty Acids. — Glycerine and mannite (propenyl alcohol) on fermentation by the enzymes of Bacillus ethaceticus and others may form ethyl alcohol, acetic acid, formic acid, succinic acid, carbon dioxide, and hydrogen Acetic, lactic, butyric, proprionic, malic, citric, succinic, and other acids on fermentation are each converted into varying amounts of the others and eventually into carbon dioxide and water. The M. pneumoniæ also ferments mannite.

Fischer refers to the various dextro- and levo-rotatory acids which may be produced in fermentations. For example, the enzymes of B. coli change dextrose into lactic acids which differ in the direction and the extent to which polarized light is rotated. The source of the nitrogen supply seems to be a determining factor in this case If ammonium phosphate is supplied, levo-rotatory lactic acid results; while if peptone is used as a source of nitrogen, dextro-rotatory acid is produced. Lactic acid produced by other fermentations is optically inactive (levo- and dextro-rotatory).

Zymogenic Bacteria in Milk and its Products. — The lactose or milk sugar which is normally present in milk undergoes decomposition by the action of the enzymes of various species of bacteria after the milk has been standing for some time at a warm temperature The acidity is evident to the sense of taste when it reaches the equivalent of 0.3 per cent lactic acid. As the acid is produced, the caseinogen of the milk is acted upon by bacterial enzymes similar to rennet, and, as a result, the casein formed is precipitated, thus producing a clot or curd. This takes place when the acid reaches a concentration of 0.35 per cent to 0.4 per cent. The resulting coagulum or curd becomes more solid as the acid increases.

A large number of species of bacteria which are present in milk produce in the process of fermentation other acids besides lactic acid, and large amounts of gases such as carbon dioxide, methane, nitrogen, and hydrogen. Bacteria do not produce as much acid in cream as in milk.

In the process of cheese manufacture, the presence of gas-producing bacteria may cause the curd to "float" and produce a poor cheese, due to the holes formed by the gas.

A curd due to the rennet enzymes of bacteria may also be produced without the formation of any acid. Occasionally milk does not sour rapidly and produces a soft, slimy curd in a weak acid solution. The condition is known to dairymen as "sweet curdling." The bacterial enzymes which produce this condition are very similar to rennet enzymes. The curd produced may be eventually softened and digested by the action of the bacterial proteolytic enzymes. Duclaux calls this digesting enzyme "casease." The chemical reactions in these zymogenic processes are very complex.

Butyric acid fermentations usually occur in milk which has become sour due to the formation of lactic acid. This process has been discussed above. The formation of butyric acid may take place, however, in a neutral or faintly alkaline medium. In butyric acid fermentation of milk, the bacteria secrete their enzymes and produce the chemical changes in the milk after the oxygen has been abstracted by lactic acid bacteria and other aërobic species. Butyric acid fermentation is a distinct anaerobic process. Butyric acid is also formed by the decomposition of casein and fats, in addition to milk sugar.

In addition to the various organic acids which may be produced in milk some of the higher alcohols may be formed.

Mucilaginous fermentation, which has been discussed previously as occurring in milk, give it a thick, slimy consistency. The bacteria in milk and the various dairy products such as cheese, butter, etc., will receive more detailed consideration in a subsequent chapter.

Bacterial Fermentations in the Arts. — This interesting subject can be only briefly considered. Some fermentive processes are of great economic importance, while others are decidedly antagonistic to certain industries.

In the " retting " of flax (linen), jute, hemp and cocoanut fiber, fermentations, similar in a measure to putrefactive processes, are important in the softening of the cellulose walls of the plants so that the fibers may be separated.

In the preparation of indigo from the indigo plant (Indigofera tinctoria) and in the curing of hides and tobacco, bacterial enzymes are important adjuncts to the processes. Bacterial enzymes are also of commercial importance, as before stated, in the preparation of vinegar (acetic acid), butyric and lactic acids, and in many dairy processes, such as cream ripening, cheese and butter making.

Bacterial fermentive enzymes are responsible for the unpleasant flavors and odors which are frequently developed in food products. They are also partially responsible for the undesirable flavors occasionally developed in alcoholic liquids.

Zymogenic bacterial enzymes are useful in conjunction with yeasts in bread making. Lactic acid fermentation occurs in the formation of ensilage. In bread making the bacterial enzymes prepare the starch (flour) by the action of amylolytic enzymes for the subsequent action of the zymogenic enzymes of the yeasts, and by the lactic and acetic acid which they generate give a pleasant flavor to the bread.

CHAPTER XX

THE SAPROGENIC AND SAPROPHILIC BACTERIA

Introduction. Definitions. — In the previous chapter it was pointed out that enzymes produced by bacteria are responsible for all the changes occurring in the media in which the organisms are growing and not the bacterial cell *in toto*.

It is a well-known fact that plants as a whole secrete only a small amount of carbon dioxide after the natural absorption of carbon and oxygen in this form (CO_2), and never liberate and very rarely absorb any nitrogen from the air. Nitrogen which has been taken up from the nitrates of the soil is returned thereto only when the plant dies and its protein compounds are decomposed. The same can be said of the greater amount of the nitrogen contained in animal cells. It is liberated on the decomposition of the animal. There is, however, in the animal a small amount of nitrogen secreted in the milk and excreted in the urine (urea, uric acid, hippuric acid, etc.). These compounds are eventually broken down into ammonia and free nitrogen by the action of bacterial enyzmes.

Those bacteria which bring about the profound decomposition or putrefaction of nitrogenous compounds are called *saprogenic bacteria.* B. vulgaris Mig. is a typical example of this class. All putrefactive processes are brought about by the action of bacterial enzymes. These enzymes are, in the main, proteolytic. There are still other bacteria which derive nutriment from and perhaps in some cases aid in breaking up still further the compounds formed by the saprogenic bacteria. These organisms are called *saprophilic bacteria.* B. coli, Sp. undula, and B. subtilis are examples of bacteria which belong to this last-mentioned class.

The saprogenic bacteria are very widely distributed. The enzyme action of the saprogenic species undoubtedly serves these organisms as a source of energy. It was supposed during the early days of bacteriological research that decomposition was due to one species of bacteria which was called Bacterium termo. It is now known that putrefaction is due to a large number of species of saprophytic bacteria. These bacteria are not always found under the same conditions. No attempt has been made to classify the putrefactive bacteria. It seems that some species are particularly common in decomposing animal material, others in decomposing vegetable material, and others in decomposing urea.

Proteolytic Enzymes. — The proteolytic enzymes of bacteria resemble in their action the trypsin of the pancreatic juice of the animal body in many particulars. These enzymes act better in an alkaline than in an acid medium. There is a proteolytic enyzme which is secreted by a large variety of bacteria which dissolves or peptonizes gelatin compounds.

This enzyme will resist a temperature of 100° C. for fifteen minutes. Wells refers to the statement of Schmailowitsch that some bacteria produce an enzyme which acts in an acid media on gelatin but not upon albumen, and changes it into proteoses and peptones. He states that those acting in an alkaline medium carry the process still further, to the point where amino acids, such as leucin and tyrosin, are produced.

The proteolytic enzymes of pathogenic bacteria in certain cases are prominent in putrefactive processes. There is no relation between the proteolytic enzyme and the pathogenicity of a species of bacteria. There is a possibility that the bacterial enzymes do play a minor part in the digestion or decomposition of the exudates in suppuration.

There are also other proteolytic bacterial enzymes which produce a coagulation of caseinogen and later a digestion of the casein of milk. Other species of bacteria produce proteolytic enzymes which are capable of acting on the fibrin of blood and the blood corpuscles, changing them into the proteoses and peptones, and later into the amino acids. Hemolysis is closely related to proteolytic enzyme action. All enzymes capable of digesting gelatin will also digest the casein of milk (Eijkman).

Nearly all the putrefactive bacteria produce proteolytic enzymes which are able to break the protein molecule down to its simplest compounds. A large number of saprophytic bacteria produce proteolytic enzymes, and it is this class which produce the majority of putrefaction. The following table from Wells's "Chemical Pathology" gives a partial list of some of the more important bacteria and other microorganisms which produce digesting proteolytic enzymes: —

PROTEOLYTIC — DIGESTING ENZYMES

	Milk Coag.	Milk Digest	Gelatin	Serum	Egg Alb.	Fibrin	Red Corpuscles
1. Bact. anthracis	+	+	+	−	+	+	+
2. Msp. comma	+	+	+	+	+	+	+
3. B. coli	−	−	−	−	−	−	−
4. M. pyo. aureus	+	+	+	−	−	−	+
5. Str. pyogenes	−	−	−	−	−	−	+
6. Ps. pyocyanea	+	+	+	+	+	−	?
7. B. violaceus	−	−	+	−	−	−	+
8. B. mycoides	+	+	+	−	+	−	+
9. B. prodigiosus	−	+	+	+	+	+	+
10. Aspergillus niger (mold)	+	+	−	−	−	−	+
11. Aspergillus oryzœ	+	+	+	+	+	−	−

The above table shows that there is a selective action by the bacterial enzymes from different species on the various protein compounds. The digestion of gelatin takes place in a definite manner among the various species of bacteria (see Fig. 30).

A few bacterial enzymes which might be considered as steatolytic have been noted in putrefying fluids. Ps. pyocyanea, B. prodigiosus, M. pyogenes var. aureus, are among the best-known bacteria which produce fat-splitting enzymes. Glycerine and the various fatty acids are among the end-products. It is a difficult matter to isolate the particular species of bacteria in putrefying fluids which produce the steatolytic enzymes.

In order that putrefaction take place, certain of the prerequisites of bacterial growth must be at hand. A certain amount of moisture is absolutely necessary. It is a familiar fact that protein material, such as meat, when dried, does not decompose Temperature is another important requirement. Low temperatures prevent the action of the putrefactive bacterial enzymes. Fischer refers to the finding of the Siberian mammoths which had been frozen in the ice for centuries and the flesh was still in good condition.

The bacteria concerned in the putrefactive processes are aërobic, anaerobic, and facultative anaerobic. The aerobic bacteria by using up the supply of oxygen and forming carbon dioxide thus provide the necessary conditions for anaerobiosis, and consequently the rapid generation of gases and disintegration of the compound. Aerobic bacteria in putrefaction are, on the whole, of secondary importance.

Mechanism of Putrefaction. — Putrefaction is primarily a process of decomposing and splitting up nitrogenous compounds by the action of the proteolytic enzymes of bacteria. It is in a measure a fermentive process. It should be remembered that in every case when an animal or plant compound is decomposing that the zymogenic or fermentive bacteria are acting on the carbohydrate compounds at the same time that the saprogenic bacteria are acting on the nitrogenous compounds. The processes usually go hand in hand. The process of true putrefaction, however, takes place only in nitrogenous compounds. A distinction is sometimes made between putrefaction and decay. The former is held to be a distinctly anaërobic process, while the latter is applied to those decompositions taking place in the presence of oxygen and due to aërobic bacteria.

Products Produced. — We will discuss as briefly as possible the results of the decomposition and so-called putrefaction of the protein molecule which contains the nitrogen of nearly all organic substances.

It may be here stated that the protein molecule can be split by many agencies, among which are superheated steam, acids and alkalies in different concentrations, and by bacterial enzymes. The changes produced by bacterial enzymes are the most pronounced, and the secondary products produced thereby are different from the cleavage products produced in other ways. In all cases, the protein molecule is changed into compounds which are closely related to the original typical protein molecule; namely, *proteoses* and *peptones*. At this point the lines of cleavage may be different and many end-products result. By the action of the bacterial enzymes of saprogenic bacteria these proteoses (albumoses) and peptones are split into a series of simple substances which seem to be the usual elementary products of the protein molecule. They are as follows: —

1. Glycocoll
2. Leucin
3. Alanin
4. Amino-valerianic acid ..... Simple amino acids of the fatty acid series

5. Aspartic acid
6. Glutaminic acid .... Dibasic acids closely related to monatomic acids

7. Phenylalanin
8. Tyrosin
9. Tryptophan ...... Aromatic constituents of the proteid molecule

10. α-pyrrolidin carboxylic acid (prolin)
11. Oxy-α-pyrrolidin carboxylic acid (oxy-prolin) } Probably from some other amino acid by rearrangement

12. Serin .... Together with 10, 11, bring protein in close relation to carbohydrates

13. Lysin
14. Arginin
15. Histidin .... Hexone bases

16. Cystin .... Sulphur exists in this form

It will be noted that the simple amino acids of the fatty acid series are glycocoll, leucin, alanin, and amino-valerianic acid. These acids are characterized by the presence of an NH_2 group attached to the carbon atom in the alpha position. The common formula is $R-CHNH_2-COOH$. On putrefaction these substances produce many compounds. The various fatty acids can be easily derived from them on the splitting off of the NH_2 group. Glycocoll on splitting produces acetic acid, and alanin on splitting produces propionic acid. Wells states that in all probability acetic and butyric acid are most commonly produced in this way. In the process of the putrefaction of these amino acids, various gases, such as hydrogen, marsh gas, ammonia, and carbon dioxide, are evolved. Acetone is, in all probability, also formed from these amino acids.

From the diamino acids (hexone bases) some very interesting substances are formed. These substances — diamins — are formed by bacterial action, and are characterized by the fact that they retain the NH_2 group, instead of splitting it off as in the foregoing case. These substances are called *ptomains*, and frequently, on absorption, produce serious intoxications in the animal body. They will be discussed in Chapter XXII. Not all ptomains are produced from this group. One of the principal ones produced is putrescin ($NH_2(CH_2)_2NH_4$).

The aromatic substances of the protein molecule are phenyl-alanin, tryptophan, and tyrosin. There are various substances formed from these bodies. Among those produced are indol, cresol, and phenol from tyrosin; indol-propionic acid, indol-acetic acid from tryptophan, and from these skatol and indol. In intestinal putrefaction, the indol and skatol are absorbed, oxidized, and combined with sulphuric or glycuronic acid, and appear in the urine as the so-called ethereal sulphates.

From the principal sulphur constituent of the protein molecule, cystin, methyl mercaptan (CH_3SH), ethyl mercaptan (C_2H_5SH), ethyl sulphide (($C_2H_5)_2S_2$), and large amounts of hydrogen sulphide (H_2S) are produced. Hydrogen sulphide, together with indol and skatol, are largely responsible for the disagreeable odor attendant on all putrefactive processes These substances are produced to a large extent in the human intestine. The process takes place in the absence of oxygen.

On the decomposition of the nuclein of the nucleoprotein, phosphoric acid and the various purin bases are produced.

The various fat compounds are also decomposed by the action of the enzymes of saprogenic bacteria. The changes produced are very similar to the fermentation of carbohydrates. Gases are evolved, and glycerine and the many fatty acids

$$\underset{\text{Palmitin}}{C_3H_5(OC_{15}H_{31}CO)_3} + 3\,H_2O = \underset{\text{Glycerine}}{C_3H_5(OH)_3} + \underset{\text{Palmitic acid}}{3\,C_{15}H_{31}COOH}$$

are produced. Butyric acid is one of the common fatty acids which is produced in fat decomposition. The lecithin ($C_{24}H_{84}NPO_9$), which is a phosphorized fat, and commonly combined with the protein molecule, can be easily split into the ptomain, cholin and this into another very toxic ptomain called neurin These ptomains will be discussed elsewhere.

As stated heretofore, in putrefaction there is also some fermentation of the carbohydrate compounds. The enzymes producing these fermentations have the power of hydrating dextrose, maltose, inulose, starch, etc. The products of this process include practically all of the fatty acids and the oxyacids, among which are lactic, succinic, and oxybutyric, etc. In addition to these, acetone, oxalic acid, and small quantities of ethyl alcohol are formed. Methane, carbon dioxide, and hydrogen are the principal gases produced.

These numerous putrefactive processes may occur in the intestinal tract of all animals. Conditions there are particularly favorable to the action of anaërobic bacteria.

The ultimate end-products of all putrefactive processes are: free ammonia (NH_3), carbon dioxide (CO_2), hydrogen (H), and water (H_2O); under certain conditions phosphoric acid (H_3PO_4), phosphoretted hydrogen (PH_3). Free nitrogen (N) is undoubtedly evolved in some cases.

The process of putrefaction is greatly influenced by the presence or absence of oxygen. The disagreeable aromatic odors are not produced by aërobic bacterial processes (decay), but are evolved only when oxygen is excluded. The presence of oxygen accomplishes rapid oxidation, and the odor is not noticeable after a short space of time.

For the purpose of summarizing, we can say that the following substances result from the putrefaction and fermentation of organic compounds in all composite decomposition processes.

1. Proteins:

    (a) Aromatic radicals — phenylalanin, tryptophan, and tyrosin, which by splitting produce indol, skatol, phenol, cresol.

    (b) Sulphur radicals — hydrogen sulphide, ethyl sulphide, ethyl and methyl mercaptan.

    (c) Fatty acid radicals — formic, acetic, propionic, butyric, valerianic, palmitic, stearic acids, acetone and various gases, such as carbon dioxide, ammonia, methane, and hydrogen. Ptomains, such as cadaverin, ethyldendiamin, and putrescin.

(d) Phosphoric acid and purin bases (from nuclein).

2. Fats:

Glycerine and all the higher fatty acids. Ptomains, such as cholin, neurin, etc., from the phosphorized fat lecithin.

3. Carbohydrates:

The following fatty acids have been isolated and probably others occur which have not been isolated, — formic, acetic, propionic, butyric, valerianic, succinic, oxybutyric. Gases, such as hydrogen, carbon dioxide, methane in the case of cellulose, and acetone.

Most plants obtain their nitrogen supply from the nitrates of the soil. The nitrogen of the soil is the key to soil fertility. As a result of the action of the enzymes of various species of saprogenic bacteria, ammonium salts are produced after the ammonia which is formed during the process of decomposition is combined with certain inorganic elements, such as sodium and potassium. Only a small amount, if any, of these ammonium salts can be used by plants as a source of nitrogen supply. By the action of the nitroso bacteria which are present in the soil, these ammonium salts are broken up and converted into nitrites. The nitrites thus formed are again acted upon by the nitrifying bacteria of the soil, and as a result nitrates are produced. In this manner the nitrogen locked in the protein molecule is again made available for plant use. This process is known as nitrification. Bacteria which have the power of abstracting the oxygen of the nitrate compound are noted in some soils. These organisms, by again breaking up this compound, which is useful to the plant, are, obviously, very detrimental to soil fertility. This class of bacteria is called denitrifying organisms.

CHAPTER XXI

Pathogenic Bacteria

Introduction. Definitions. — Those bacteria which produce morbid changes in the animal or plant body, under natural conditions or under conditions artificially produced by inoculation, are called *pathogenic bacteria*. The term is relative and applicable only within certain limits Some of the ordinarily harmless bacteria, when introduced into the body of the animal or plant in large numbers, produce morbid affects. There is, also, no one pathogenic bacterium which will produce diseased conditions in all animals or plants. Some varieties of bacteria are pathogenic for one species of animal or plant and non-pathogenic for others.

The term *pathogenic* has come to be usually applied to a bacterium, or other microogranism, which produces disease under normal conditions.

Many saprophytic bacteria are pathogenic for man and for some species of animals and plants. These bacteria may accidentally gain entrance into the tissues of the body or may be introduced for experimental purposes. Bacteria of this class are called *facultative parasites*. There are still other bacteria which give all the evidences of being parasites, normally, but often, for varying periods of time, may live as saprophytes. As examples of this last-mentioned class of bacteria, Msp. comma and B. typhosus may be given. Bacteria of this class are called *facultative saprophytes*.

There are other species of bacteria which are not able to

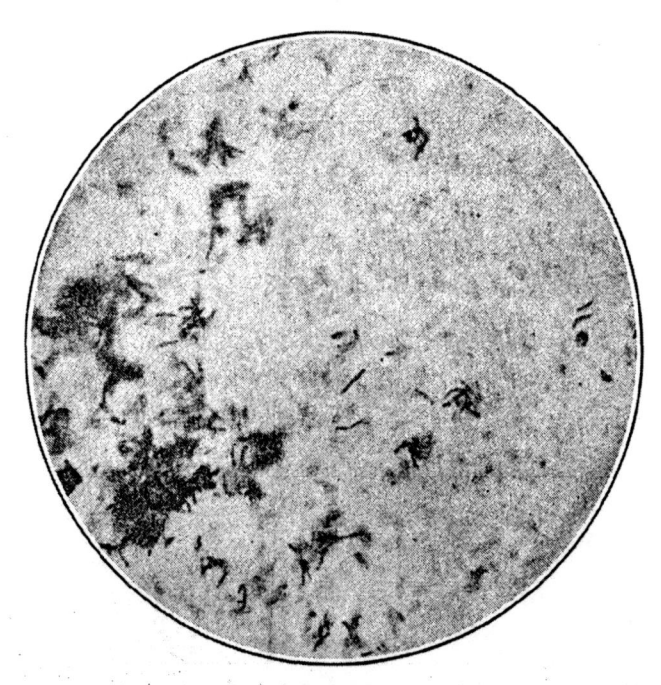

FIG. 46.—Bact. tuberculosis in human lung. After Muir and Ritchie.

exist for any length of time outside of the bodies of the animal which they infect. These bacteria are called *strict* or *obligate parasites*. Bact. tuberculosis and Bact. lepræ are examples of this class. It should be noted in this connection that bacteriologists have been able to cultivate some of these strict parasites on special artificial media which is made to resemble, as nearly as possible, the pabulum on which these microorganisms grow naturally.

It is supposed that at one period of time all pathogenic bacteria were saprophytes, but, having their biological charac-

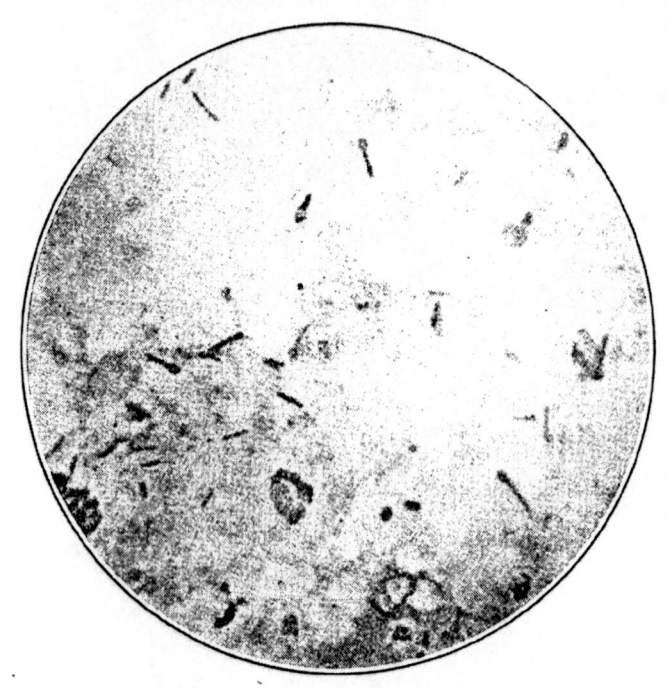

FIG. 47.—Film preparation of discharge from a wound in a case of tetanus, showing B. tetani in "drumstick" spore formation. After Muir and Ritchie.

ters modified, they have become parasitic on account of natural selection and environment.

Experiments have been made with various species of bacteria, and it has been shown that it is possible to modify bacteria to such an extent that many of the strict parasites can be made to become saprophytes, and conversely. Some saprophytic bacteria may be indirectly pathogenic by reason of the fact that they may frequently multiply in various food products, such as meats, milk, cheese, etc., and, by their saprogenic processes, produce poisonous protein substances

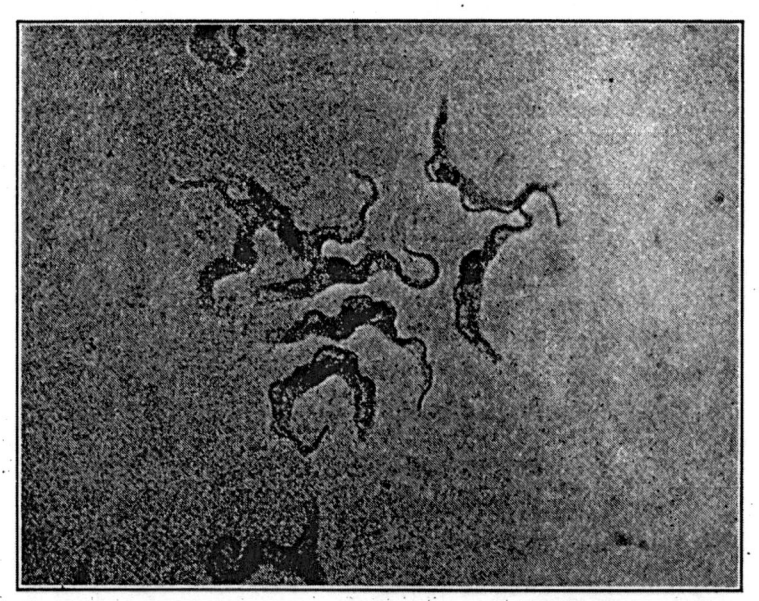

Fig. 48.—Trypanosoma bruci of nagana. The trypanosome is carried by the tsetse fly. After Williams.

called ptomains. These ptomains, when taken into the body and absorbed by the lymphatics and blood, give rise to serious intoxications. These substances will be considered more in detail later.

The injection of certain species of true saprophytic bacteria under the skin of some of the experimental animals is often attended by the production of abscesses, necrosis, and general gangrene.

232 BIOLOGY OF SPECIALIZED GROUPS

All the above-mentioned facts and experiments serve to demonstrate the conclusion which can be definitely stated; namely, that the limits of the "pathogenic bacteria" are not definite.

Diseases. Infectious and Contagious. — All diseases pro-

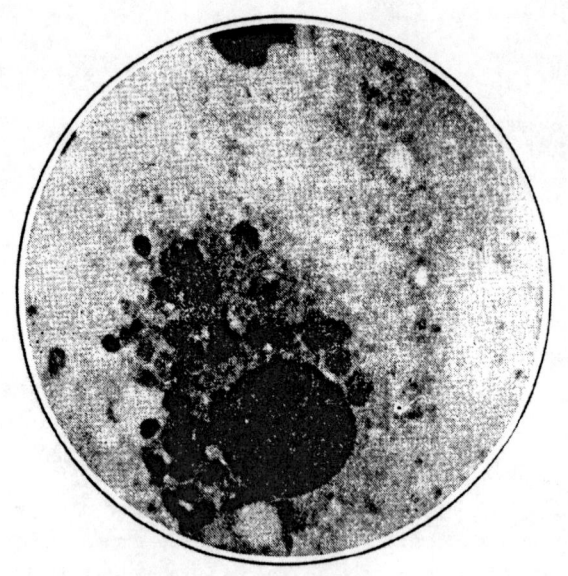

Fig. 49. — Leishman-Donovan bodies of kala-azar. It is supposed that at certain stages these bodies are flagellated similar to Figure 48. Williams.

duced by bacteria and other microörganisms are called *infectious diseases*. Many definitions have been suggested by pathologists for the term "infection." According to Ziegler, infection is "the entrance of bacteria into the body and their increase there." As McFarland says, this usually means an entrance into the tissues of the body and a multiplication of the bacterial cells in the tissues. Some pathogenic bacteria produce disease conditions without entering the tissues of the body. For example, Msp. comma produces poisonous effects on the mucous membrane of the intestines without entering the tissues.

The mere entrance of the bacteria into the body or the tissues of the animal or plant is only a part of the process of infection. In addition there must be some injury to the body cells. As has been mentioned above, the harmless saprophytic bacteria may be present in the body of an animal and never produce any morbid effects until, for some reason or other, the resistance of some of the body cells is reduced. The term "infested" has been applied to those conditions where so-called harmless bacteria are present in the body normally. These bacteria may enter the tissues of the body under certain conditions and produce an infection. Adami calls this process subinfection.

It has been stated that all diseases due to bacteria are infectious. A certain proportion of these infectious diseases are also *contagious;* that is, they may be transmitted by direct contact of the infected individual with healthy individuals, or by indirect contact through the agency of fomites. *Contagion* has to do with the manner of transmission of a disease, and *infection* with the nature of the cause of the disease. For example, smallpox and diphtheria are infectious, contagious diseases, while tetanus and anthrax are purely infectious diseases.

Infectious diseases may be arbitrarily divided into specific and non-specific diseases. *Specific infectious diseases* are those

234   BIOLOGY OF SPECIALIZED GROUPS

which are produced by a definite bacterium or microörganism. The symptomatology of these diseases is equally specific. The definite bacterium or microörganism *is the only* exciting cause of this class of diseases. Diphtheria, typhoid fever, bubonic plague, are types of specific infectious diseases. The

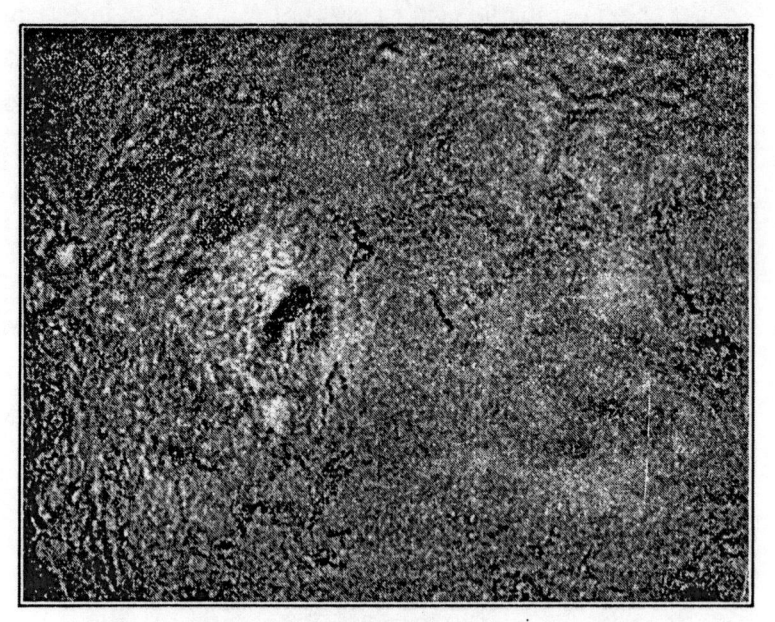

FIG. 50. — Treponema pallidum of syphilis in tissue. Williams.

etiological agents in these diseases are Bact. diphtheriæ, B. typhosus, and B. pestis, and natural infection of a body with these bacteria usually produces a definite pathological condition and symptomatology. Some infectious diseases, in which the etiological agent is not known, are called specific infectious diseases. Hydrophobia, smallpox, and chickenpox are examples of this class.

Non-specific infectious diseases are those which are not caused by any one definite bacterium. The various inflammatory processes which characterize so many diseases (see table below) are examples of pathological conditions which are not specific and may be due to a variety of microörganisms. For example, M. pneumoniæ, B. coli, Str. pyogenes, and many other bacteria may produce inflammation in various parts of the body. Infections, for example, with Str. pyogenes, may produce, depending upon the avenue of infection, diseases such as erysipelas, puerperal septicemia, septicemia, tonsillitis, abscesses, peritonitis, etc. These diseases are widely different in their symptomatology. The following incomplete tables will serve to give an outline of the various common infectious diseases: —

PARTIAL LIST OF SPECIFIC INFECTIOUS DISEASES DUE TO BACTERIA

Disease	Etiological Bacterium
Gonorrhœa	Micrococcus gonorrhœæ
Chancroids	Bacillus chancroides mallis
Meningitis, cerebro-spinal, epidemic	Micrococcus meningitidis intracellularis
Typhoid fever	Bacillus typhosus
Relapsing fever	Spirillum obermeieri
Malta fever	Micrococcus melitensis
Dysentery, bacillary	Bacillus dysentariæ Shiga
Tuberculosis	Bacterium tuberculosis
Glanders	Bacterium mallei
Tetanus	Bacillus tetani
Influenza	Bacterium influenzæ

Disease	Etiological Bacterium
Anthrax	Bacterium anthracis
Leprosy	Bacterium lepræ
Diphtheria	Bacterium diphtheriæ
Asiatic cholera	Microspira comma
Bubonic plague	Bacillus pestis
Swine plague	Bacillus cholera suis
Malignant œdema	Bacillus œdematis maligni
Symptomatic anthrax	Bacillus chauvæi
Chicken cholera	Bacterium cholera gallinarum
Botulismus	Bacillus botulinus
Strangles	Micrococcus equi

PARTIAL LIST OF SPECIFIC INFECTIOUS DISEASES NOT DUE TO BACTERIA

Disease	Etiological Bacterium	
Actinomycosis	Streptothrix actinomyces	⎫
Mycetoma	Streptothrix maduræ	⎬ Molds
Farcin du Bœuf	Streptothrix farcinicus	⎭
Blastomycosis	Odium coccidoides	⎫ Yeasts
Odiomycosis (Thrush)	Odium albican	⎭
Malaria	Plasmodium malariæ	⎫
Dysentery	Amœba coli	
Texas fever	Piroplasma bigeminum	
Infectious jaundice	Piroplasma commune	
Syphilis	Trepenema pallidum	
Nagana	Trypanosoma bruci	
Dourine	Trypanosoma equiperdium	⎬ Protozoa
Mal de Caderas	Trypanosoma equinum	
Surra	Trypanosoma evansi	
Sleeping sickness	Trypanosoma gambieneis	
Rat disease	Trypanosoma lewisi	
Kala-azar	Trypanosoma X	
Filariasis	Filaria sanguinis hominis, and other worms	⎭

Partial List of Nonspecific Infectious Diseases and the Bacteria which may Produce Them

Disease	Etiological Bacterium
Pneumonia (Pneumonitis)	Micrococcus pneumoniæ
Conjunctivitis	Streptococcus pyogenes
Iritis	Bacillus typhosus
Rhinitis	Bacillus coli
Pharyngitis	Bacillus proteus vulgaris
Laryngitis	Bacterium welchii
Enteritis	Bacterium tuberculosis
Tonsillitis	Bacterium pneumoniæ Friedlander
Otitis	Micrococcus pyogenes var. aureus, etc.
Adenitis	Micrococcus intracellularis meningitidis
Pleuritis	Pseudomonas pyocyanea
Myocarditis	Micrococcus tetragena
Arthritis	Micrococcus gonorrhœæ
Endocarditis	
Ostitis and periostitis	
Cystitis and urethritis	
Nephritis	
Endometritis	
Salpingitis and oöphoritis	Saprogenic bacteria in some conditions
Vaginitis	
Orchitis	
Meningitis	
Appendicitis	
Peritonitis	
Bursitis	
Dermititis	
Neuritis	
Myositis	
Stomatitis	
Etc.	

The above-mentioned inflammations may be either acute or chronic and may be attended by suppuration (pus formation).

It should be remembered that all of the non-specific diseases above-mentioned are not always produced by microorganisms. Mechanical, physical, and chemical factors may be responsible in certain rare instances.

The diseases (non-specific) tabulated in the foregoing list may be caused by a variety of bacteria. Not every disease men ioned is caused by all the bacteria tabulated. Some diseases are caused by a large variety of bacteria (ten species in some cases), while other morbid conditions are caused by only a few species. Some of the bacteria mentioned also produce specific infections when attacking the body at definite points, *e.g.* M. gonorrhœæ in the genito-urinary tract, B. typhosus in the intestines, etc. They, however, not uncommonly produce non-specific infections.

Partial List of Infectious Diseases of Unknown Etiology, Specific and Non-specific

Pertussis (Whooping cough)
Parotitis, epidemic (Mumps)
Spotted fever, Rocky Mountain
Yellow fever
Rheumatic fever (Rheumatism)
Typhus fever
Scarlet fever (Scarlatina)
Aphthous fever (Foot and mouth disease)
Hydrophobia (Rabies)
Smallpox (Variola)
Cowpox, Vaccination (Vaccina), same organism
Chicken pox (Varicella)

Measles
Rubella (Röthelin)
Dengue (Breakbone fever)
Beri-beri
Trachoma

Rinderpest
Rhinoscleroma
Sheep pox
Distemper
Swine erysipelas

The Means of Transmission of Bacteria from One Individual to Another. — The transmission of pathogenic bacteria and other microörganisms from one individual to another takes place in different ways. We will briefly call attention to a few well-recognized facts in this connection.

It has been known for years that a patient suffering from diseases such as gonorrhœa, chancroids, syphilis, leprosy, or external suppurating lesions could transmit the disease by direct contact with the abraded skin or mucous membrane of the diseased person or some article having been in contact with the diseased individual. In these cases the bacteria pass directly by contact from one infected wound to another and infect it. Tuberculous lesions have also been noted to be developed in the skin by direct inoculation from operations and necropsies performed on tuberculous individuals. Then again there are other diseases, for example, such as scarlet fever and smallpox, which can be transmitted by the agency of fomites; that is, articles which have been in contact with the diseased individual, such as eating utensils, bedclothing, books, etc.

It has been recently pointed out that typhoid fever, which was heretofore supposed to be transmitted only through the agency of water which has been contaminated by sewage or infectious substances coming in contact with water, may be carried by normal persons who have had an attack of typhoid fever at some time previous. Cases are on record where B. typhosus has been carried for eighteen years after an infection by a domestic and then transmitted by personal uncleanliness to several members of the family in which she was employed. B. typhosus is frequently observed in the gall bladder in persons having had the disease for long periods. Flies may also carry B. typhosus from feces to various food products, and other individuals may then be infected.

In bubonic plague the disease is transmitted among the rats, which are very easily infected with B. pestis by means of the bite of the rat flea. A few observations are on record showing that these rat fleas may also bite and infect man. Frequently the flea deposits the bacteria on the skin and by scratching the organisms are inoculated. Some disease-producing bacteria are largely water-borne, such as B. typhosus. The same is also true of B. dysenteriæ and the Msp. comma of Asiatic cholera.

In diseases like malaria, yellow fever, and some forms of filariasis mosquitoes act as the carriers of the infection. In malaria the hematozoan undergoes certain periods of its life cycle in the mosquito. In yellow fever this is probably the case also, but as the etiological organism is not known we cannot formulate definite information in this regard.

Protozoan diseases, such as Texas fever, African relapsing fever, are carried by means of the ticks, and the infectious organism is transferred in some cases from mother to young. In tropical protozoan diseases, such as nagana and sleeping

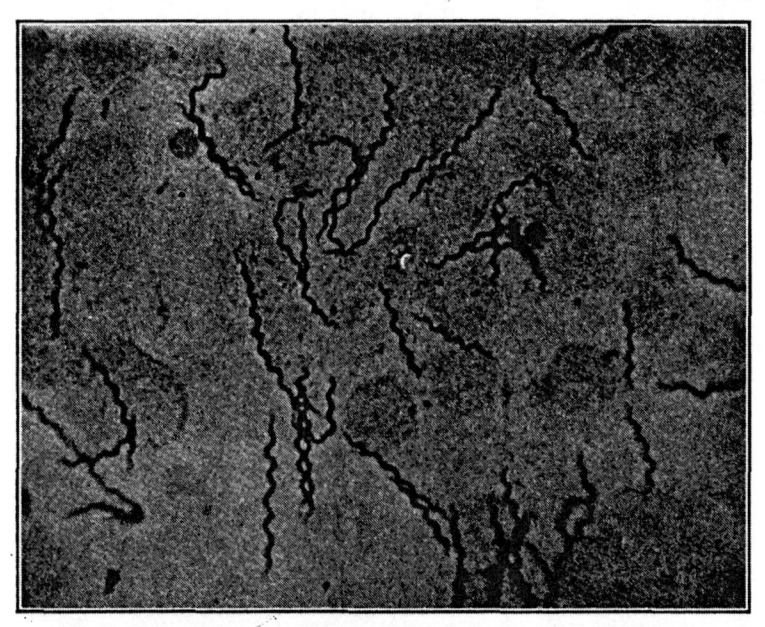

FIG. 51. — Spirochæta obermeieri of relapsing fever. Williams.

sickness which are due to trypanosomes, the tsetse flies are factors in the transmission of the disease. These protozoan diseases are transmitted by bites of the flies.

Bedbugs, common fleas, and lice may also be capable of transmitting certain infectious diseases. Bact. tuberculosis has been found in the bedbug. It has also been stated recently that the louse transmits the microörganism of typhus fever.

It is also a well-known fact that healthy persons may carry on their mucous membranes such organisms as the

R

M. pneumoniæ and Bact. diphtheriæ without producing any effect. These same organisms may become virulent when taken into a susceptible individual. The organisms may be transferred from one to the other by direct or indirect contact.

CHAPTER XXII

Pathogenic Bacteria (*Continued*)

Mode of Action of Pathogenic Bacteria. — Pathogenic bacteria produce morbid conditions in the animal body by the following general methods. Frequently there is a combination of two or more of the methods in one disease condition in the body.

(*a*) By mechanically clogging the capillaries of the blood vessels, thus preventing the oxygen and nutriment from reaching the vital tissue cells. In anthrax, which is caused by Bact. anthracis, a large portion of the pathogenesis is produced by this mechanical method. Mycotic emboli are often formed in the capillaries.

(*b*) By the production of soluble toxins or poisons by the action of bacteria inside the body, which when absorbed by the blood, lymphatics, or nerve tissue and carried to the various cells of the body produce morbid changes within them. In diphtheria, for example, the toxins generated by Bact. diphtheriæ are responsible for the disease.

(*c*) By the destruction of tissue cells at the focus of the infection, thus incapacitating these cells from performing their normal functions. In tuberculosis, the destruction of tissue by Bact. tuberculosis is one important part of the disease process. Progressive gangrene is also due in part to the destruction of tissue by bacteria.

Diseased conditions of this nature may also be produced in the body by bacteria which cannot directly be called pathogenic.

(*d*) By the production of poisons or toxins by saprogenic bacteria acting on food products outside the body. When taken into the body through the digestive tract and absorbed, these poisonous substances present give rise to serious intoxications. Similar morbid conditions may arise on account of the action of saprogenic bacteria within the intestines. The poisonous substances produced are called ptomains. Meat poisoning, milk and ice cream poisoning, are examples of diseased conditions arising from the action of ptomains.

Occasionally, after parturition a portion of the placenta is retained within the uterus, and it may be acted upon by saprogenic bacteria. Ptomains generated and absorbed in this region usually produce pronounced intoxications.

Two principal factors are involved in the production of a disease by bacteria: (1) The entrance of bacteria into the tissues of the body and their multiplication This factor, it will be recalled, constitutes *infection*. (2) The elaboration of poisonous products by the bacteria which may act on the tissues immediately surrounding them or on the entire body. The latter factor constitutes what is known as poisoning or *intoxication*. In most morbid conditions both of these factors are concerned. In only a few cases is one factor alone involved.

In the case of the infection of the body and the multiplication within the body of Bact. anthracis, the pathogenic effects are probably principally mechanical and due in the main to the rapid multiplication of the bacteria. In this case there is also some form of toxin produced by the bacterial cells.

The products of the metabolism of the pathogenic bacteria will receive consideration later.

Proof of Etiological Relationship. — In order to prove that a definite microörganism is the etiological factor of a specific disease, Robert Koch devised the following postulates or rules which if fulfilled establishes the connection between a microörganism and a disease.

(*a*) The microörganism must be found in the tissues or body of the animal or plant with the disease.

(*b*) The microörganism must be isolated in pure culture from the body of the diseased animal or plant.

(*c*) It must be grown successfully on culture media.

(*d*) It must be able to produce the disease in a healthy animal or plant in approximately the same form and giving the same symptomatology as in (*a*). It must also again be found in the tissues of the experimental animal or plant.

The majority of pathogenic bacteria fulfill these laws, but there are some microörganisms which undoubtedly produce specific infectious diseases which do not fulfill the postulates of Koch. The following table gives a partial list of the microorganisms which produce specific infectious diseases but which are unable to fulfill Koch's laws: —

Bacterium lepræ (Leprosy).
Treponema pallidum (Syphilis).
Spirochæta obermeieri (Relapsing fever).
Amœbi coli (Amœbic dysentery).
Plasmodium malariæ (Malaria).

There are other bacteria, as, for example, the M. gonorrhœæ, which fulfill all but one or two postulates. In this case M. gonorrhœa will not produce the disease when inoculated into animals. There are still other bacteria which have been proved to be the etiological agents in diseases which do not comply with all the laws. The constant association of definite microörganisms with diseases showing the same symptomatology has led to these organisms being regarded as specific.

Effects of Pathogenic Bacteria on the Body. — The following tabular outline is given by Muir and Ritchie and portrays in a very general way the action of the pathogenic bacteria on the animal body.

A. Tissue Changes.
(1) Local changes. In region of the bacteria.
Position (a) At primary lesion.
   (b) At secondary foci.
Character (a) Tissue reactions.
   (b) Degeneration, acute or chronic.
(2) Changes produced at a distance from the bacteria directly by the absorption of toxins.
   (a) In special tissues

(1a) As a result of damage — nerve cells and fibers, secreting cells, vessel walls, or

(2a) Changes of a reactive nature in the blood-forming organs (Bones, spleen, etc.).

(b) General anatomical changes due to malnutrition or increased waste.

B. Changes in Metabolism.

Occurrence of fever, errors of assimilation and elimination.

The effects of bacterial action in the body, briefly stated, are as follows: (a) Degeneration and necrosis; (b) regeneration, reactive and defensive changes. Degeneration and necrosis are due to the susceptibility and vulnerability of the tissues. In the latter process (b) in all probability the phagocytes and the body fluids are both responsible.

The position of the lesions in the body is not easily explained by any mechanical means. Without doubt the microörganisms or their toxins and special varieties of tissue cells enter into chemical combination with each other. There is a selective action on the part of the bacteria or their toxins for these special tissues. The affinity of the tetano-spasmin of the tetanus toxin for nerve cells is a case in point.

In acute infections by bacteria there is usually a locus of inflammation at the focus of the infection. Hemorrhage, œdema, and in some cases suppuration may be attendant conditions.

In chronic infections, as, for example, the infective granulomata (glanders, tuberculosis, actinomycosis, syphilis, and leprosy), there is only a small amount of vascular change but a comparatively large amount of tissue hyperplasia This hyperplasia (increase in tissue cells) is principally noted in the connective tissues.

The general lesions in the body due to the toxins of bacteria are usually those of cloudy swelling and, sometimes, fatty degeneration of parenchymatous organs, such as the liver, kidney, etc. Capillary hemorrhages due to hyaline changes in the arterial capillaries are also noted.

Marked changes in the metabolism of the body are noted in bacterial infections. Fever may be due either to the destruction of tissue or the formation of antibodies, etc. Paralysis, coma, spasms, are not uncommon in infections where the nervous system is markedly affected Disturbances of the secretory functions of the various glands of the body are also noted.

The Poisonous Products of Bacteria. — The poisonous chemical substances produced by bacteria may be grouped into four classes as follows: —

(*a*) Products of the decomposition of the media on which the bacteria are growing. *Ptomains* and some other bodies are produced in this way.

(*b*) Soluble poisons, synthetically produced by the bacterial cells and secreted by them into the surrounding media. The true *toxins* are produced in this way.

(*c*) Poisonous products synthetically produced by the bacteria which are not secreted outside the cell wall. These poisons are specific substances. On account of being intracellular, these toxic substances are called *endotoxins*.

(*d*) Poisonous proteins which are constituents of the protoplasm of the bacterial cell. These proteins are not in any sense soluble or specific and are not definitely known to be responsible for any morbid condition in the body. They may be concerned in tuberculosis. These poisonous products are called *toxic bacterial proteins*.

Ptomains. — These substances were the first bacterial products to be recognized. They were assumed to be alkaloidal in nature, and on account of the fact that poisonous plants owe their effects to alkaloidal substances, some observers were inclined to believe that ptomains were responsible for disease.

Ptomains are basic nitrogenous substances and are found in the media on which certain species of bacteria are growing. It was soon determined that ptomains from pathogenic bacteria were not alone able to produce the morbid effects noted in experimental animals. The most highly poisonous ptomains are produced by the so-called non-pathogenic bacteria (saprogenic bacteria). Only a small amount of research work has been done on the subject of ptomains during recent years.

Ptomains are formed by the action of various species of saprogenic bacteria on protein material. They owe their basic nitrogenous character to the amino groups which they contain. It has been determined that ptomains may be produced by the action of saprogenic bacteria on dead pathogenic bacteria, or other bacteria. It is not known whether or not any ptomains are produced by intra-cellular bacterial processes. The ptomains are closely related to the amino acids, and Wells states that in all probability they are produced by secondary changes (enzyme action) on these acids. Ptomains are themselves susceptible to the action of saprogenic and saprophilic bacteria They are noted to decrease in amount in some cultures and this fact is accounted for by reason of their susceptibility to the action of other bacteria. Ptomains are distinct from toxins, as will be pointed out later.

Ptomains only produce disease in the animal body when they are introduced in the food products in which they have been formed by the process of decomposition. They are also produced in the body by the retention and the decomposition of protein material, such as a portion of the placenta in the uterus after parturition The toxic condition resulting from the absorption of ptomains is known as sapremia.

There are many different ptomains which have been isolated, divided into groups, and named. All the ptomains have very complex formulas. There is one group of ptomains which is of special interest, and this is the cholin group. This group will be briefly considered. The group includes cholin and related substances as follows: —

Cholin . . . . $CH_2OH - CH_2 - N(CH_3)_3 - OH$.
Neurin . . . . $CH_2 = CH - N(CH_3)_3 - OH$.
Mucarin . . . . $CH(OH)_2 - CH_2 - N(CH_3)_3 - OH$.
Betain . . . . $COOH - CH_2 - N(CH_5)_3 - OH$.

Cholin is a substance which is present normally in all cells. It forms the nitrogen portion of the lecithin molecule. The source of this ptomain in decomposing protein material is therefore evident. It is stated by various writers that it is broken down in the animal body especially when nervous tissue, which is rich in lecithin, is disintegrated. Cholin is said to be present in the cerebro-spinal fluid and in the blood in certain degenerative nervous diseases. For example, it has been reported in the blood in cerebral syphilis, epilepsy, and dementia paralytica. Cholin is only slightly toxic, but the next member of the group, neurin, into which cholin can be transformed, is very toxic. Wells suggests that intoxications in the gastro-intestinal tract which are often ascribed to " food intoxications " may be due to cholin being split off from the lecithin of the food by the action of saprogenic bacteria and the cholin thus formed being changed into neurin which, when absorbed, gives rise to intoxication.

Cholin and neurin are closely related in structure and physiological action to muscarin, an alkaloidal substance first derived from mushrooms. A ptomain identical with muscarin has been isolated from decomposing fish, and the name muscarin has also been applied to it. Neurin and muscarin are very poisonous ptomains. Betain, the last member of the group, is only slightly toxic. It is also derived, for the most part, from the lecithin of the cells.

Toxins. — As has been stated, certain bacterial cells have the power of secreting poisonous synthetic products into the surrounding media. These substances are called soluble toxins or toxins. There are very few bacteria which have the power of producing these toxins. Bact. diphtheriæ, B. tetani, Ps. pyocyanea, and B botulinus are practically the only bacteria which produce toxins of this character, with the possible exception of some species which produce toxin-like hemolytic products These substances are referred to below.

Certain animals, such as snakes, eels, lizards, scorpions, etc., by activity of a particular group of gland cells produce soluble toxins, venoms, etc. Immunization with these animal toxins produces antibodies. In some toxins, as, for example, tetanus toxin, two distinct toxins can be separated — tetanospasmin, which has an affinity for nerve tissue, and tetanolysin (hemolysin), which destroys the red blood cells. In diphtheria, in all probability, there are also two toxins generated — the principal toxin, to which most of the diphtheritic infection is due, and another toxic substance, which is formed slowly by the bacteria and called by Ehrlich a toxon. The paralysis noted late in some cases of diphtheria is ascribed to these toxons.

The chemical constitution of toxins is unknown. A great amount of research work has been done and is being done at the present time along this line. Toxins are very labile substances and are easily destroyed by comparatively low moist heat, light, chemicals, and by oxygen, even in the amount found in the air. All oxidizing agents, including the enzymes of the body and of bacteria, destroy toxins. They are not affected by chloroform, toluol, phenol, etc., and are precipitated by the majority of the heavy metals. On account of their marked lability, chemical analyses cannot be made with accuracy. It is possible that as physical chemistry is developed, more information will be gained in regard to these substances. Investigations are being carried on at the present time by some of the noted physical chemists. Many facts have been learned about toxins by means of animal experimentation.

It is, however, established that toxins are not true proteins as they give none of the reactions for these substances. They seem to be more closely related in their various reactions to the enzymes. For example, it is impossible to isolate them pure, and they are not like proteins but seem like enzymes to be collodial substances of high molecular composition. Both toxins and enzymes pass through porcelain filters, but have their strength much reduced. They rarely pass a dialyzing membrane. They are both destroyed by 80° C. moist heat, but will withstand 100° C. dry heat and low temperatures for some time. They rapidly deteriorate on standing, and this seems to be due to the destruction of one part of the enzyme or toxin molecule. The toxin and enzyme molecules are made up of two distinct chemical parts or groups. One part combines with the substance attacked (haptophore), and the other portion produces the toxic or fermentive effects and the destruction of the substance (toxophore or zymophore group).

The part of the toxin or enzyme molecule which is affected by the various agents is the toxophore or zymophore group, and the molecules thus become what are called toxoids or fermentoids. Enzymes act equally well on liberation after being combined with substances on which they have acted, while toxins differ in that they are rendered inert after combining with any substance. An enzyme can, therefore, as far as amount goes, produce more effect than the toxin. Both toxin and enzyme are toxic or poisonous to animals. Their injection produces a reaction in animals and certain antibodies are produced. The bodies are considered below.

It can be readily seen from the foregoing that there are many points of resemblance between the enzyme and the toxin.

Toxins differ from ptomains in that they are specific substances produced by definite bacteria, while one distinct ptomain can be produced by the action of several species of bacteria. Antibodies can be produced against toxins, but not against ptomains. Toxins are secretions of the bacterial cells, while ptomains are produced by cleavage of the media on which the bacteria are growing. Ptomains are comparatively stable substances and can be subjected to chemical analysis. Toxins are very labile and cannot be analyzed chemically.

Endotoxins. — The majority of bacteria produce endotoxins, and it is to these poisonous chemical substances that the majority of diseases are directly due. In all probability, the endotoxin is a secretion of the bacterial protoplasm within the cell wall. It is not thrown out through the wall into the surrounding media like the soluble toxins, but is stored up within the cell. These endotoxins are liberated by the action of the enzymes in the body which they attack, or by autolysis (self-destruction by enzymes) of the bacteria themselves. The various species of pyogenic (pus-producing) micrococci, M. pneumoniæ, B. typhosus, Msp. comma, and many other bacteria, produce endotoxins. The filtrate (porcelain filter) of cultures of these bacteria is only slightly toxic. The bodies of the bacterial cells are extremely toxic when injected into animals, proving that the poisonous substance is contained within the cell wall. Endotoxins can be extracted by pressing out the intra-cellular substances by means of a high power hydraulic press, or by grinding the bacteria after they have been rendered brittle by liquid air. Immunization of animals with bacteria-producing endotoxins yields in the body fluids of the animal injected not antitoxins, but increased bactericidal substances, agglutinins, precipitins, opsonins, etc. The failure to secure antibodies which will combat the action of the endotoxins directly (antiendotoxins) has seriously impeded the progress of serum therapy.

The following toxic substances are produced by some of the higher plants. They are not unlike bacterial endotoxins except that antibodies may be produced against them by immunization. They are called phytotoxins.

Ricin from the seeds of Ricinus communis (castor oil bean).
Abrin from the seeds of Abrus precatorius (jequerity bean).
Crotin from the seeds of Crotin tiglium.
Robin from the leaves and bark of Robina pseudoacacia (locust).

CHAPTER XXIII

Pathogenic Bacteria (*Continued*)

Toxic Bacterial Proteins. — It has been found that after bacteria have been washed free of all soluble toxin and have been freed of all endotoxin, that the remaining cell wall and cell protoplasm possesses some toxic properties. When injected into an experimental animal these products produce inflammation, necrosis, and pus formation. The effects are not in any sense specific, and injection in different animals may produce different results. The toxic substances of this nature are not confined to pathogenic bacteria alone, but it is not infrequent to find that non-pathogenic bacteria, which have been treated as mentioned above, possess the same properties (B. prodigiosus, etc.). These toxic substances are separate and distinct from endotoxins and soluble toxins, as is shown in the fact that they resist a temperature of 110° C. for ten minutes when in one per cent sulphuric acid solution. The bacterial proteins can be isolated in this way. The substances are undoubtedly protein in nature and in all probability some form of nucleo-protein. Wells thinks that they may possibly be derived from the endotoxins by some indirect chemical process.

There are some diseases, notably tuberculosis and anthrax, leaving out of consideration the mechanical effect of the bacteria in the latter case, which do not seem to be due to any soluble toxins or any endotoxins which the respective organisms might produce. It has been suggested that there may be some relation between their toxic effects and the protein substances which are contained within their cell protoplasm.

Anaphylaxis to Bacterial Proteins. — It has been shown by various workers that an animal body may be made to become hypersensitive to most all proteins, including those derived from bacteria. The condition of hypersusceptibility to proteins is designated as anaphylaxis (Gr. against protection). If an animal receives a small injection of a definite protein, like egg white, horse serum, etc., and then again after at least 8 to 13 days receives a somewhat larger injection of the same protein, the animal usually dies or is seriously intoxicated. The same symptoms result when bacterial proteins are used. There is a possibility that an individual may be hypersensitized to a bacterial protein, and later when infected with the homologous bacteria in larger number may offer no resistance whatever. Anaphylaxis may be transmitted from mother to young *in utero*. In this way the individual may seem to be naturally hypersensitive to the protein concerned.

Bacterial Hemolysins. — It is a well-established fact that many bacteria, pathogenic and non-pathogenic, produce toxic substances which destroy red blood corpuscles. The filtrates of certain bacterial cultures, such as M. pyogenes vars. aureus and albus, Str. pyogenes, B. typhosus, Ps. pyocyanea, etc., contain these hemolytic substances. Bacterial hemolysins are closely related to the toxic bacterial proteins, but are, perhaps, more closely related to the soluble toxins. They can, for all practical purposes, be regarded as modified toxins which have a special affinity for red blood corpuscles. These hemolysins are divided into distinct chemical molecules, a *complement* or thermolabile substance, and an *amboceptor* or thermostable substance, as have been noted in the bactericidal substances in the serum.

Hemolysins are contained in the secretions or extracts of animal and plant cells, such as snake venom, eel serums, and the various phytotoxins above mentioned. The mechanism of hemolysis (blood destruction) is very similar to bacteriolysis (bacterial distraction).

Antitoxins. — Practically all cells of the body possess physiological receptors (side chains), composed of definite chemical radicals connected with a central group of atoms or molecules. These side chains have open valencies and are capable of uniting with various foreign substances, such as food, poisons, etc. The classical example used to demonstrate a central group and its side chains is the benzene ring and the substances which may be formed from it: —

$$\text{Benzol} \qquad \text{Benzoic Acid} \qquad \text{Benzoate of Soda}$$

The above graphic representation shows the benzol molecule having a central group of C_6 with lateral side chains of H connecting with each atom of C. When one of these side chains of H is replaced by COOH, benzol is converted into benzoic acid. If to this acid radical Na is united, supplanting an H in the OOH of this radical, sodium benzoate is produced.

When toxins are generated in the body by pathogenic bacteria or when they are introduced artificially for the purpose of producing active immunity, the toxin molecule combines with the various side chains of the cells. There is first a chemical combination between that chemical group of the toxin molecule, which is known as the haptophore, with a corresponding group (side chain) in the cell known as the haptophile. Later the so-called chemical toxophore group of the toxin molecule unites with the corresponding group (side chain) in the cell called a toxophile group. The union of the toxin with the cells is a definite chemical union which is stable in some cases (tetanus) and not so stable in others (diphtheria). The cell is usually stimulated only when the haptophore group unites with it, and is injured only when, in addition, the toxophore group unites with it. The union of the toxin molecules with the various cells of the body for which it possesses an affinity, causes a reaction and an increased generation of chemical side chains, not in the cell injured, as was first thought, but by cells which have been indirectly injured by the removal from active work of those cells injured by the toxin molecule. In other words, there has been a compensatory hyperplasia of chemical side chains, just as we have a hyperplasia of tissue cells in chronic inflammations. When a certain number of cells have been stimulated by the toxin, the chemical side chains from the other cells begin to be secreted into the blood, lymph, and body fluids. These secreted side chains constitute the antitoxin molecules.

The exact chemical nature of the antitoxin molecule is not known. This is also true of the toxin molecule. It has been shown that the antitoxin of diphtheria is closely associated with the serum-globulin, but this is not *prima facie* evidence of the antitoxin being a globulin. The antitoxin molecule is evidently of very large dimensions. Most antitoxic molecules do not pass through a porcelain filter of the smallest caliber. The molecules behave like colloids, being electro-negative and therefore move toward the anode of the electrical field. The antitoxin molecules are larger than the corresponding toxin molecules. In their reactions, antitoxins resemble the known protein substances more closely than toxins. They are not as labile as the toxin, but may be altered and destroyed with comparative ease.

In the commercial preparation of antitoxins healthy horses are immunized to increasing doses of toxin or mixtures of toxin and antitoxin. After a certain period, varying from two to six months, the horses are bled to the extent of five or six liters of blood, and the blood serum which separates out on standing contains the antitoxin (discharged side chains). This antitoxin is standardized against toxin which has been previously standardized against standard antitoxin. Dried standard antitoxin is stable.

The union between the toxin molecule and the antitoxin molecule is a definite chemical combination. Antitoxin is produced in the largest quantities in the spleen and bone marrow of all susceptible animals.

When a body is naturally infected by a pathogenic bacterium, or is immunized with living or dead pathogenic bacteria which produce endotoxins, there is developed in the blood serum and other body fluids of the infected animal a variety of substances. As has been previously stated, the body fluids contain no distinct antitoxins. The fluids contain the following substances.

Antibacterial Substances. — These properties are manifested by the ability of the blood serum and body fluids to destroy the vitality of the bacteria without destruction of the cell substance (bactericidal), or to disintegrate in addition the bacterial cell (bacteriolysis). Bacteriolytic action may be due to autolysis of the bacteria themselves or to the direct action of the serum. Two important molecular groups are concerned in a bacteriolytic and bactericidal reaction. The action of these chemical groups may be shown by the following experiments.

If an antibacterial serum, be it bactericidal or bacteriolytic, is heated to 60° C. for twenty minutes, then placed in contact with the specific bacteria *in vivo* or *in vitro*, the bacteria will not be affected. On the other hand, if some normal blood serum be added, the bacteria will be markedly effected and killed, and in bacteriolytic serums will be disintegrated. In addition the experiment shows the presence of an extremely labile substance in the bactericidal serum which was replaced by the fresh normal serum. This substance is called the *complement*. There is present in the serum also a stable substance which resists heat and all external agents This substance is called the *amboceptor* or immune body. These chemical substances can be definitely separated from each other. It has been shown by experiment that the chemical group which is called the amboceptor must first unite with the bacterial cell before the complement can combine and destroy it. Anti-complements and anti-amboceptors may be produced on immunizing with these bodies. Complements may also be changed into complementoids by heat. The amboceptor-complement reaction will be mentioned later in the consideration of other immune substances.

Agglutinins. — Agglutinins are substances which are found in the blood serum of some normal and immunized animals, and which have the power to produce a clumping of the specific microörganism causing some infections. Group agglutinins, that is, agglutinins for bacteria related to the species producing the agglutinin, may also be present in small amounts in the serum. These may be removed by diluting the serum. The agglutinin in the serum enters into chemical combination with the so-called agglutinogen which is present in the bacterial cell, and the resulting chemical reaction produces an agglutinate of the bacteria. Agglutinins are produced under similar conditions to the antitoxins. They are discharged chemical side chains. Agglutinoids may be produced by heating or adding certain chemicals to the agglutinin, and anti-agglutinins may be produced by immunization with agglutinin. The phenomenon of agglutination is made use of in the so-called Gruber-Widal reaction for typhoid fever and also in the diagnosis of glanders.

Opsonins. — In some infections (pyogenic, etc.) due to bacteria which produce endotoxins, bactericidal substances are not always easily produced. Without doubt phagocytosis by the polymorphonuclear and mononuclear leucocytes, and other cells of the body is of great importance in combating certain infections. There are present in normal serums specific substances called opsonins. These opsonins are increased during an infection and by the process of immunization by vaccination. The phagocytes during an infection can only ingest the etiological microörganism after they have come in contact with the opsonins of the blood serum. This has been positively demonstrated. The nature of the reaction between the opsonin and the bacteria and other infectious microörganisms is not known. The opsonins prepare the bacteria for phagocytosis, or, to use the latest terminology, the bacteria are "sensitized." The more opsonins the more phagocytic action will take place, and therefore the more infecting bacteria will be destroyed. The opsonins have no direct effect on the leucocytes or other phagocytes.

The normal opsonins may be increased by immunizing the animal body with killed bacteria, thus causing the cells of the body to react and secrete more opsonin, as is the case in antitoxin formation.

Precipitins. — If the blood serum of an animal which has recently had an infection, or been artificially immunized, is brought in contact with a filtrate of bacterial culture of the same species of bacteria which caused the infection, or the species which was used in the process of immunization, a definite chemical reaction results. This reaction is characterized by the precipitation of certain of the protein substances in the filtrate which are evidently derived from the bacterial cells The substances in the serum are called precipitins. The reaction is nearly a specific one , that is, precipitation is rarely accomplished by a serum when placed in contact with a filtrate produced by bacteria other than those used in the process of immunization, or present in the infection. Occasionally, for example, the serum of an animal immunized to B. typhosus will precipitate the filtrates of other members of the so-called Typhoid-Colon Group, such as B. coli, B. paratyphosus, etc. This fact indicates that there is a close chemical relationship between these bacteria. Specific precipitins have been obtained for practically all protein substances such as blood, milk, and egg albumen with serums produced by immunizing animals with these foreign substances. Precipitins are also specific for the bloods of various animals. Precipitins are distinct from agglutinins although they are both frequently present in the same serums.

In the chemical reaction the precipitin of the serum must enter into chemical combination with a substance in the filtrate derived from the bacteria called precipitinogen, and, by thus combining, a definite chemical precipitate is formed. Precipitation, like agglutination, does not take place in the absence of salts (electrolytes). Nothing definite is known in regard to the chemical structure of the precipitins. They are probably protein substances. They are precipitated in the euglobulin part of the serum, like most antibodies, and cannot be separated from the serum proteins. On heating serums containing precipitins they are changed into precipitoids. The combining group is uninjured, but the active group (zymophore), which causes the precipitation, is destroyed.

Antienzymes. — Some pathogenic bacteria produce enzymes (M. pyogenes var. aureus, etc.) in small amounts. Immunization of animals with these enzymes produces antienzymes in the serum of the animal. Little is known in regard to the antienzymes. There is a possibility that in certain cases they may inhibit bacterial growth. The subject of bacterial enzymes has been considered in another chapter (Chap. XV).

Table of Antibodies which may be produced by Immunization

Antitoxins for bacterial toxins of:
  Bact. diphtheriæ (Diphtheria).
  B. tetanus (Tetanus).
  B. botulinus (Botulism).

Ps. pyocyaneus (Blue-green pus).

B. feseri (Symptomatic anthrax).

Anticytotoxins for the various toxic parenchymatous cells of the body.

Antihemolysins for the hemolysins of bacteria.

Antileucocidin for the leucocyte poison of the pyogenic micrococci, etc.

Antitoxins for animal toxins.

Antivenin against venom of snakes.

Antitoxin for poison of the scorpion.

Antitoxin for the poison of certain species of spiders.

Antitoxins for serum poisons of some species of fish, eel, turtle, salamander, and wasp.

Antitoxins for plant toxins.

Antiricin for poison of castor oil bean.

Antiabrin for the poison of the jequerity bean.

Antirobin for the poison of the locust, leaves and bark.

Anticrotin for the poison of the crotin oil bean.

Antipollen for the poison in the pollen of various plants.

Antiserums for:

Msp. comma (Asiatic cholera).

B. typhosus (Typhoid fever).

M. pneumonia (Pneumonia).

B. pestis (Bubonic plague).

Antienzymes for the enzymes of various zymogenic bacteria.

Vaccines and Agents influencing the Opsonins

Vaccines have been prepared of the etiological agents in:
Smallpox.
Tuberculosis.
Anthrax.
Symptomatic anthrax.
Hydrophobia.
Practically all bacteria which produce endotoxins, such as,
  Msp. comma (Asiatic cholera).
  B. typhosus (Typhoid fever).
  M. pyogenes var. aureus (Pus infections).

It should be remembered that only a few of the antibodies above mentioned are of use as therapeutic agents.

Factors which influence and modify Infections. — The conditions which modify an infection in the body by bacteria or other microörganisms may be briefly stated as follows: —

(1) The virulence of the infecting agent.
(2) The number of the infecting organisms.
(3) The avenue of the infection.
(4) The subject or individual infected.

(1) *Virulence.* — By this term is meant the ability of an organism to produce disease. This property varies, and may be increased or decreased. The virulence of a pathogenic bacterium may be increased by passing it through a series of susceptible animals, or growing it in celloidin sacs placed in

the abdominal cavity or under the skin of a susceptible animal. The virulence may be decreased by growing the bacteria on culture media, and by growing the cultures at a comparatively high heat. Virulence depends upon the ability of the bacteria or microörganisms to grow in the body and to subsequently form toxic substances.

(2) *Number.* — The number of bacteria or other microorganisms necessary to produce an infection in the body and overcome its resistance varies with the species. For example, it has been found that the introduction of one single Bact. anthracis is all that is necessary to produce anthrax. This one bacterium, of course, soon multiplies very rapidly in the body. Observations have been made on tuberculosis, and it has been demonstrated that at least eight hundred and twenty of Bact. tuberculosis are necessary to produce the disease experimentally in a guinea pig. In all probability, in man and animals it requires only a few bacteria to start a tubercular infection naturally.

Watson-Cheyne found on experimentation with B. vulgaris that six million bacilli injected under the skin produced no lesion, eight million produced an abscess, fifty-six million a phlegmon, and that two hundred and twenty-five million were necessary to produce a fatal result in two hours.

It has been also demonstrated that two hundred and fifty million of M. pyogenes var. aureus were required to produce an abscess, and one billion were necessary to cause death in an experimental animal, such as a rabbit.

These few experiments show that the internal resistance of the body is greater against some infecting organisms than others. There is, however, a limit to the number of microorganisms which may be introduced into the body without producing any pathological condition.

It should be remembered that the phagocytes of the body aid materially in combating infections. They are able to destroy only certain species of bacteria and certain numbers of bacteria, without the body becoming infected. It will be readily seen, therefore, that the number of bacteria influences and modifies the infection.

(3) *The Avenue of Infection.* — By this expression is meant the point and channel of infection. It makes a decided difference in the symptomatology and subsequent results if the avenue of infection differs when a definite microörganism is the etiological factor. For example, Bact. tuberculosis when entering the body through the respiratory or digestive tract may produce tuberculosis of the lungs or tuberculosis of the intestines and accessory organs and, furthermore, usually terminates fatally. If Bact. tuberculosis infects the skin, a distinctly local disease known as lupus results which may persist indefinitely without ending fatally. The Str. pyogenes when it enters the superficial tissue of the body produces erysipelas and abscesses, and, when present in the circulatory system, produces septicemia. M. pneumoniæ may produce pneumonia, abscesses, conjunctivitis, otitis, and meningitis, depending upon its point of entrance and the tissue attacked.

(4) *The Subject Infected.* — The susceptibility of individuals to infections varies with the (1) species, (2) with race and individual idiosyncracies, and (3) with the age of the individual. The species of animal which is attacked by a pathogenic microorganism may be resistant (immune) or susceptible. An animal may be naturally immune to infection or may have acquired immunity by having a disease or by vaccination with a pathogenic microorganism in a modified form For example, animals are immune to such diseases as gonorrhœa, leprosy, etc., which affect man. They do not naturally contract such endotoxic diseases as typhoid fever, Asiatic cholera, but may be artificially infected by the bacteria when introduced artificially. Tuberculosis is more common among the negro race than among other races. Diminished vitality of the body due to exposure, use of drugs, injury, loss of sleep, overwork, and disobedience of other normal hygienic conditions influence the results of an infection. There are certain diseases, for example, diphtheria, which is more common in younger life than in adult life. Tuberculosis is a disease which is more common in early life (25-30) than at any other period of life. There is evidently more susceptibility to infection at certain periods of life.

In regard to source of the infectious microörganisms, it may be briefly stated that pathogenic bacteria and some other infectious organisms, etc., may be normally present in the nose, mouth, intestines, respiratory tract, on the skin, and may also be introduced through the agency of food and drink.

Immunity to Pathogenic Bacteria. — Immunity is resistance to disease. The absence of such resistance characterizes susceptibility. The subject of immunity in all its phases is being carefully investigated at the present time by many scientific workers. It is one of the most interesting of the comparatively unexplored fields of science. Only a very brief outline of the subject is given below.

The following table will be serviceable as an outline: —

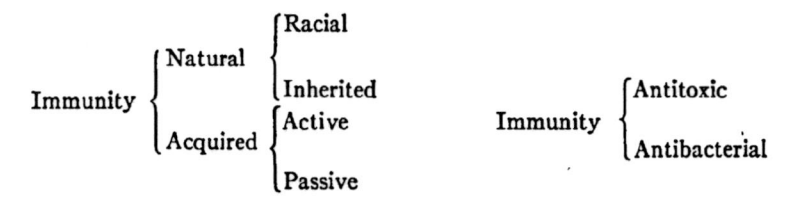

Immunity { Natural { Racial, Inherited }, Acquired { Active, Passive } } Immunity { Antitoxic, Antibacterial }

Natural immunity is the immunity which certain species or races of animals and plants possess against pathogenic bacteria and other disease-producing microörganisms. For example, man is immune to chicken and hog cholera, and the horse is immune to typhoid fever and Asiatic cholera. The lower animals do not have malaria, yellow fever, scarlet fever, or measles. The negro, as a race, is more immune to yellow fever than the white race.

Acquired immunity is that resistance which is acquired by having a disease, by being vaccinated, or by injections with antiserums. That immunity which is acquired by having the disease, or by vaccination, is called *active*, and that acquired by being inoculated with an antiserum, as, for example, an antitoxin, is called *passive* immunity. Vaccination is the injection into the body of the modified and attenuated bacteria or virus of a disease so as to produce the disease in a much less severe form than normally. In active immunity there is a reaction on the part of the body cells, while in passive immunity the cells do not react and the antibody exists inactive until combined with the toxic substances of the microorganisms. Acquired immunity to certain infections may, to some extent, be inherited according to the latest work on this subject.

Immunity may be either antibacterial, that is, against bacteria (endotoxins), or antitoxic, that is, against the toxins secreted by the bacteria. The term immunity is a relative one. Large numbers of pathogenic microorganisms, or large amounts of toxin, always produce some effect on the animal body when injected for the purpose of experiment.

The Theories of Immunity. — (1) Exhaustion Theory. It was claimed at one time by Pasteur that in acquired immunity the bacteria or infecting agents present in one infection used up all the pabulum necessary for the vital activity of the organisms, and that in natural immunity these substances were never present. Infection is, therefore, impossible.

(2) Noxious Retention Theory. This theory held that some substances of a noxious character were present in the body normally in some cases, or were retained in the body as a result of a previous infection. A second infection was, therefore, impossible for this reason.

(3) Phagocytic Theory. Metchnikoff claims that the

activity of the phagocytes (leucocytes, etc.) in the body are responsible for the immunity. It is very probable that immunity to certain diseases depends on the phagocytes.

(4) Chemical Theory. Ehrlich and others hold the view that certain chemical substances which are present to a limited extent in all normal serums and cells are increased after having an infection or vaccination and are responsible for both natural and acquired immunity of the body. These substances are bactericidal substances, agglutinins, precipitins, opsonins, etc., and antitoxins.

Immunity can be most satisfactorily explained on the basis of the phagocytic action of the body cells and the chemical action of certain substances in the body fluids (Nos. (3) and (4).

CHAPTER XXIV

Bacterial Diseases of Plants

Introduction. — Most of the scientific research on the pathogenic bacteria has been done on those species which produce disease conditions in man and animals. Few important investigations of any consequence were made prior to the last decade on the subject of bacterial diseases of plants. Recently bacteriologists have been paying more attention to this subject. The United States government has established in the Department of Agriculture a Bureau of Plant Industry. This bureau is actively engaged among other things in making pathological and physiological investigations of plants. In laboratories in other parts of this country and abroad research is now being carried on along the lines of plant pathology.

Early Conception. — It was held for some time by certain writers, and is still held to a limited extent by some investigators (Fischer, Ward), that bacteria do not cause primary infections of plants. The only exception to this condition of affairs, it is held, is in the case of the bacterial nodules which develop on the roots of the leguminous plants. Fischer, for example, in his " Vorlesungen über Bakterien " makes the following statements. He calls attention to the anatomy of the plant, and shows that bacteria can only enter through the stomata and lodge in the intra-cellular spaces under natural conditions. He argues that the bacteria can derive no nutriment from the material contained in the spaces between the cells, and therefore cannot produce any disease in the plant. He holds the opinion that pathogenic bacteria cannot dissolve the cellulose wall of the plant cell. Furthermore, the statement is made that the only spores which can possibly germinate in the aqueous material in the intra-cellular spaces are those of the parasitic fungi (Hyphomycetes, etc.), since they possess reserve food material. These fungi, it is claimed, may dissolve away the cell wall, penetrate the cell with the hyphæ, and thus produce a morbid condition therein (rusts, etc.).

Fischer and some others think that the bacterial infection of the plant is secondary to infection by fungi. He states that the uninjured plant is impermeable to the attacks of bacteria, and that even in the injured plant only those cells which are attacked by the hyphomycetes, etc., are available for bacterial action. The fact that bacteria are present in diseased plants in enormous numbers is, of course, recognized, but Fischer and others think that they are existing only metatrophically.

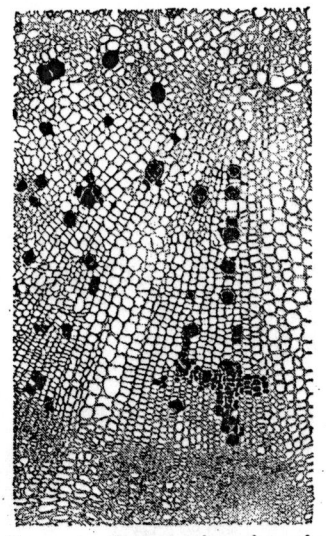

FIG. 52.—Cross section of turnip leaf inoculated with Bact. campestre. (Pure culture inoculation with needle.) After Smith.

Present Conception. — Against the opinion of these few investigators will be found the majority of pathologists and bacteriologists. It is now agreed by the leading authorities that there are distinct bacterial diseases of plants.

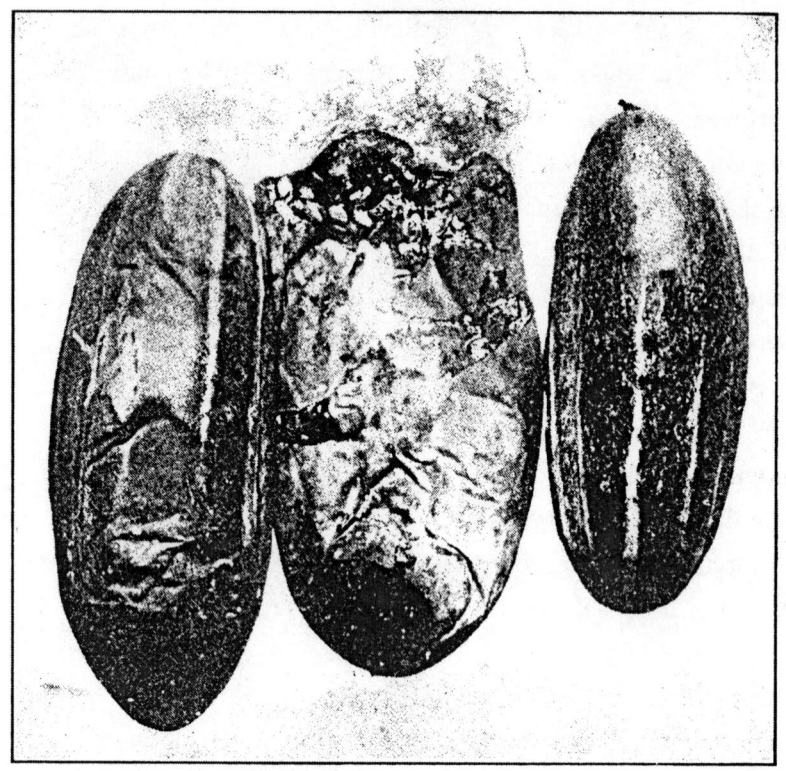

Fig. 53. — Soft rot of green cucumbers inoculated with B. carotovorus. (Pure culture inoculation.) After Smith.

These diseases can be produced in the various species of healthy plants by inoculation with definite species of bacteria (Fig. 53).

Species of bacteria have been repeatedly isolated from diseased plants and reinoculated into healthy plants producing the identical disease. These experiments are conclusive, and no substantiation exists for the foregoing statements of Fischer, *et al.* No preinvasion by a fungus is necessary. It is not uncommon, however, to have a distinct fungus disease in plants (rusts, etc.).

It must be recognized that the signs or symptoms of bacterial diseases in plants are in the main quite similar. This is particularly true of the bacterial rots. Sometimes careful study is necessary in order to discriminate between these various "rots" (Fig. 53). Some of the bacterial diseases of plants have been proved to be transmitted from plant to plant by means of the bites of insects.

FIG. 54. — Bacterium campestre in turnip root. (Vascular occlusion.) After Smith.

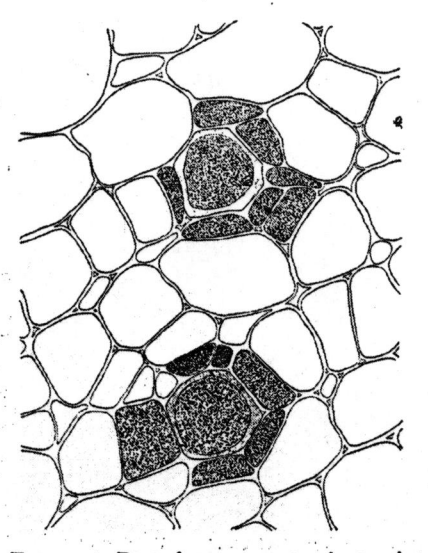

It has been noted that the bacteria which produce the various plant diseases secrete an enzyme which dissolves the cellulose of the cell wall. The action of these enzymes is slow in comparison with those of the bacteria pathogenic to animals. About one hundred and twenty-five separate diseases of plants have been recognized thus far.

278   BIOLOGY OF SPECIALIZED GROUPS

Method of Infection. — In plants, as in animals, bacteria usually cannot enter the body unless it has been injured in some way and an avenue of infection thus provided. The healthy uninjured animal or plant body is usually impregnable as far as bacteria are concerned. The resistance of the

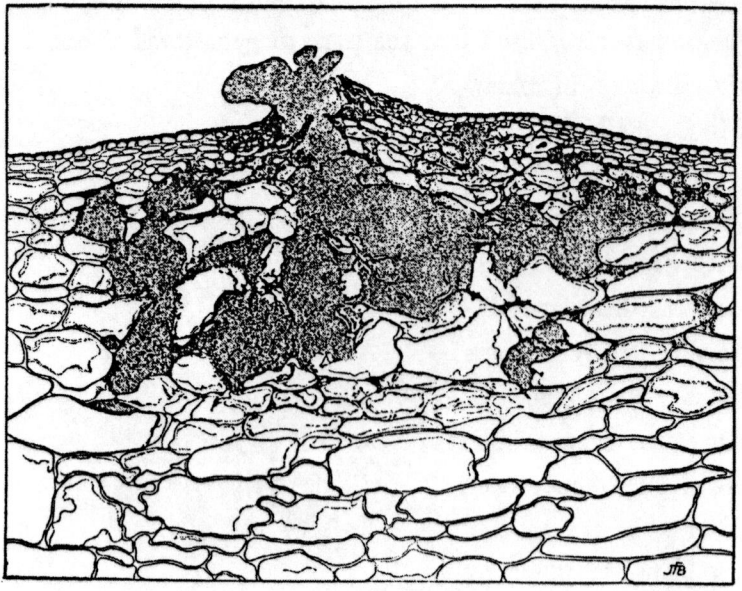

Fig. 55. — Bacterium pruni in green plum. (Cavity formation.)   After Smith.

body must be lowered before infection is possible. In the case of plants, the resistance or vitality of the plant is usually lowered and the avenue of infection provided by the sting of an insect, a frost bite, or a bruise. This is particularly noticeable in the case of the fruits of plants which have become infected. A few cases of bacterial disease are on record where no lesion of the plant could be found.

FIG. 56. — Olive knots (tumors). (Culture inoculation.) After Smith.

Often specific systems in a plant are affected, and these alone. For example, the vascular system may be occluded (Fig 54). At other times the bacteria invade the intracellular spaces and form cavities (Fig. 55) At other times there is a compensatory hyperplasia of cells and, as a result, tumors are formed (Fig. 56).

The following partial list gives a few of the bacterial diseases produced in plants and some of the bacteria which produce them The bacteria are in some instances not specific and certain species of bacteria may cause disease in several species of plants.

Tobacco wilt	Pseudomonas solancearum
Cucumber wilt	Bacillus ariodeæ
Melon wilt	Bacillus tracheiphilus
Tomato wilt	Pseudomonas solancearum
Blight or spots on green apples, quinces, prunes, pears, plums, etc.	Bacillus amylovorus
Potato rot	Pseudomonas solancearum
Turnip rot	Pseudomonas campestre
Carrot rot	Bacillus carotovorus
Diseases of the leaves and stems of cotton, sweet corn, broom corn, cabbage, etc.	{ Pseudomonas vascularum Pseudomonas campestre Pseudomonas malvacearum }
Bacterial olive knots (tumors)	Pseudomonas stewarti
Disease of walnuts, flowers of plants, etc.	{ Pseudomonas hyacinthi Pseudomonas jugulandes }

PART VII. DISTRIBUTION OF BACTERIA

CHAPTER XXV

BACTERIA OF THE SOIL

Distribution according to Habitat. — Some plants are localized and appear only under certain conditions, while others are more cosmopolitan, and what is true of plants and animals is true also of bacteria. It is a matter of some considerable importance to know the relation of bacteria to certain locations. At first thought it might be supposed that bacteria were evenly distributed in nature, but this, as has been said, is not true.

Bacteria of the Soil. — The bacteria find conditions favorable for growth in the soil, and the upper layers of the surface of the earth teem with them. The greasy feel which the earth has and with which everyone is familiar is due, in large measure, to the bacteria which it contains. Of course, certain parts of the surface soil are much more abundantly supplied with bacteria than other parts; the laws governing this will be discussed as we proceed, but in a general way the number of organisms in any particular soil depends upon the amount of food substance, or humus, which is present. A great many organisms are associated with putrefaction and decay, and where these processes are actively going on enormous numbers of bacteria are found (Fig. 57).

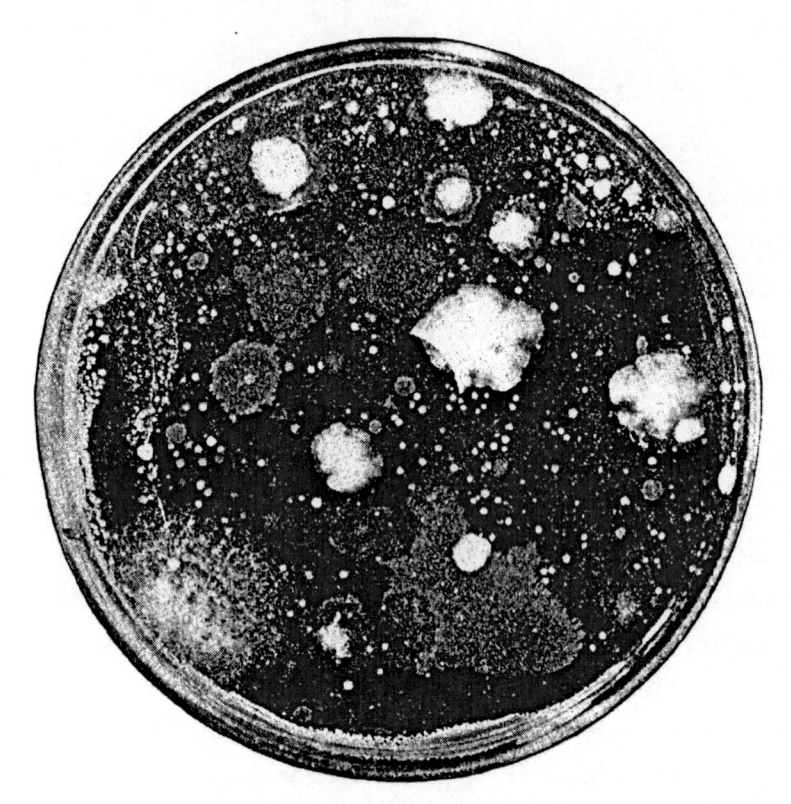

Fig. 57. — Colonies of soil bacteria. After Lipman.

Quantitative Distribution of Bacteria in the Soil

The number of bacteria in different soils is determined by the character of the soil. In some soils they are comparatively few, in others the numbers are enormous. The number of bacteria in various soils, both in a vegetative and spore condition, are shown in the following table: —

BACTERIA IN SURFACE LAYERS OF SOIL

Kind of Soil	Bacteria per Gram	Spores per Gram
Virgin soil, Woods	660,000	360,000
Virgin soil, Grass plot	780,000	480,000
Virgin soil, Pasture	810,000	480,000
Made Soil, College Hill	630,000	360,000
Made Soil, Hillside	920,000	475,000
Made Soil, College Hill	1,740,000	680,000
Made Soil, Bank of Lake	2,120,000	1,120,000
Cultivated Soil, Roadside	2,400,000	600,000
Cultivated Soil, Grain field	2,880,000	1,026,000
Contaminated Soil, Street	6,410,000	3,600,000
Contaminated Soil, Barnyard	8,640,000	4,400,000
Contaminated Soil, Hotel yard	10,920,000	4,800,000

There is a marked vertical distribution of the bacteria in the soil. The greatest number are in the first six inches and after a depth of one foot the number falls off very rapidly. Comparatively few bacteria, either in the vegetative or spore state, are found at depths over five or six feet.

The Species of Bacteria. — The bacteria of the soil are mainly saprophytic in nature and are associated with the processes of putrefaction and decay. A great many are also merely saprophilic; that is, they require dead organic matter, but are not largely concerned in its decomposition. There are a few pathogenic or disease-producing bacteria which have their home in the soil, such as the B. tetani and B. feseri (symptomatic anthrax). A great many more disease-producing bacteria simply pass a short but variable time in the soil, in an inactive condition. There has been a great deal of discussion as to whether or not pathogenic bacteria can grow in the soil, and it is still an open question how long these bacteria can persist in the soil if they do not grow. There is, perhaps, no good reason *a priori* why disease-producing bacteria might not grow in the soil. In certain localities, at least, there would be an abundance of food, and at certain seasons of the year there is sufficient heat. Some pathogenic forms will grow in media made from soil extract, but the evidence that bacteria can grow in the natural soil is very slight, and the chief reason why they do not grow, it is easy to imagine, is because of the antagonism of what may be termed the soil bacteria. Disease bacteria are preserved in the soil for a considerable period of time, and this is especially true of those bacteria which have spores. Soil which has become contaminated with the Bact. anthracis is dangerous soil for many years. The sporeless forms live for a much shorter time, and ordinarily they cannot cope with the unfavorable conditions which surround them except for a brief time. The practical importance of this problem comes out in the question of the persistence of disease bacteria in human or animal cadavers. The popular notion is that a cemetery is a dangerous place and many epidemics have been traced, in the popular mind, to close proximity to such places, or to contamination of water from them, etc. Whenever a grave is opened that contains the body of a person dead of an infectious disease, or an attempt is made to move a cemetery, fear is invariably aroused among people living in the neighborhood. There is very little evidence, however, to show that any of the bacteria of human disease can live for any length of time in the soil. Bact. anthracis without spores live only a few days, B. typhosus and Msp. comma only a few weeks, and the Bact. tuberculosis not over a few months. The antagonism of other forms is undoubtedly a potent factor in their early destruction. It is easily seen, then, that with the exception of the B. tetani, whose distribution in the soil is practically worldwide, that the disease-producing bacteria have only a very local distribution, and these localities bear a definite relation to some preexisting case of disease. Other soil bacteria of a very great importance are the legume and nitrifying bacteria. A discussion of the biology of these is found elsewhere.

The Legume or Nitrogen-fixing Bacteria. — This group of soil bacteria has already been referred to and their biology discussed, but it is desirable in this connection to emphasize their importance as nitrogen gatherers. Nitrogen is an essential plant food. When the supply is limited in a soil, it is found necessary to replace it. Nitrogen fertilizers are, at the present time, very expensive. It has been known for a very long time that certain leguminous plants were able to increase the nitrogen supply of the soil, and it was later found that this activity was associated with the presence of nodules on these legumes (Fig. 58). It is now known that the nitrogen fixation is brought about by the bacteria which produce these nodules. The knowledge which has been gained in recent years has opened up a number of problems, the solution of which would be of the greatest importance to agriculture. Some soils seem to lack the proper kind of nodule bacteria, and it is necessary that fields where leguminous crops are to be grown, such as clover or alfalfa, should be inoculated with the particular bacteria (Fig. 59). Attempts have been made to put up cultures of these bacteria in a form which would make them available for the farmer. Up to the

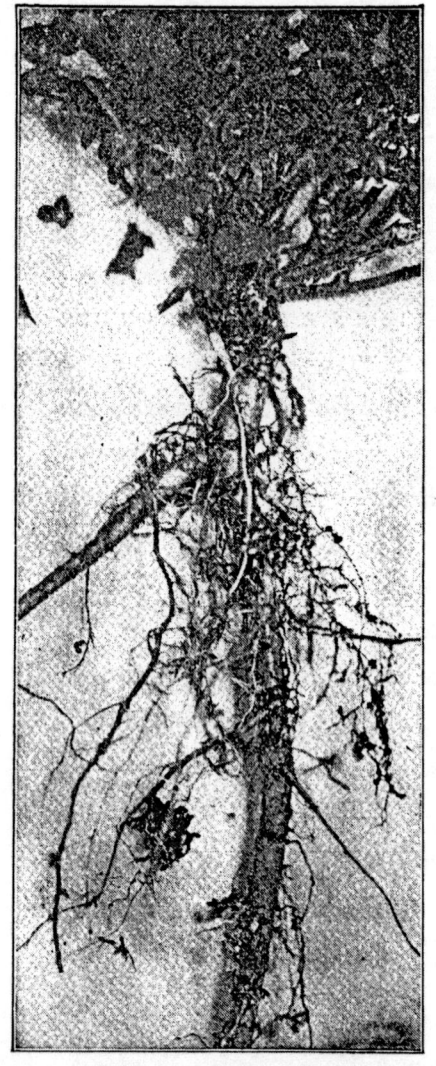

FIG. 58. — Tubercles on the roots of an old alfalfa plant. After Lipman.

present time, however, efforts in this direction have largely failed, and recourse must be had to the transference of these bacteria through the natural soil in which they are found rather than by means of artificial cultures. Another problem, perhaps utopian in nature, is to adopt these legume bacteria to a life on the roots of other kinds of plants. For instance, if we could teach the legume bacteria to grow on the roots of corn, there seems no reason why we could not raise three hundred bushels of corn to the acre where we now raise sixty.

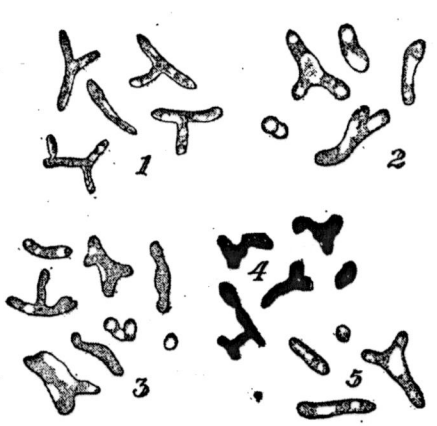

FIG. 59.—Bacteroids from legumes. (1) From Melilotus alba; (2, 3, and 5) from Medicago sativa; (4) from Vicia villosa (Harrison and Barlow). After Lipman.

Some bacteria are able to fix the nitrogen of the air independent of any symbiotic relation with the legumes. It is quite likely that it will develop that these organisms are, or may become, very important agents in the maintenance of soil fertility. Already attempts have been made to cultivate these bacteria and put them up in commercial form. If it should turn out that this is possible, these living nitrogen gatherers could be bought in the market and sown on the field, where they would fix for plants the nitrogen from the inexhaustible supply in the air.

The Nitrifying Bacteria. — They are exceedingly important organisms from the standpoint of the cycle of nitrogen in nature. The saprogenic and saprophilic bacteria break down the organic matter to the form of ammonia. This is available to a limited extent, if at all, to the green plants. The conversion of the ammonia formed during the process of putrefaction into the nitrates is a matter of greatest importance in soil fertility. This change is effected by the nitrifying bacteria. In order that they may do their work, certain conditions must exist The soil must be readily permeable to air, since these bacteria are oxidizing organisms. Drainage and methods of cultivation are of very great importance in this connection. In order that nitrification may proceed successfully, it is necessary that the acids produced by them be neutralized by bases. A soil to encourage nitrification must, then, have suitable bases. The question of soil fertility is then, in its last analysis, a bacteriological problem.

Denitrifying Bacteria. — The denitrifying bacteria are frequently found in the soil. Their action is just the reverse of the nitrifying bacteria; that is, they reduce the nitrates back to ammonia. In this way the nitrogen is lost as food for the higher plants. Such bacteria are, then, very undesirable from the agricultural standpoint. It is very fortunate that the conditions which are demanded by the nitrifying bacteria are those which are most unfavorable for this class; hence, conditions which favor nitrification interfere or prevent the activity of the denitrifying bacteria.

CHAPTER XXVI

BACTERIA OF THE AIR

Introduction. — Air practically always contains bacteria. In crowded cities, dusty streets, and elsewhere, the numbers may be very large. On high, snow-capped mountains and over the sea at some distance from the shore the bacteria are very few. The bacteria are not constant in their presence in the air, but vary at different times of the year and under different conditions. It has been supposed in the past that the bacteria of the air frequently include those of great disease-producing power, and it has been supposed that certain diseases could be carried for long distances through the air. Modern views, however, seem to indicate that the bacteria of the air are far less dangerous than was formerly thought.

Condition in Air. — The bacteria of the air are not in a state of active growth, but are in a dormant condition while in the air. A moment's reflection will show that this is of necessity so. Bacteria would be quite unable to get their food in a dried condition. Furthermore, the bacteria are usually attached while in the air to some dust particle, and very frequently they ride on these dust particles in small masses and not as individuals.

Origin of Bacteria. — The air bacteria are derived very

largely from the soil layers beneath. A great many different kinds of bacteria find their way into the air, but a great many of them are unable to withstand the desiccation to which they are subjected, so that certain forms die off and others remain. Thus there is established a more or less characteristic bacteriological flora. The extreme minuteness of the bacteria permits them to remain in the air for long periods of time.

Bacteria cannot be dislodged from a moist surface. They would not be blown into the air, for instance, from the surface of water. The only way that water bacteria can get into the air would be to have them shot into it by the bursting of bubbles of gas. This question is one of considerable practical importance, due to the discussion which has frequently occurred in regard to the bacteria in sewer air The air from sewers is usually low in its germ content, due to the fact that the sewage, and the walls of the sewers, are moist. These considerations, as well as those discussed elsewhere, lead to the belief that sewer air is not as great a factor in the production of disease as was formerly supposed. It is quite likely that in cases where it was supposed to be the cause of disease it was merely a concomitant circumstance. Furthermore, the bacteria of disease are not likely to occur in the breath of those suffering from disease for the same reason. They are very frequently shot from the mouth of diseased persons during fits of coughing and sneezing, and, to lesser extent, during talking, in little droplets of sputum. When these "droplets" dry, then the bacteria in them may get into the air.

Quantitative Distribution. — The number of bacteria in the air varies with different conditions, as has already been indicated. They are found to be very sparse in the air over snow-covered mountains, and over large bodies of water. They are comparatively few in the country air and very abundant in the air of cities, or other parts of the country where there is a great deal of dust. Their distribution will depend upon the character of the surface of the soil, the amount and direction of wind, the action of the sunlight, etc.

Seasonal Distribution. — Season has an influence upon the number of bacteria in the air. Conditions which favor dryness, and hence dust, increase the number of bacteria. Rains not only keep down the dust but they wash the air free from bacteria. The same is true of snow, so that when the air is washed by rain or snow it is much freer from bacteria than at other times.

The Species of Bacteria in the Air. — Bacteria found in the air are mostly saprophytes and are harmless. There are certain parasitic bacteria, however, which may be air-borne. One of the best examples of air-borne, disease-producing bacteria is Bact. tuberculosis. That this germ can be transported through the air from one individual to another is beyond question, and most people believe that this disease is transmitted, largely if not entirely, through the bacteria which get into the air from dried sputum. The work of Cornet and others has shown experimentally that this is possible. Recent work by a considerable number of investigators, following the lead of Ravenel, has shown that the distribution of tuberculosis may be accounted for in other ways, to a certain extent at least Bact. diphtheriæ may be distributed through the air, and this germ can undoubtedly live for long periods of time in the air. Other diseases that were formerly supposed to be airborne, such as influenza, are now accounted for, so far as their distribution is concerned, in other ways. In a considerable number of other diseases, such as the acute exanthemata, which includes smallpox, measles, and scarlet fever, evidence seems to point to the air as a vehicle of transmission. It should be noted that in the past it has been largely true that we have attributed to the air an important rôle when we have been largely or completely ignorant of the cause and means of distribution of these diseases. As our knowledge has become more exact, we have found that the air has had less to do with it than was formerly supposed. Whether this is generally true or not only time can tell. But we do not have at the present time any convincing evidence that any disease is either in whole or in part largely spread through the air. Of the saprophytes which persist in the air for long periods of time and constitute very largely the bacterial flora of the air, the micrococci are the most prominent. Among these are many brilliant chromogenic forms. In addition to bacteria there is always present a considerable number of mold spores and yeast cells.

CHAPTER XXVII

BACTERIA OF WATER AND SEWAGE

Introduction. — Water always contains bacteria. It was supposed some years ago that such waters as distilled water and that from deep wells were sterile, but since Burbon Sanderson, in 1871, showed that many bacteria existed in distilled water, it has been recognized that there are always bacteria present in a water supply. Many of these bacteria are perfectly harmless so far as man is concerned, and exist in the water composing a natural flora. None of the bacteria found normally in water are harmful to man. Some of these, however, may cause trouble by growing in the water pipes, filling them up, as in the case of the Crenothrix. Certain bacteria that cause a good deal of difficulty may also get into the water, especially from human sewage. One of the great problems of sanitation is to protect the water supplies from sewage contamination, or in case they become contaminated to purify them.

Number of Bacteria in Water. — The number varies from a very few bacteria per cubic centimeter in the water from deep wells or springs to a very great many in a surface water, especially if this is contaminated with sewage. A good idea of the number of bacteria in different waters may be obtained from the following table: —

Number of Bacteria in Various Waters

Source	Number of Bacteria per cc.	
Rain water	4 3	outside of Paris, Miquel.
Rain water	19	inside of Paris, Miquel
Snow	3	to 300, Janowski
Snow	2	glacier in Norway, Schmelck.
Hail	40	Madison, Wisconsin.
Hail	21,000	Bujwid
Hail	729	Fountain
Lake waters	500	to 2000, Lake Mendota, Wisconsin.
Lake waters	150,000	Lake Geneva, near shore, Fol and Dunant.
Lake waters	38	Lake Geneva, middle
River water	27,000	to 200,000, Seine
River water	20,000	Rhine.
River water	75	Rhone at Lyons.
Sewer water	38,000,000	Koch.
Ground water	850	to 1620, shallow well, Rubner.
Ground water	300	to 400, deep wells, London, Franklin.
Ground water	18	to 33, deep wells, Vienna, Kowalsky.
Ground water	15	to 50, Madison, Wisconsin.
Ground water	0	to 60, springs, Frankfort-on-the-Main
Ground water	9	to 3425, springs, Zurich, Cramer.

The Origin of Bacteria in Water. — Some bacteria come from the air, being washed from the sky with the dust. The majority of bacteria get into surface water from soil washings. The number which get in depends upon the conditions surrounding a body of water; for example, a great many more bacteria get in from a cultivated soil when this makes up the watershed than from a virgin soil; more, and particularly more dangerous kinds, when the watershed is inhabited than when it is uninhabited. Many of the bacteria which get into the water are capable of growing there and forming what is known as the water bacteria, or the normal bacterial flora of the water. Many of these bacteria are able to grow even in waters that contain very little organic matter. Certain species of bacteria can practically always be found in a water supply. In spite of the fact, however, that they seem to be well adapted to life in water they do not grow beyond certain limits. One would naturally think that if bacteria existed in water fitted for their development that they would soon increase to enormous numbers, but this is not true. Protected from the contamination which comes from the soil, the bacterial content of a surface water remains quite constant and would give a comparatively low count. When these same waters are separated from their natural condition, as, for instance, when they are bottled ready for analysis, the number of bacteria in them increases rapidly to an enormous extent. This indicates that there is in natural waters a germicidal substance which hinders the excessive multiplication of water bacteria. Just what this bactericidal property is due to is an open question.

The Species of Bacteria in Water. — Certain bacteria find their optimum conditions for development in water. These are the bacteria which are ordinarily spoken of as "water bacteria." They have been extensively studied by a number of investigators, but are not important, so far as we know, in affecting the potableness (drinkableness) of the water. Other kinds of bacteria make their way into the water and usually quickly disappear. Those which are most important in this connection are from sewage in general, and human sewage in particular. Among these sewage bacteria which get into water are B. coli, B. typhosus, B. dysenteriæ, and Msp. comma. Bacillus coli is the common inhabitant of the human intestine. It is also found in the intestine of other animals, particularly those which are domesticated. Its presence in surface waters in very small numbers, for example, less than one to a cubic centimeter, may possibly be accounted for by the presence of the excreta of animals not closely associated with man. But when present in greater numbers than indicated above, they constitute, by practically common consent, evidence of dangerous sewage contamination. The presence of B. coli in water may, then, be regarded as an indication of pollution. In fact, its presence or absence in water, as determined by an analysis, is used very largely in forming an opinion in regard to the potableness of a water supply. Not infrequently, the disease-producing bacteria mentioned above, B. typhosus, B. dysenteriæ and Msp. comma, get into sewage-polluted waters, and very serious epidemics are frequently traced to sewage-polluted waters. In the case of typhoid fever, probably at least sixty per cent of the cases are water-borne. One of the first typhoid epidemics to be carefully studied was that which occurred in Lawsen, Switzerland, in 1872. Here, from August to October, a hundred and thirty cases of typhoid fever developed in a population of 780. This epidemic was very definitely traced to the water supply connected with an underground stream which became contaminated with the discharges of typhoid fever patients. In 1885, the Plymouth epidemic occurred which has become a classical example of a water-borne typhoid epidemic. In that year, more than one thousand cases developed in a very short period of time out of a population of 8000 (Fig. 60). It was conclusively shown that the disease was caused by the discharges of a typhoid patient living and nursed on the banks of the stream from which the water supply of the city was taken. Many other epidemics have been definitely traced to an infected water supply, and the time must soon come when no city will think of taking water for drinking purposes which comes from a source that is not properly protected from sewage contamination. The dangers that come to cities taking their water supply from an infected source is well illustrated in those cities situated on the Mohawk and Hudson river valleys.

Asiatic cholera is also a water-borne disease. Fortunately, Asiatic cholera has been kept out of American and European countries for many years, and it is hoped that it will never return in epidemic form. If it does, however, it will travel, as it has in the past, largely through water. That it is a water-borne disease is very strikingly shown by the facts developed in Germany in 1893. Hamburg and Altona are two contiguous cities. Hamburg took its water supply from the River Elbe. Because it had its intake situated somewhat

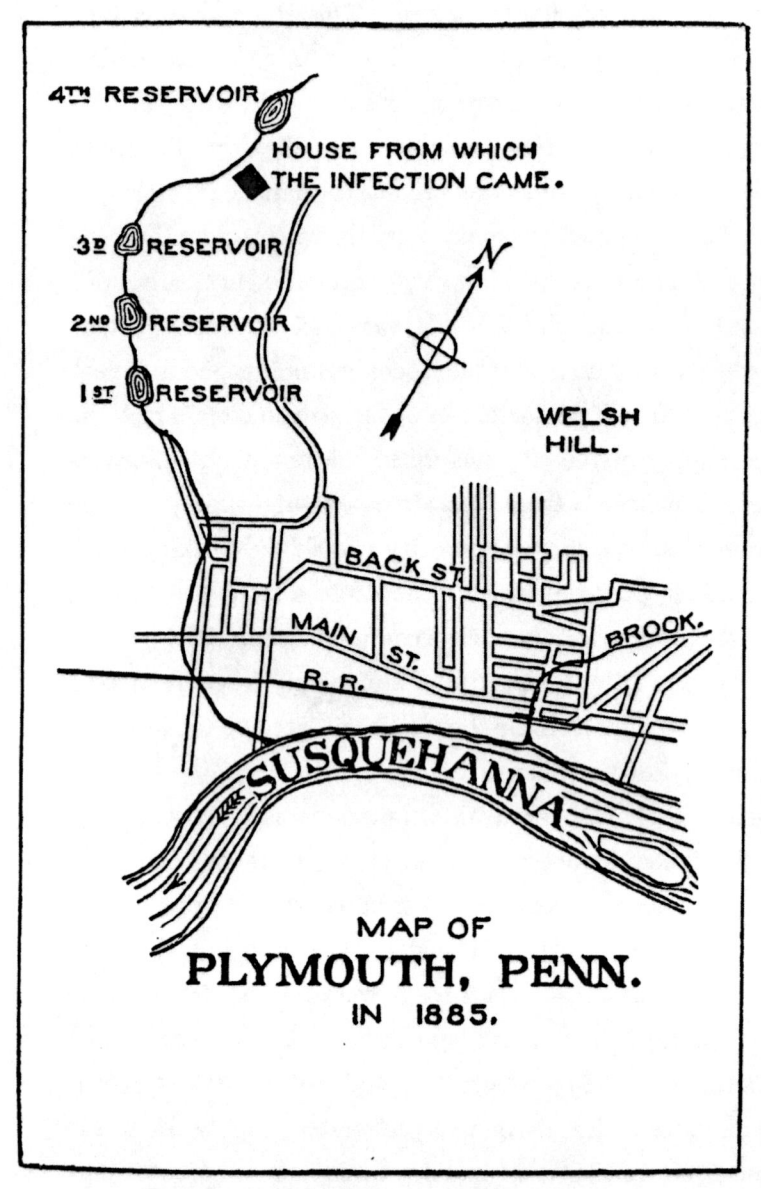

FIG. 60. — Plymouth epidemic of typhoid fever.

above the city, the water was used in a raw state. Altona, on the other hand, was obliged to take its water, if at all, from th's river, after the sewage of 800,000 people had been poured into it. The water was therefore filtered. In 1893, during the cholera epidemic, the cases were very frequent in Hamburg, where raw water was used, and very few in number in Altona, where filtered water was used. The character of the water supply was the only difference between these two places which could account for the distribution of the cases. To complete the proof that this Hamburg epidemic was water-borne, in the winter, after the disease had disappeared from Hamburg, it broke out explosively in Altona, because, as was later ascertained, the sand filter had cracked on freezing, allowing the unfiltered water to pass into the city main.

Water Analysis. — The efficiency of the bacteriological water analysis is becoming more and more evident as its use increases and the technique becomes perfected. Its value, supplementing that of a chemical analysis, was first demonstrated by Frankland's work on the filtered water of London. Chemical analysis was unable to detect the purification accomplished by a sand filter, and these filters were about to be discarded in London as inefficient when Frankland showed that so far as the removal of bacteria was concerned, their efficiency was very high, *i.e.* over ninety-nine per cent. Filters can only be efficiently controlled by proper bacteriological analyses. In the sanitary examination of water, the bacteriological determinations are becoming recognized as of great value. In a bacteriological water analysis the number of bacteria per cc. is determined by plate cultures. It is impossible to judge the character of a water by the number of bacteria it contains alone, but the bacterial content is frequently a matter of importance taken in connection with other factors. The number of different kinds of bacteria present in water is also important, but, as in the quantitative analysis, does not give information which can be used alone It is very rare that B. typhosus or Msp. comma can be detected in the water. The reason for this is, among others, that the analysis is usually not attempted until considerable time has elapsed since the introduction of these bacteria into the water. These bacteria live for only a short time in water under ordinary conditions and, therefore, have probably disappeared or become extremely few in number at the time of an analysis, and again it is a very difficult matter to separate B typhosus from other closely related bacteria What is sought for in a water analysis is the presence of B. coli. This is usually done by introducing the water to be examined in varying amounts from one tenth of a cc. to ten cc. into special culture media. The culture medium most generally used is dextrose bouillon in fermentation tubes. The presence of this bacterium is determined in what is frequently called the presumptive test by its ability to ferment the sugar in the dextrose broth of the fermentation tubes, with the production of certain amounts of gas of a definite formula, the production of red colonies on lactose litmus agar, the nonliquefaction of gelatin, and the production of indol.

In water analyses, an important part is the collection and transportation of the samples. The sample must be collected in sterile bottles and in such a way as to avoid contamination, and examination must be made either immediately or the sample must be kept packed in ice so as to prevent the changes which otherwise take place.

The Purification of Water. — As the population of the country increases, the necessity of purification of water supplies for certain portions of the population, at least, becomes imperative. The purification of water is at the bottom a bacteriological problem. It may be accomplished in a number of different ways; by sedimentation, which may take place naturally in some waters, or as a result of the addition of chemicals in others. It is secured also, and most frequently, by filtration methods. This is accomplished by what are known as continuous sand filters, used largely in Europe, by means of mechanical sand filters, developed and widely used in America, and by intermittent sand filters, developed in America and very successfully used on grossly polluted waters. In the continuous sand filter the efficiency depends upon the formation of a slime layer on the surface of the filter, so that this filter is really a living filter. In the mechanical filter, the efficiency is due to a precipitate produced on the sand by the addition of chemicals to the water. Its advantage over the continuous filter comes from the fact that it works much more quickly, and hence occupies less space. In the intermittent sand filter, the purification depends largely upon the action of the nitrifying bacteria which develop in the interstices of the filter between the flushings when the material is filled with air.

Sewage. — By sewage is meant the liquid waste from laundry, kitchen, and water closet. It contains organic matter and enormous numbers of bacteria. Winslow found 712,000 per cc. in winter and 11,487,500 per cc. in summer. Many different species occur. Three groups are of particular interest. One group is composed of the putrefactive bacteria, B. vulgaris, etc. Another group is composed of those bacteria which are characteristic of sewage, — such forms as B. coli, B. cloacæ, B. welchii, and Str. pyogenes are included. The third group, and from a public health standpoint the most important, is the disease-producing bacteria, as B. typhosus, Msp comma, and B. dysenteriæ.

The Purification of Sewage. — The savage and barbarian are little concerned with this problem. Their refuse is thrown in a pile, and when it becomes offensive they move on. Civilized man moves the refuse. In the case of single dwellings and small communities this has been done by burying or putting it into a cesspool. In larger communities it has been washed into an adjacent body of water. As the population increases it is found that these methods are unsatisfactory for the care of the growing volume of sewage. Recently bacteriological methods of sewage purification have been developed. In order to purify sewage its organic matter must be destroyed, and the pathogenic bacteria which it may contain, killed. All satisfactory methods are fundamentally bacteriological. Whether buried, treated by the dry-earth system, the cesspool, the stream, or better methods, sewage is purified or rendered harmless by bacteria. The modern methods most frequently used are the intermittent filtration, broad irrigation, and the septic tank and contact bed methods. Their importance is in the inverse order from that in which they are enumerated.

Intermittent filtration is used successfully in certain localities where the coarse material needed in their construction, such as gravel, broken stones, or cinders, are available. One acre purifies the sewage for one thousand people. The most favorable location is along a river bed. These beds, although they must be much more extensive than those required for water, may cost less. Sewage may be purified by this method so that it is indistinguishable from pure water, except perhaps by the amount of sodium chloride. The aërobic bacteria are especially active in this filter. *Broad irrigation* or sewage farming is successfully practiced where the proper soil exists (dry and porous). The amount of land required is from ten to twenty times as great as is required by the intermittent filter. The sewage is run down one side of the field in a ditch, and in lateral ditches or furrows it flows through growing crops towards a stream. The sewage is applied intermittently as above. This method is used in Berlin and Paris, and also extensively in England and to some extent in North America. It is economical, since several crops can be raised instead of one. It is perfectly satisfactory from a sanitary standpoint. The *septic tank* was first built by Cameron of England. This tank is a tight cement chamber through which the sewage slowly flows. The point of entry is below the surface, so as not to disturb the scum that soon forms, and not near enough the bottom to interfere with the sediment. The rate of flow for the sewage is such that it requires about twenty-four hours to pass through the tank. The anaerobic bacteria find conditions favorable for their activity and gradually liquefy the solid matter. This reduction may amount to 80 per cent. The work of the anaerobic or putrefactive bacteria in the septic tank is supplemented by the work of the aërobic bacteria in the *contact filter beds* These are filled with coarse material, such as cinders and coke. The beds are covered with the effluent from the septic tank for a few hours and are then drained and allowed to stand a few hours. This process is repeated several times a day. This method of sewage disposal is most satisfactory and is widely used at the present time. The amount of land required is small, the attention required slight, and the degree of purification high.

The use of chemicals, such as chloride of lime, for the purpose of sterilizing the effluent of the septic tank or polluted waters is being advocated. This method may be of the greatest service in treating water supplies during epidemics of water-borne diseases, especially typhoid fever.

CHAPTER XXVIII

BACTERIA OF MILK AND ITS PRODUCTS

Introduction. — Milk is one of the most important of the food products. It is an excellent food for man, and it is just as good food for microbes, and since milk is usually sold in its raw state it happens that it frequently contains enormous numbers of bacteria. Some of these bacteria produce no change whatever in the milk, and their presence is a matter of indifference. Certain other bacteria produce changes in the milk itself, causing it to spoil. These are undesirable, although they may in no way affect the health of the consumer. Still another class of bacteria sometimes found in milk are disease-producing, and against the presence of these in milk the consumer should have absolute protection.

The Bacteria in the Udder. — It was formerly supposed that milk in the udder of the cow was sterile, but we now know that it is practically impossible, even under aseptic conditions, to secure sterile milk. The number of bacteria in the milk taken under the best conditions varies from two hundred to a thousand bacteria per cc.

The Number of Bacteria in Market Milk. — The number of bacteria found in market milk varies greatly from a few thousand per cc. to many million per cc. In what may be considered the highest grade of milk on the market, namely, certified milk, the number is usually limited in the contract to ten thousand bacteria per cc., and, practically, a considerable amount of this milk is delivered to the home of the consumer with only a small fraction of this number present. Other milk collected under less ideal conditions, but constituting what would be considered a good milk, has tens or hundreds of thousands of bacteria per cc. A number of cities have limited the number of bacteria permissible in good milk to two hundred and fifty thousand, and others to five hundred thousand.

A good many milks produced under poor conditions, or kept, after being collected, for long times under unfavorable conditions, contain enormous numbers of bacteria For instance, Park found in New York City an average in twenty samples 5,669,850 bacteria per cc. as the milk was received in the city.

From tenements, midwinter, 1,977,692.

From well-to-do districts, midwinter, 327,500.

From tenements, Sept., 15,163,600.

From well-to-do districts, 1,061,400.

The Source of Bacteria in Milk. — Attention has already been called to the initial bacterial content of milk, and it perhaps ought to be added that the attempt is sometimes made to reduce this by discarding the fore milk, or the first few cubic centimeters drawn from each teat, but while there are more bacteria in the fore milk than in other parts of the milking, the difference is not so great that the discarding of the fore milk makes any great improvement in the general character of the whole milking. So that whether the fore milk is retained or discarded is a matter of little importance in the total number of bacteria.

Contamination from the Animal. — The coat of the animal is a fruitful source of bacteria in milk. Dirty animals introduce an enormous number of bacteria. When particles of manure are dislodged and fall into the milk during the process of milking, they carry with them great numbers of bacteria, and these are of an especially undesirable kind. When the animals are not kept clean, the number of bacteria which fall into the pail is great. Every particle of dust has a number of bacteria riding on it, and the same thing is true of the hairs of the animal. This source of contamination can be prevented to a considerable extent by, in the first place, keeping the animals clean, and, where possible, currying them frequently at some other time than just before milking, keeping the hair of the hind quarters clipped short, and furthermore by moistening the udder and flanks of the cows with a damp cloth just before milking. It is also desirable to use a small-topped milk pail, and many of them are now so constructed that they prevent, largely, the entrance of bacteria and dirt into the pail during the process of milking. The use of these pails also prevents the entrance of bacteria from the next source to be considered.

The Entrance of Bacteria into the Milk from the Air. — If milk is to be produced under as good conditions as possible, it is desirable that the air of the stable, where the milking is done, should be as free from bacteria as possible. This means that the cows should not be fed with dry food just before or during the milking time, since the shaking up of the hay and other dry fodder is the means of getting into the air a great amount of dust and its concomitant bacteria. This can be prevented by avoiding the use of dry foods and by using the small-top milk pail. The cleanliness of the milking utensils is another point to be considered.

Cleanliness of Milking Utensils. — The milking utensils need to be so constructed that the seams are all rounding, so that it is impossible for milk, or milk and water, to remain in the seams by capillary attraction. Care is usually exercised now by the manufacturers to see that all of the seams are well rounded out with solder. Utensils ought to be not only carefully cleaned, but they must be allowed to dry, and they ought to dry completely very shortly after they have been washed. Otherwise the water which is left, particularly if there is quite a little milk in it, affords a culture medium for the growth of bacteria, and it may well happen that between milkings the water left in a milking utensil may literally teem with bacteria, and when these same utensils are used in milking, they add very considerably to the germ content of the milk.

The Milker. — The milker affects the bacterial content of milk in more ways than one. In the first place, the dirty suit of clothes, or a suit used in the stable or in the garden, may introduce a good many bacteria, and for this reason in the production of a high-grade milk the milker should have a clean suit of clothes. In many dairies the milker wears a white duck suit, clean at each milking, or at least once a day. In other cases special suits are worn, but are not washed so frequently. The hands of the milker may effect the bacterial content of the milk. There is a habit among the milkmen of milking a few streams on to their hands and then milking wet, as it is called. This is a disgusting practice and should be discontinued. The milkman ought to wash his hands before beginning to milk, and in some dairies it is done before milking each cow. For those who object to milking dry the hands may be moistened with vaseline. It appears also that some milkers can get a much better milk from the same cow under the same conditions than others. For example, it has been shown that dairy students milked more efficiently than the ordinary force, the difference being due to the fact, no doubt, that the students understand and pay heed to the rationale of the process.

The Care of the Milk. — Care in collecting milk is necessary in order to keep the initial germ content low, but the subsequent care of the milk is quite as important. Milk is an ideal food for microbes, and they grow with great rapidity if they are given conditions favorable to development. When the bacteria are in the milk, about the only thing that they need in order to grow rapidly is the proper temperature. The milk furnishes everything else. It is absolutely necessary, then, in order to keep the germ content low, to prevent the bacteria from multiplying rapidly in the milk. The effect of temperature upon the rate of growth in bacteria is indicated by the fact that if milk is kept at 50° F. for twenty-four hours, a single germ may increase fivefold. If these same bacteria are kept in milk at a temperature of 70°, the increase is 720 fold. In the production of the milk, then, it is desirable that the milk should be cooled immediately and the cooling ought to be sufficient to take the milk below the temperature at which bacteria readily grow. Where it is possible, a cooling apparatus should be installed and the milk cooled to nearly the freezing point as quickly as possible, at least within a fraction of an hour from the time of milking. And the milk should be kept cool until it is ready to be used. It should be iced during delivery and be kept cool after it is delivered to the home. This is especially true of milk to be used for infant feeding.

CHAPTER XXIX

Bacteria of Milk and its Products (*Continued*)

The Species of Bacteria in Milk. — Of the bacteria which get into milk there are a good many different species. They may be grouped in the present consideration into those bacteria which produce little or no change in the milk, even though they may multiply to a considerable extent, and this would include the bacteria usually found in the udder, most of the bacteria from the air, etc. Another group of bacteria produce certain fermentations in the milk, causing the precipitation of the casein due to the formation of acids and enzymes, the production of gas which interferes with the use of milk for the manufacture of cheese, or the production of disagreeable odors and tastes and unnatural colors, and even sliminess. Another group of bacteria that sometimes get into milk are disease-producing.

Lactic Acid Bacteria. — Lactic acid bacteria always find their way into milk. They get into the milk usually from some contaminating influence, and the number that get in may be very small, but the lactic acid bacteria find milk the culture medium par excellence, and although they are few in number at first they soon outgrow the other forms, and milk left to itself almost invariably undergoes lactic acid fermentation.

This fermentation is undesirable in that it produces a taste which is objectionable to most people and produces a physical change in the milk which is ordinarily objectionable. Methods of preservation are aimed almost entirely against this fermentation. This does not mean of course that the fermentation of milk by the lactic acid bacteria produces a harmful change in milk. Metchnikoff has called attention to the fact that the Bulgarians make use of sour milk as a beverage, and he suggests that lactic acid organisms may serve a very useful purpose in the intestines of man since they antagonize the putrefactive bacteria which have a very undesirable influence on health by forming metabolic products that are detrimental. In the production of butter, at least in this country, we are dependent upon the fermentations caused by these bacteria. One of the great problems, then, of the dairyman is the production of a milk in which the lactic acid fermentation is held in check for a reasonable length of time; and it is possible, with the greatest care, to produce a milk which will remain sweet for many days.

Slimy Milk. — Slimy milk may be produced as the result of bacterial growth. Some bacteria grow in milk, and secrete a mucilaginous substance which causes the milk to assume a slimy character. Sometimes this slime causes long strings or ropes to appear in the milk. This is an undesirable fermentation, although not dangerous to health. Very frequently it may be carried from one farm to another through the creamery or cheese factory products; that is, through the skim milk or whey. If one patron brings infected milk to a creamery and then another takes away the milk or whey which contains these organisms in the same cans in which they bring their milk the next morning, infection is likely to be distributed and may become widespread.

Blue Milk.—Epidemics of blue milk sometimes occur. This is due to the growth in the milk of a bacterium that produces a blue coloring substance. An epidemic of this kind was described and shown to be communicated from one lot of milk to another as long ago as 1838, by Steinhoff.

Red Milk.—Milk sometimes appears red or bloody, due to the growth of certain bacteria in it. B. prodigiosus sometimes gets into the milk from the air and produces there its characteristic red color. A yeast is widely distributed in the air which produces a reddish pink color. These changes of course are to be sharply differentiated from the presence of blood in the milk. In the latter case the red color appears immediately upon milking, while in the former it only results from the growth of bacteria, and hence would appear only after a period of incubation of a greater or less length (Fig. 61).

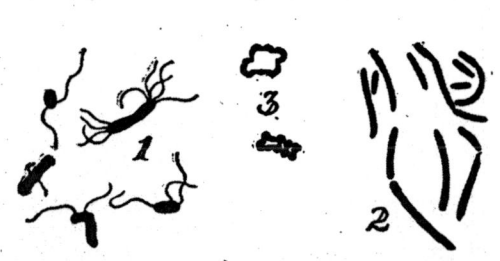

FIG. 61.—Bacteria producing milk faults. (1) B. cyanogenus (blue milk). (2) B. lactorubefaciens (red milk). (3) Coccus lactis viscosi (ropy milk). After Lipman.

The Disease-producing Bacteria in Milk. — A third group of bacteria which unfortunately are sometimes found in milk are those capable of producing human diseases. Some of these bacteria are derived directly from the cow, as Bact. tuberculosis, for example. In other cases the infectious agent enters after the milk is drawn. From the standpoint of public health this group is far more important than any other group of bacteria found in milk. In the case of the bacteria which are derived directly from the animal it would seem possible to protect the public when they are sufficiently aroused to demand protection. In those cases where the disease-producing bacteria enter after the milk is drawn, the problem is more difficult, because it seems quite impossible to detect mild cases of such diseases as typhoid fever, diphtheria, and scarlet fever in those that handle milk. It seems likely that occasional epidemics may occur for a good many years, although rigid inspection could quickly bring these epidemics to a minimum.

Disease Bacteria derived directly from the Animal. — Tuberculosis is very common among dairy cattle. It is also the most common disease of man, and that it may be transmitted from cattle to man seems beyond doubt. When milk from tuberculous cows is inoculated into guinea pigs, the disease is produced, as a number of investigators have found long ago. Russell, for example, found that 1 cc. of milk killed a rabbit. Bact. tuberculosis is present in milk not only when there is an apparent disease of the udder, but also when cattle appear in perfect health. When cattle are suffering from tuberculosis the bacilli appear in the fæces, so that not only are diseased cattle likely to have tubercle bacilli in their milk, but other cattle in the same herd, from particles of manure which are very likely to get in during milking process.

A number of bacteriologists, headed by Koch, have denied the intertransmissibility of this disease. The works of recent years, especially that of Ravenel, and more recently by the English and German Commissions, and by Park, have shown that a considerable portion of tuberculosis in children is due to bovine infection. And the question at the present time is not whether the disease is intertransmissible or not, but what proportion of human tuberculosis comes from bovine sources. It is certainly incumbent on those responsible for the rearing of children to use milk from cattle free from tuberculosis when this is possible. If not, it would seem better to use milk from a herd rather than from a single untested cow, "for Bollinger and Gebhardt showed milk which produced disease in guinea pigs was innocuous when diluted with healthy milk fifty to one hundred times its volume. Therefore, there is less danger in mixed herd milk than that of a single cow, unless it is positively known that she is unaffected with the disease."

The detection of tuberculosis is so easily and accurately done by the use of tuberculin that there is no excuse for having milk contaminated with the tubercle bacilli. All that is needed is an aroused public sentiment.

Pathogenic Bacteria which enter Milk after it is Drawn.
Typhoid Fever. — Frequent epidemics of typhoid fever have been traced to milk supplies. From 1857–1899 a hundred and ninety-five such epidemics have been recorded. The germ gets into the milk in one of several ways. For instance, the milker may be suffering from typhoid fever either in a mild form, or he may be a " germ carrier." In either case he contaminates the milk directly. In the second place the contamination may occur indirectly by the person milking or handling the milk also acting as nurse, or the transmission may be more indirect, as, for instance, by the use of polluted water in the cleaning of milk vessels. As an example of the first method of infection indicated above, the epidemic at Somerville, Mass., in 1892, may be cited. Thirty-five cases of typhoid fever occurred in this place; thirty of these upon investigation were found to be the consumers of milk from a particular dairy. At this dairy the son of the milkman handled and delivered milk while suffering from an indisposition which was not diagnosed as typhoid fever until after the investigation.

At the University of Virginia in 1893 there occurred fourteen cases of typhoid fever. All of the patients lived at a particular hotel and used the same milk. Upon investigation it was found that the milk came from a dairy situated on a creek. This creek received sewage from the main university sewer. It was also found that a negro having typhoid fever had thrown the dejecta on the bank of the creek. The milkman used the water of this creek to wash the udders of the cows during milking. In 1895 an epidemic of typhoid fever occurred in Stamford, Conn. Altogether there were three hundred and seven cases. This epidemic was thoroughly investigated. It was found that the greater number of patients were in the habit of drinking milk, that practically all of them took milk from a single dairyman, and that, while the premises were in good condition and no typhoid fever could be detected on the place, the cans, after they were washed in the house, were taken to a well to be rinsed. This well was situated in a plowed field, and was covered with loose boards. The field was manured with night soil, and it is believed that the B. typhosus present in the soil was carried on the feet of the men, and got into the water through the cracks in the board cover.

Cholera Asiatica. — Cholera can undoubtedly be carried through a milk supply, although the fact that the Msp. comma is very susceptible to acids undoubtedly makes it quite impossible for this germ to grow in milk to any extent, or even to live for any length of time. Practically only one epidemic has been traced to milk, and this is the well-known Simpson case. Cholera suddenly appeared on shipboard in the harbor of Calcutta. It was found that ten men obtained milk from a native. Of these, five were sick with cholera but recovered, four were sick and died, while one who drank only a little milk escaped.

Diphtheria. — A considerable number of epidemics has been traced to milk supplies. From 1877–1898 thirty-six epidemics of diphtheria, caused by infected milk, are described. Klein and some others believe that cows may suffer from this disease, and that the germs may be thus transmitted from the animal to man. Most investigators have been unable to obtain evidence which would confirm this belief, and it is generally recognized that the Bact. diphtheriæ must get into milk after the milk leaves the body of the animal in one of the first two ways indicated under typhoid fever. An epidemic which is characteristic of this disease occurred in Hightstown, N J, in 1892. There were twenty-eight cases and four deaths. All these cases occurred within one week, and all of them used milk from one particular dairy. Upon investigation it was found that a German boy who assisted in milking was suffering from diphtheria at the time and was, therefore, the means of distributing the disease.

Scarlet Fever. — A considerable number of epidemics of scarlet fever have been traced to milk supplies. From 1867–1899 ninety-nine epidemics of this kind were reported. As a typical example of such epidemics the one which occurred in Buffalo, N.Y., may be cited. Twenty cases occurred in the city and were found to be all in the families of those taking milk from a particular farm. Upon investigation it was found that four persons who lived at this farm had had scarlet fever, and that one, a convalescent, had helped in the milking and the handling of the cows. This was stopped, and no more cases developed.

CHAPTER XXX

THE BACTERIA OF THE HUMAN BODY

Introduction. — The healthy human body at all times is infested or inhabited by a great variety of bacteria. In the majority of cases these bacteria are harmless, although pathogenic bacteria may occasionally be present. When present, these pathogenic bacteria do not always necessarily enter the tissues of the body and produce an infection. Bacteria are present on the skin and mucous membranes and in all the cavities of the body which are in communication with the exterior. Some species are quite constant in their presence, while others are found only occasionally. It should be remembered that the conditions requisite for bacterial growth are organic food, a certain amount of moisture, and a temperature varying from $15°$ C. to $40°$ C. These conditions are all present in the human body. It is possible that the non-pathogenic bacteria may serve in some unknown way to protect the body against invasion by the pathogenic organisms. This point has not been thoroughly investigated.

Bacteria of the Skin and Exposed Mucous Membranes. — A great variety of species of bacteria and large numbers of them are found on the exposed surfaces of the body. The secretions of the subaceous glands of the skin and the desquamated cells of the epidermis furnish the necessary nutritive substances.

The number of bacteria present on the skin is influenced by the heat and moisture of the body, the clothing worn, the occupation of the individual, and the degree of cleanliness observed.

Disinfection and sterilization of the hands has received careful attention in recent years by surgeons and bacteriologists. It has been found that the hands, notwithstanding the fact that they are exposed to all sorts of outside influences and that they are frequently cleansed and freed of desquamated epithelial cells, are covered with as large a number of bacteria as those surfaces of the body which are not exposed and not cleansed so often. Foster found that it was impossible to remove all the bacteria in a short time by the use of soap, water, and brush. It is claimed at the present time that constant washing of the hands with sterile disinfecting soap, water, and brush for twenty minutes is necessary to remove all the bacteria. Bockhart and Fürbringer have found large numbers of bacteria under the finger nails. The foregoing statements serve to illustrate the prevalence of the bacteria on the skin and how difficult it is to remove them.

The bacteria usually found on the surfaces of the body belong almost entirely to the Coccaceæ and the Bacteriaceæ. The micrococci are perhaps the commonest inhabitants. The pus cocci are quite numerous at all times.

Hohein has investigated the number of bacteria in plate cultures made from underclothing of various kinds and worn for different periods of time. Sterilized materials were placed in direct contact with the body surfaces. On linen, wool, and cotton the colonies which developed varied in number from 28 to 600 in one day and from 4180 to 6799 in two days. In four days the number of colonies could not be counted.

Maggiora and Bordoni-Uffredussi have investigated the species of bacteria found on the epidermis of the feet. The former has isolated twenty-two non-pathogenic species from the feet. Some of these when grown artificially produced disagreeable odors.

Miquel reports that the wash water from the laundries on the Seine River contains more bacteria than the water of the Paris sewers.

The conjunctiva of the normal eye possesses a large variety of bacteria. It is claimed that these bacteria come primarily from the air, and the species found in the eye have also been repeatedly isolated from this source. Micrococci, pathogenic and non-pathogenic, compose the majority of the organisms present.

Bacteria of the Genito-urinary Tract. — Other exposed membranous surfaces of the body also show a large number of bacteria. For example, the mucous secretions from the surfaces of the vulva and vagina of the female and the secretions found in the meatus urinarius of the male and female show a great many species of bacteria. The uterus, Fallopian tubes, and bladder in healthy individuals contain no bacteria.

The secretions of the female genito-urinary tract at certain times seem to be slightly germicidal. For example, in the later stages of pregnancy and at parturition in the healthy person very few bacteria, if any, are found on the surfaces which come in contact with the secretions. The species found are usually non-pathogenic. Under certain conditions the genito-urinary organs of the male and female may be subjected to severe infections.

Bacteria of the Nose. — The mucous membrane of the nose usually contains a great variety and a large number of bacteria. They are derived principally from the inspired air. The hairs and mucous secretions of the nose and upper respiratory passages catch the bacteria, and as a result practically none reach the alveoli of the lungs immediately. Consequently the expired air is usually sterile. The nasal mucus exerts a very slight germicidal action on some bacteria. Pathogenic bacteria, such as Bact. diphtheriæ and M. pneumoniæ, are frequently found on some normal nasal mucous membranes. The nose and mucous secretions of diseased individuals often contain pathogenic bacteria. This is sometimes the case in individuals suffering from tuberculosis and other infectious diseases.

Bacteria of the Mouth. — A large amount of work has been done upon the bacteria which are usually present in the mouth. The mouth is lined by a mucous membrane composed of stratified squamous epithelial cells and is constantly kept moist by the saliva. The saliva contains an amylolytic ferment called ptyalin. This ferment converts starch into sugar. The conversion of the starch materials into sugar by the ptyalin is undoubtedly favorable to bacterial action. Furthermore, the stratified squamous epithelium lining the mouth is continually being thrown off, and this material furnishes excellent nitrogenous food for the bacteria which may be present.

The teeth are, of course, bathed in saliva all the time. There are always present in the mouth numerous irregular depressions of the mucous membrane, and these together with the spaces between the teeth serve as lodging places for particles of food which are kept moist by the saliva. The saliva is said by some writers to be slightly antiseptic, but this action is of no practical consequence. The temperature of the mouth is relatively high (98.6° F. or 37° C.), and it is at once evident that a better place for the incubation and growth of bacteria cannot be found. The main prerequisites for bacterial growth are at hand, namely, moisture, heat, and organic food.

The average mouth contains a great variety of species of bacteria. Certain of the saprogenic or putrefactive bacteria, the chromogenic or pigmented bacteria, the aërogenic or gas-producing bacteria, and the pathogenic or disease-producing bacteria may be present. One writer describing the bacteria of the mouth says that almost every organism which has been described in any position has been found in the human mouth. As a matter of fact, about fifty species of bacteria have been isolated and cultivated from the mouth. The connection of the mouth with the exterior accounts for the large flora present. The bacteria usually enter by inhalation through the mouth, by food or by drink. They may be introduced indirectly by being inhaled through the nose and also postnasal discharges containing bacteria may find their way into the mouth.

There are a large number of species of bacteria whose presence in the mouth is accidental, and there are also several species which are found rather constantly. To the latter class of organisms the name " mouth bacteria " has been given by some investigators. As far as is known these bacteria produce no deleterious effect on the body. Bacteriologists have been unable to cultivate these " mouth bacteria," and consequently very little is known about their biology. The origin of these bacteria is unknown.

A large amount of research work on the bacteria of the mouth was done by Miller in the early periods of bacteriological work. The following bacteria were isolated and named by him: Leptothrix[1] innominata, Leptothrix buccalis maxima, Iodococcus-vaginatus,[2] Spirillum sputigenum, Spirochæta dentium, and Bacillus buccalis maxima. Leptothrix buccalis maxima is the organism supposed to have

[1] Leptothrix is a term which was applied to filamentous bacteria.
[2] Iodococcus is a coccus form of bacteria not unlike the micrococci.

been seen by Anton von Leewenhoek and described by him as an animalcule in a communication to the Royal Society of London in 1683.

The above terms are not used at the present time. The bacilli, cocci, and spirilli found in the mouth were supposed by Miller to be intermediate stages in the development of Leptothrix buccalis. Fischer says that the term Leptothrix should only be applied collectively to the mouth bacteria. Miller and others have isolated a large number of species of bacteria from the mouth, but the identity of all these organisms has not been completely established.

The common saprogenic and zymogenic bacteria are nearly always present in the mouth. The following pathogenic bacteria are quite often found in the mouth of normal individuals: M. pneumoniæ, M. pyogenes var. aureus and var. albus, St. pyogenes, M. sputi septicus, Sar. tetragena. The pathogenic bacteria which occasionally find access to the mouth are as follows: Bact. diphtheriæ, Bact. mallei, Bact. tuberculosis, B. tetani, Ps. pyocyanea, and certain of the pathogenic fungi such as Actinomyces var. bovis and var. hominus, Oïdium albicans, and various varieties of saccharomycetes.

Many of the bacteria found in the mouth have the power of producing organic acids. One of the principal acids produced is lactic acid. One of the bacteria which is prominent in the production of this acid is Bact. acidi-lactici. This is the bacterium which causes the souring of milk, and in all probability is introduced into the mouth in milk.

Dental Caries. — Among the bacteriological processes which take place repeatedly in the mouth of all individuals is caries or the decay of the teeth The subject of caries has been studied by physicians and dentists for centuries. There are many theories as to the cause of this condition. The foremost is the chemical and parasitic theory, which may be briefly stated as follows: the theory holds that decay of the teeth results primarily from the action of the organic acids produced by bacteria, first, on the enamel, and second, on the dentine and pulp, and that as soon as the dentine is softened the various putrefactive bacteria infect the tooth and cause rapid disintegration and decomposition.

It will be recalled that the crown of the tooth is covered with enamel, which is the hardest tissue in the body Underneath the enamel is the dentine, which is the principal constituent of the tooth. This substance is traversed by small microscopic tubulæ, which run almost parallel to the long axis of the tooth. These minute tubes are filled with pulp and empty into a central perpendicular pulp cavity. The acids produced by the bacteria dissolve the enamel and change it into a cheesy mass. About 92 per cent calcium salts and 42 per cent of organic material are lost on account of the acids secreted by the bacteria (Fischer).

When the soft mass produced by the action of the bacteria upon the enamel is washed off, as it is by the saliva, there is usually a slight excavation produced in the underlying dentine, which serves as a lodging place for the saprogenic bacteria. The dentine is next decalcified and softened. It is an interesting observation that it takes longer for the bacteria to produce a complete change in the soft dentine than in the hard enamel. Once the dentine is softened the bacteria follow the tubules and enter the pulp cavity, destroying tissue as they go. It is possible after this stage is reached for various pathogenic microörganisms, such as the pus cocci, actinomyces, etc., to effect an entrance through the carious portions of the teeth and produce a generalized infection in the body.

Fischer refers to the fact that bacteria not unlike those occurring in the mouths of people in this day were found in the hollow teeth of some of the Egyptian mummies, and this goes to show that bacteria have been inhabitants of this region of the human body for centuries.

Bacteria of the Stomach and Intestines. — Since the mouth contains such a large variety of bacteria it is to be expected that some of these organisms will constantly pass down into the stomach with food and drink.

The bacteria find the healthy stomach an unfavorable place for growth. The gastric juice in the normal stomach contains a quantity of free hydrochloric acid (HCl). The experiments of Strauss and Wurtz and others demonstrate the fact that the normal gastric juice is decidedly germicidal. It owes this property to the free hydrochloric acid it contains, and not to any ferment. It has been repeatedly demonstrated by different observers that the normal gastric juice is free from bacteria and in fact is capable in certain instances of killing such microörganisms as those of Asiatic cholera and typhoid fever in from one hour to two hours. The vegetative forms of Bact. anthracis have been killed in from fifteen to twenty minutes and Bact. tuberculosis in from thirty-six to forty-eight hours. The gastric juice has practically no effect on the spores of Bact. anthracis, and the various species of pus cocci are also very resistant to its action. A large number of the non-pathogenic bacteria are also resistant to the action of gastric juice and pass through the stomach unharmed into the intestine. Bacteria may pass through the stomach into the intestines in particles of food and thus escape the germicidal action of the gastric juice. It is probable that Bact. tuberculosis and the endospores of all spore-producing bacteria readily pass through the stomach to the intestine.

In certain conditions, however, there are a large number of bacteria developed in the stomach. This is especially true as a result of diseases in which the functional activity of the stomach is lowered and the gastric juice is reduced in amount or becomes feebly acid or neutral. (Stenosis of pylorus, carcinoma.) Usually fermentation is set up in the stomach by some of the bacteria present. This is the condition in some forms of dyspepsia.

Abelous investigated the power of a large number of the bacteria found in the healthy stomach to digest fibrin, and the ability of others to convert starch into dextrose. The experiments were made *in vitro*. His conclusions were, that although digestion of fibrin and conversion of starch into dextrose did take place as a result of bacterial action, the time required for such reactions was so long that there was no basis for assuming that any of the bacteria were concerned in the process of digestion in the normal stomach.

In the intestine a large variety and an immense number of bacteria are constantly present. Some of these bacteria are present in the intestine constantly, while others occur only occasionally. The intestinal contents being alkaline in reaction and the temperature constant and relatively high, most of the bacteria present find optimum conditions. A great many of the bacteria found in the intestine are the saprogenic or putrefactive organisms. The species of bacteria encountered in the intestine are for the most part anaërobes or facultative anaërobes. The strict aërobic bacteria are not capable of multiplying to any great extent in the intestine on account of the scarcity of oxygen. On the inside of the intestine, in contact with mucous membrane, aërobic changes may take place to a limited extent. B. coli is one of the many microörganisms which is facultatively anaërobic and a natural inhabitant of the intestinal tract.

The end-products of the zymogenic and saprogenic processes which take place in the intestine vary with the character of the food in the intestine on which the bacteria are acting. If protein material similar to meat is acted upon, the process is essentially saprogenic, and the end-products produced include amino acids, aromatics, and gases, such as leucin, tyrosin, indol, skatol, hydrogen sulphide, and ammonia. If vegetable material containing a large amount of carbohydrate is acted upon by the bacteria, usually the zymogenic or fermentive processes are predominant, and among other substances organic acids are produced.

The intestines of carnivorous and omnivorous animals contain a greater number of bacteria than the herbivorous animals, and there are considerably more in the large than in the small intestine (De Giaxa).

It is claimed by certain investigators, among them Gillepsie, that although the majority of bacteria are of no use in gastric or pancreatic digestion, yet some are of great use in controlling putrefaction in the lower parts of the small intestine. Some of the organisms which are able to pass through the stomach, as stated above, produce organic acids during their metabolic activity. These acids, it is claimed, serve to reduce the alkalinity of the contents of the small intestine and consequently, in a measure, control the putrefactive processes due to other bacteria. Saprogenic bacteria are more active in an alkaline than in an acid medium. In the large intestine the alkalinity is so marked that the acids formed by bacteria are of no consequence in preventing saprogenic processes. In all probability this action on the part of acid-forming bacteria is of little consequence. They are certainly not necessary auxiliaries in the process of digestion if they do possibly aid indirectly in certain instances. The products of metabolism of the intestinal bacteria for the most part are not in any way useful to the human body. Fischer says that the fresh human fæces contain 75 per cent water and 1 per cent bacteria.

The intestinal tract of the infant at birth is sterile, but in a very short period of time after birth (12 to 18 hours), before any nutriment has been taken, bacteria appear in the meconium, and as soon as milk is ingested they increase rapidly in numbers. Seven different species of bacteria have been isolated from the intestine of the infant before any nutriment has been taken. These bacteria probably come from the air. B. coli and Bact. acidi-lactici are some of the first organisms to be noted in the intestine, and the former usually remains an inhabitant of the intestinal tract throughout life.

It has been shown by careful experiments, after removing a guinea pig fœtus from the pregnant mother by Cæserian section under strict aseptic precautions, feeding the young animal with sterilized food, and using every means to prevent contamination, that, after eight days, when the animal was killed, the intestine was sterile. The experiment serves to illustrate that bacteria have little or nothing to do with intestinal digestion at this period at least, and that they are not present in the intestines at birth.

The saprophytic bacteria in the normal intestinal tract are absolutely harmless as long as the mucous membrane which lines the canal is uninjured. If this be injured, some of the bacteria may enter into the tissues and produce serious diseased conditions. They may accomplish this alone or in connection with some of the pathogenic species which occasionally invade the intestine. For example, B. coli is a frequent cause of pyogenic or pus infections in the intestine, and in connection with B. typhosus, for example, may do much to increase the severity of the infection.

Besides the many non-pathogenic bacteria which are present in the intestine normally, at certain times pathogenic bacteria may invade these parts of the body, grow, and produce most virulent infections. B. typhosus, B. dysentariæ, Msp. comma, are among this class of microörganisms.

INDEX

A

Abiogenesis, 8-13.
Acetic acid bacterium, 172.
Acetic acid fermentation, 208-209.
Acid-fast bacteria, 98. -
Acids, fermentation of the fatty, 211-212; produced by bacteria, 174-175; which are produced by action of bacterial enzymes of saprogenic bacteria, 222.
Aërobes, class of bacteria known as, 131; obligate and facultative, 132.
Aërotropism, 141.
Agar as a culture medium, 74-75.
Agglutinins, 262-263.
Agglutinoids, 263.
Air, bacteria of the, 289-292.
Alcohol, bacterial pigments soluble in, 195; insoluble in, 195-196.
Alcohols produced by process of fermentation, 206; fermentation of the higher, 211-212.
Algæ, relationship between fungi and, 121; relationship of bacteria to the blue-green, 122-123; relationship of bacteria to the true, 123.
Alkalies produced by bacteria, 175.
Amboceptor, or immune body, 262.
Amino acids of fatty acid series, 222.
Amphitrichous class of flagellate bacteria, 31.
Anabolism vs. catabolism, 166 ff.
Anaërobes, 31; obligate and facultative, 132.
Anaërobic culture methods, 132-133.
Analysis of water for bacteria, 299-301.
Anaphylaxis to bacterial proteins, 257.
Anilin dyes for staining, 6, 95-96.
Animal kingdom, question of classifying bacteria in, or in vegetable kingdom, 115-116.
Animal life, spontaneous generation theory, 8-13.

Antagonism between species of bacteria, 164.
Anthrax bacillus, size of, 29.
Antibacterial substances, 261-262.
Antienzymes, 182, 265-267.
Antiseptic action of chemical substances, 146 ff.
Antiseptics, chemicals which are, 146-154; action of, on fermentation, 205.
Antiserums, 266.
Antitoxins, 258-261, 265-266.
Aromatics, fermentation of the, 211-212.
Arthrospores, 50.
Arts, bacterial fermentations in the, 214-215.
Asiatic cholera, 297-299; carried by milk, 317.
Assimilation, 165, 166.
Association, bacteria affected by, 164.
Autoclave, the, 82-83.
Autolysis of bacteria, 181-182.
Autolytic bacterial enzymes, 181-182.

B

Babes-Ernst granules, 58.
Bacilli, defined, 17.
Bacillus dentrificans, dimensions of, 29.
Bacillus prodigiosus, history of, 196-197.
Bacteria, discovery and history of the study of, 2-7; morphology of, 14 ff.; form and structure of, 14-41; two orders and two suborders of, 15 ff.; lower bacteria, 15-21; higher, 21-24; involution forms among, 24-27; dimensions of, 27-29; average weight of, 29; locomotion of, 29-35; four classes of flagellate bacteria, 31; rapidity of movement of, 35; capsules surrounding, 35-37; mass

333

INDEX

grouping of (Zoogloea, Pellicles, Colonies), 37-41; reproduction of, by fission, 42-46, by spore formation, 46-50, rate of multiplication of, 43-46, food of, 44-45, 67, histology of the bacterial cell, 52-60, minute structure of the bacterial cell, 52-65, question of nucleus in cells, 59-60, chemical structure of cells, 60-65, study of, by cultivation, 66 ff, sterilization and disinfection of, 77-84, methods of isolation, 86-92, microscopical examination of, 94-101, classification of, 102-114, taxonomy of, 102-126, relationship of, 115-126, definition of, 116-117, points of resemblance to other forms of life, 117-120; physiology of, 127 ff, relations between their environment and, 127-164; water necessary to growth of, 129-131; oxygen and, 131-133; influence of temperature on, 134-140; classification according to effect of heat on, 135-136, action of chemicals on, 140-154; relation of light to, 155-159; effect of electricity on, 159-162, lack of effect of Rontgen rays on, 162-163, effect of movement on, 163; effect of pressure on, 163, effect of association on, 164, metabolism of, 165-170; nitrifying, 183-185, prototrophic, 183-189, nitrogen-fixing or legume, 185-186, 285-287; sulphur bacteria, 186-188, iron bacteria, 188-189, chromogenic, 190-197; photogenic, 198-201; zymogenic, 202-215, saprogenic and saprophilic, 216-227, pathogenic, 228-273; specific and nonspecific infectious diseases due to, 235 ff, mode of action of pathogenic, 243-245, distribution of, 282-332, of the soil, 282-287; species of, 283-285, of the air, 289-292, of water and sewage, 293-304, of milk and its products, 305-318; of human body, 319-332
Bacteriaceæ Migula, 107-108
Bacterial cells, dimensions of, 27-29.

Bacterial diseases of plants, 274-280
Bacterial sheaths, 37
Bacteriology, definition and history, 1-7
Bacteriopurpurin, 187-188.
Bacterium anthracis, 18-19
Bacteroids from legume bacteria, 185-186
Beggiotoaceæ group, 23
Berkefeld system of filters, 78
Binary division, reproduction by, 42-43
Blood serum as a culture medium, 72
Blue milk, epidemics of, 313
Bouillon as food for bacteria, 67, 68-71
Bread-making, zymogenic bacterial enzymes of use in, 215.
Brownian movement of bacteria, 35
Butyric acid fermentation, 209-210, in sour milk, 213-214

C

Capsules surrounding bacteria, 35-37.
Caramelization of sugar media, 83
Carmine for staining, 95
Catabolism, 166, 167-168
Catalase, example of intra-cellular enzyme, 178
Cells, minute structure of bacterial, 52-65
Cellulose in cell walls, 63-64
Cheese, zymogenic bacteria in, 213.
Chemical changes, produced by enzymes, 177-178, resulting from decomposition and so-called putrefaction of the protein molecule, 221-227. *See* Metabolism
Chemical composition of food, 129
Chemicals, used for disinfection, 84; action of, on bacteria, 140-154; disinfecting qualities of, 146 ff
Chemical structure of bacterial cell, 60-65.
Chemical substances, poisonous substances produced by bacteria, 248 ff.
Chemical theory of immunity, 273.
Chemotaxis, 141-143, 144 ff.
Chemotropism, 141-143, 144 ff.
Chlamydobacteriaceæ, 22.

INDEX

Chloride of lime as a disinfectant, 147.
Cholera, 297-299, 317.
Cholera red reaction, the, 176.
Chromatophorous bacteria, 191
Chromogenic bacteria, 190-197.
Chromoparous bacteria, 191
Cider, aid of acetic acid bacteria in making, 209.
Cilia on bacteria, 29 ff.
Cities, abundance of bacteria in air of, 291.
Cladothrix group, 24
Cladothrix odorifera, 189
Classification of bacteria, 102-114, 119-120.
Cocci, definition of, 15; dimensions of, 27-29; direction of division, in reproduction by fission, 43.
Cohn, Ferdinand, 5, 30
Cold, slight value of, in destroying bacteria, 78-79 See Temperature and Thermal death point.
Colonies of bacteria, 39-41.
Colors in chromogenic bacteria, 190 ff.
Comma bacillus, the, 19-20.
Complement; substance called the, 262.
Conidia, 22.
Contagious diseases, 232-239.
Cover-glass preparations, 94-95.
Crenothrix polyspora, 188-189.
Culture media, 66-76.
Culture methods, 85-92, 132-133.
Cultures, testing disinfection by, 154.
Cyanophyceæ (blue-green algæ), relationship of bacteria to, 122-123.

D

Definition, of bacilli, 17; of bacteria, 117.
Denitrifying organisms, class of bacteria called, 226-227; found in the soil, 288
Dental caries, 326-327.
Diamino acids, substances formed from, by bacterial action, 222, 223.
Digesting enzymes, 217-220.
Dilution methods of isolation, 87-88.
Dimensions of bacterial cells, 27-29.

Diphtheria traced to milk supplies, 317-318.
Diplococci, 16.
Diseases, infectious and contagious, 232-239; Koch's postulates establishing connection between microörganisms and, 245; of plants, 274-280; distribution of, by air-borne bacteria, 291-292. See Milk and Water
Disinfectants and disinfecting, 146-154.
Disinfection, process of, 77 ff, 84; test of, by means of cultures, 154.
Distribution of bacteria, 282-332.
Double stains, 100.
Dunham's solution for study of bacteria, 71.

E

Ectoplasm layer of bacterial cell, 53-54.
Eggs as a culture medium, 72.
Electricity, effect of, on bacteria, 159-162.
Endospores. See under Spores.
Endotoxins, 249, 254-255.
Entoplasm, the, 54.
Environment, effect of, on bacteria, 127-164.
Enzymes, bacterial, and their mechanism of action, 176-180; autolytic bacterial, 181-182; and ferments, 202-206; proteolytic, 217-220; immunization of animals with, resulting in antienzymes, 265.
Epidemics, 295-299; caused by milk supplies, 316-318.
Esmarch roll, the, 89.
Eubacteria, 15, 104; suborders of, 105-111.
Eurythermic organisms, 138.
Exhaustion theory of immunity, 272.
External conditions, bearing of, on bacteria, 127-164

F

Facultative parasites and saprophytes, 228-229.
Fermentation, an enzyme process, 202-204; organized and unorganized

agents of, 204-206; definition of process of, 205-206, lactic acid, 206-208; acetic acid, 208-209, butyric acid, 209-210; methane and mucilaginous, 211, of the higher alcohols, aromatics, and fatty acids, 211-212, in the arts, in retting of flax, preparation of indigo, curing of hides and tobacco, bread-making, etc, 214-215

Ferments, organized and unorganized, 204-206

Filtration, sterilization by, 78, of water, 301-302, of sewage, 302-304

Fish, phosphorescence of, due to photogenic bacteria, 198-200

Fission, reproduction by, 42-43

Flagella on bacteria, 29 ff, do not interfere with process of fission, 45-46, chemical structure of, 65, special stain devised for, 98

Flame, sterilizing by a direct, 79

Fluid cultures, 92.

Food of bacteria, 44-45, 67, 118, classification according to, 128-129, amount required, 128-129; of photogenic bacteria, 199-200

Formaldehyde as a disinfectant, 148-150

Fractional methods of isolation, 86

Freezing, all bacteria not killed by, 79 See Temperature and Thermal death point.

Fungi, relationship of bacteria to, 120-122.

G

Gases, produced from metabolism of bacteria, 174; which may be produced by process of fermentation, 206.

Gelatin culture medium, 73-74

Gelatin plate method, Koch's, 6, 89-91.

Gelatin stab culture, 91-92

Genito-urinary tract, bacteria of the, 321-322.

Germicidal action of some chemical substances, 146 ff.

Gonidia, 22, 51, 121, 187.

Gram's stain, 97

H

Habitat, distribution of bacteria according to, 282

Hanging drop preparations, 94

Haplobacteria, 15, form types of, 15-21, reproduction among, 42-50

Haplobacterinæ, 105-109

Heat, value of, in destroying bacteria, 79, 134-137 See Temperature.

Hematoxylin for staining, 95

Hemolysins, bacterial. 257-258

Higher bacteria (Trichobacteria), 21-24, reproduction among the, 50-51

Histology of the bacterial cell, 52-60

Homothermic organisms, 138

Human body, bacteria of the, 319-332

I

Illusions, certain historical, due to bacteria, 196-197

Immunity, to pathogenic bacteria, 271-273, theories of, 272-273

Indigo, bacterial enzymes of use in preparing, 214

Indol, production of, by bacteria, 175-176

Infections, factors influencing and modifying, 267-270; effect of property of virulence, 267-268, number of bacteria necessary to produce an infection, 268-269, avenue of infection, 269; susceptibility of individuals to, 270; method of infection in case of plants, 278-280.

Infectious diseases, 232-239

Intermittent filtration of sewage, 303.

Intermittent method of sterilization, 80-81

Intestines, bacteria of the, 329-332

Involution forms, 24-27; production of, by fission of cells before reaching adult stage, 43

Iron bacteria, 188-189.

Isolation, methods of, 86-92; of photogenic bacteria for studying, 201

INDEX

K

Kircher, early bacteriologist, 2.
Koch, Robert, 6–7; development of culture methods by, 85; rules of, to prove connection between a microorganism and a disease, 245

L

Lactic acid bacteria, 172; in milk, 311–312; produced by bacteria of the mouth, 325.
Lactic acid fermentation, 206–208.
Leeuwenhoek, Anthony Van, 2–4.
Legume bacteria, 185–186, 285–287.
Life processes of cells, general character of, 165–166.
Light, effect of, on bacteria, 155–159.
Lime as a disinfectant, 147.
Locations, relation of bacteria to, 282.
Locomotion of bacteria, 29–35; effect of chemicals on, 141–142.
Loeffler's alkaline methylene blue for staining, 97
Loeffler's blood serum, 72.
Lophotrichous class of flagellate bacteria, 31.
Lower bacteria (Haplobacteria), 15–21; reproduction among, 42–50.
Luminosity, power of, in certain bacteria, 198.

M

Mass grouping of bacterial cells, 37–41.
Membranes, mucous, bacteria of, 319–321, 322.
Mercuric chloride as an antiseptic, 147.
Merismopedia, 16
Mesophilic bacteria, 135–136.
Metabolism of bacteria, 165–170, products of, 171–182.
Metachromatic granules, 55, 57–59.
Metatrophic bacteria, 167.
Methane and mucilaginous fermentation, 211.

Methods used in studying bacteria, 66–101.
Microbiology, 1.
Micrococci, 16
Micrococcus progrediens, size of, 29.
Microscope, bacteriological, 6; history of the, 93–94.
Microscopical examination of bacteria, 93–101.
Microspira, 19
Migula, classification of bacteria by, 103–104 ff.
Milk as food for bacteria, 71; bacteria of, 212–214, 305–318
Molds, relationship of bacteria to, 121, 123–124.
Monotrichous class of flagellate bacteria, 31
Morphology of bacteria, 14 ff.
Mouth, bacteria of the, 322–325.
Movement, of bacteria, 29–35; effect of chemicals on, 141–142; effect of movement on bacteria, 163.
Mucilaginous fermentation, 211; in milk, 214.
Muller, O. F., 4–5.
Multiplication of bacterial cells, rate of, 43–46. See Reproduction.
Myxobacteriaceæ, relationship of bacteria to, 124.

N

Neutralization of bouillon in preparation as bacterial food, 69.
Nitrification, process known as, 226–227.
Nitrifying bacteria, 183–185.
Nitrogen-fixing bacteria, 185–186, 285–287.
Nitrogenous substances produced by bacteria, 175–176.
Nitroso-bacteria, 183–184.
Nonalbuminous culture media, 75–76.
Nose, bacteria of the, 322.
Noxious retention theory of immunity, 272.
Nucleus in bacterial cell, question of, 59–60.

O

Opsonins, 263-264; vaccines and agents influencing the, 267
Osmotic pressure in bacterial cells, 55-56, plasmolysis by, 129
Oxidative changes, 174
Oxygen, varying effects of, on bacteria, 131-133, 141-142, necessary for production of light by bacteria, 200

P

Parachromatophorous bacteria, 191
Parasites, bacteria called, 128, facultative, 228, strict or obligate, 229-230
Paratrophic bacteria, 167
Pasteur, Louis, 5, 12-13
Pasteur-Chamberlain porcelain filter, 78
Pathogenesis of photogenic bacteria, 201.
Pathogenic bacteria, 228-273; mode of action of, 243-245; effects of, on the body, 246-248; immunity to, 271-273, entrance of, into milk, 316-317
Pellicles, 38-39.
Peptones, 221.
Peritrichous class of flagellate bacteria, 31.
Phagocytic theory of immunity, 272-273
Phosphorescence caused by bacteria, 198.
Photogenic bacteria, 198-201.
Physiological methods of isolation, 86-87
Physiology of bacteria, 127 ff.
Phytotoxins, 255
Pigments, bacterial, 191-196.
Plants, relationship of bacteria to, 119-120, bacterial diseases of, 274-280
Plasmolysis, study of structure of cells by, 54-55, 129
Plasmoptysis, phenomenon of, applied to bacterial cells, 57.
Plenciz, Marcus Antonius, 4.
Pleogony, theory of, 27, 103.
Pleomorphism, 24-27, 103.

Poikolothermic bacteria, 137-138.
Polar granules, 55, 57-59
Porcelain filters, 78
Potatoes as culture medium, 71-72.
Precipitins, 264-265
Pressure, effect of, on bacteria, 163
Protein molecule, results of decomposition and so-called putrefaction of, 221-227
Proteins, anaphylaxis to bacterial, 257
Proteolytic enzymes of bacteria, 217-220
Proteoses, 221
Protista, group of microorganisms, 116
Protoplasm of bacterial cells, 53-57
Prototrophic bacteria, 167, 183-189
Protozoa, relationship of bacteria to, 125-126
Pseudomonas indigofera, size of, 28-29
Pseudozoogloea, 38-39
Psychrophilic bacteria, 135-136
Ptomains, production and grouping of, 231, 248, 249-251
Pure cultures, 85-86
Purification, of water, 301-302; of sewage, 302-303
Pus cocci, size of, 29
Putrefaction, due to saprogenic and saprophilic bacteria, 216-217, mechanism of, 220-221; results of, of protein molecule, 221-227.

R

Rapidity of movement of motile bacteria, 35.
Rate of multiplication of bacterial cells, 43-46
Redi, Francisco, 9.
Red milk, 313.
Reduction substances, 173
Regenerators, 150
Relationship of bacteria, 115 ff ; to plants, 119-120; to Eumycetes, or fungi, 120-122; to Cyanophyceæ, or blue-green algæ, 122-123; to the Euphyceæ, or true algæ, 123; to Myxomycetes, or slime molds, 123-124; to Myxobacteriaceæ, 124; to protozoa, 125-126.

Reproduction of bacteria, 42-51; by binary division or fission, 42-43; among the Trichobacteria, 50-51.
Resemblance of bacteria to other forms of life, 117-120.
Respiration, 165, 168-170.
Rigor, state of, 136.
Röntgen rays, lack of bactericidal properties of, 162-163
Ross, Alexander, 9.

S⁻

Sand flea disease due to photogenic bacteria, 201.
Saprogenic bacteria, 216-227.
Saprophilic bacteria, 216-227.
Saprophytes, bacteria called, 128, 228-232; facultative, 229; found among air-borne bacteria, 291-292.
Sarcina, 16.
Scarlet fever, epidemics of, traced to milk supplies, 318.
Schulze, Franz, 10.
Schwann, Theodore, 11.
Season, influence of, upon air-borne bacteria, 291.
Septic tank, the, 304.
Sewage, bacteria of, 302-304.
Sewers, bacteria in air from, 290.
Sheaths, 21, 37.
Silver salts as antiseptics, 147.
Skin, bacteria of the, 319-321.
Slime, bacterial masses composing, 38.
Slimy milk, bacteria in, 312-313.
Soil, bacteria of the, 282-287.
Sour milk, butyric acid bacteria infecting, 210.
Spallanzani, Lazzaro, 10.
Species of bacteria, 283-285.
Sphærotilus group, 24.
Spirilla, definition of, 19-21; direction of division, in reproduction by fission, 43.
Spirillaceæ Migula, 108-109.
Spirochætes, 20.
Spontaneous generation theory, 8-13.
Spore formation, reproduction by, 46-50; chemical structure of, 65.

Sports, 47.
Staining methods, applied to study of granules, 57-59; advantages of, in examination of bacteria, 94 ff.
Staining, principles involved in, 99-101.
Stains, varieties of, 95-98.
Staphylococci, 16.
Steam, sterilizing by, 80-84.
Stenothermic bacteria, 138.
Sterilization, process of, 77-84.
Stomach, bacteria of the, 327-329.
Streptococci, 15
Streptothrix actinomyces, 22.
Strict, or obligate, parasites, 229-230.
Structure of the bacterial cell, 52-65.
Subcultures, 91-92.
Subinfection, process called, 233.
Sugar-free bouillon, 70-71.
Sulphur as a disinfectant, 147-148.
Sulphur bacteria, 15, 104, 111-114, 186-188
Sunlight, disinfecting and sterilizing properties of, 78; effect of, on bacteria, 155 ff.
Symbiosis of bacterial organisms, 164.

T

Taxonomy of bacteria, 102-126.
Temperature, influence of, on bacteria, 134-140; rate of, for production of light by bacteria, 200. *See* Cold *and* Heat.
Tetracocci, 16.
Thallophyta, classification of bacteria as, 119-120.
Thermal death point, the, 134-135, 138-140.
Thermophilic bacteria, 136.
Thiobacteria (sulphur bacteria), family of, 15, 104, 111-114, 186-188.
Thiothrix group, 23-24; an example of colorless group of sulphur bacteria, 186-187.
Toxic bacterial proteins, 249, 256-257.
Toxins, 248, 251-254.
Transmission of bacteria from one individual to another, 239-242.
Trichobacteria, 21-24; reproduction among the, 50-51.

340 INDEX

Trichobacterinæ (higher bacteria), sub-orders of, 109-111
Trophotropism, 141
Tuberculosis, distribution of, by bacteria in the air, 291-292, among dairy cattle, 314-315
"Tyndallization," 80-81
Typhoid epidemics, 296-298, due to milk, 316-317

V

Vaccines, 267
Vegetable kingdom, classification of bacteria in, 115-116
Vegetables as culture media, 71-72
Vegetative forms of bacteria, 46-50
Vinegar, acetic acid fermentation in manufacture of, 209
Virulence, property of, 267-268

W

Walls of bacterial cells, 52-53, chemical composition of, 63-64
Water, requisite for growth of bacteria, 129-131; germicidal action of sunlight on, 157-158, effect of motion of, on bacteria, 163, bacterial pigments soluble in, 194-195, pigments insoluble in, 195-196, prevalence of bacteria in, 293-294, origin of bacteria in, 294-295, species of bacteria in, 295-298
Water analysis, bacteriological, 299-301
Weight of average bacterium, 29
Will-o'-the-wisp phenomenon, 198-199
Wine, aid of acetic acid bacteria in making, 209

Y

Yeasts, relationship of, to bacteria, 121-122, concerned in fermentive processes, 206

Z

Zeit, quoted on effect of electricity on bacteria, 160-162
Ziehl's carbol fuchsin for staining, 97
Zoogloea, formation of, 35-36, 37 ff.
Zymogenic bacteria, 202-215

A Laboratory Guide in Elementary Bacteriology

By WILLIAM DODGE FROST, Ph.D.

Assistant Professor of Bacteriology, University of Wisconsin. Third Revised Edition. Interleaved. Illustrated. New York, 1904

Cloth, 395 pages, 8vo, $1.60 net

The object of this book is to give adequate directions for the performance of certain fundamental exercises in bacteriology. The general directions contain the essential part of the exercise which does not permit of any considerable variation, while the special directions embrace such features as are most subject to modification, as, for instance, the particular organism to be used, the kind of medium, the incubation, temperature, etc.

A Manual of Determinative Bacteriology

By FREDERICK D. CHESTER

Bacteriologist of the Delaware College, Agricultural Experiment Station, and Director of the Laboratory of the State Board of Health of Delaware

Cloth, 401 pages, 8vo, $2.60 net

The present tables serve only for purposes of identification, and not necessarily for those of classification. To the student working in the laboratory the determination of unknown bacteria has been almost impossible. With the use of the present manual it is believed that the teacher can place a given culture in the hands of his pupil and expect him to determine it, as is done with other organic forms. The work does not claim to be a text-book on bacteriology, but aims only to supplement the latter.

PUBLISHED BY

THE MACMILLAN COMPANY
64–66 Fifth Avenue, New York

The Practical Methods of Organic Chemistry
By LUDWIG GATTERMAN, Ph.D.
Professor in the University of Freiberg   Translated by William B. Schoeber, Ph D., Assistant Professor of Organic Chemistry in Lehigh University   New York, Second Edition   *$1.60 net*

Methods of Organic Analysis
By HENRY C. SHERMAN, Ph.D.
Adjunct Professor of Analytical Chemistry in Columbia University   New York, 1905

Cloth, 243 pages, $1.75 net

Theoretical Organic Chemistry
By JULIUS B. COHEN
London, 1907   *Cloth, 560 pages, 12mo, $1.50 net*

Although this is written from the English standpoint, yet it has received a continually increasing use since its first introduction to American professors of Organic Chemistry. The book seems to be particularly well adapted to American needs, and of about the right size and grade of difficulty   It probably most nearly approaches the perfect text-book for use with a college class in this subject of any now published.

Practical Organic Chemistry for Advanced Students
By JULIUS B. COHEN
London, 1907   *Cloth, 272 pages, 12mo, $0.80 net*

This book, although not aiming to be a complete laboratory guide, is intended to provide a systematic course of practical instruction which shall serve to accompany the author's "Theoretical Organic Chemistry." The combination of these two books will be found most satisfactory.

PUBLISHED BY
THE MACMILLAN COMPANY
64-66 Fifth Avenue, New York

An Introduction to Zoology

By ROBERT W. HEGNER, Ph.D.

Instructor in Zoology in the University of Michigan

Only a few animals belonging to the more important phyla, as viewed from an evolutionary standpoint, are considered. They are, however, intensively studied in an endeavor to teach the fundamental principles of Zoology in a way that is not possible when a superficial examination of types from all the phyla is made. Furthermore, morphology is not specially emphasized, but is coordinated with physiology, ecology, and behavior, and serves to illustrate by a comparative study the probable course of evolution. The animals are not treated as inert objects for dissection, but as living organisms whose activities are of fundamental importance. No arguments are necessary to justify the "type course," developed with the problems of organic evolution in mind, and dealing with dynamic as well as static phenomena.

"I have read your chapter (The Crayfish and Arthropods in General) and can express my satisfaction with reference to the general arrangement of the matter, as well as with reference to the detail. The whole treatment is up to date, taking account of the modern advancement in our knowledge of the crayfishes, and, chief of all, the more important features in the natural history of these animals are very properly separated from the unimportant ones. I think this chapter gives the essence of what we know about crayfishes, and any student might use the book advantageously. In fact, I know no other text-book which gives such a wealth of information upon so few pages." — PROFESSOR A. E. ORTMANN, Carnegie Museum.

"The plan is very satisfactory, and the book will be very instructive for class use. I am very glad that you have chosen the bee as your insect type." (Chapter XII.) — DR. E. E. PHILLIPS, Department of Agriculture, Washington, D.C.

PUBLISHED BY
THE MACMILLAN COMPANY
64-66 Fifth Avenue, New York

Bacteria in Relation to Country Life
By JACOB G. LIPMAN, M.P., Ph.D. $1.50 net

"A discussion of the problem of health and comfort in the country as affected by these minute organisms which float in the air we breathe and in the water we drink and perform an important work in the soil from which our food is extracted" — *Review of Reviews.*

"Much space, almost a third of the book, is quite properly given to the relation of bacteria to the soil and to the growth of plants This part of the subject is very interesting reading and shows clearly how complex the problems of scientific farming have become and how worthy of expensive experimentation Scarcely less interesting, although exceedingly brief, is the discussion of the sewage problem" — *New York Evening Post.*

Diseases of Economic Plants
By F. L. STEVENS, Ph.D.
Professor of Botany and Vegetable Pathology of the North Carolina College of Agriculture and Mechanic Arts, and Biologist of the Agricultural Experiment Station, and
J. G. HALL, M.A.
Assistant in Vegetable Pathology in the North Carolina Agricultural Experiment Station

Cloth, 513 pages, 12mo, $2.00 net

This is designed as a text-book to meet the needs of that class of students of our Agricultural Colleges and Agricultural High Schools who wish to learn to recognize and treat plant diseases without the burden of long study as to their causes. It indicates the chief characteristics of the most destructive plant diseases of the United States, caused by cryptogamic parasites, fungi, bacteria, and slime moulds, and gives information regarding the best methods of prevention or cure of these diseases While, in the main, non-parasitic diseases are not discussed, a few of the most conspicuous of this class are briefly mentioned, as are also diseases caused by the most common parasitic flowering plants.

Text-book of Plant Diseases
Caused by Cryptogamic Parasites
By GEORGE MASSEE
London, Third Edition, 1907 *Cloth, 458 pages, 12mo, $1.60 net*

PUBLISHED BY
THE MACMILLAN COMPANY
64-66 Fifth Avenue, New York

CPSIA information can be obtained
at www.ICGtesting.com
Printed in the USA
LVOW09*1451050117
519873LV00012B/237/P

9 781373 132741